Unified Assembl

ARM A32 ASSEMBLY LANGUAGE

Guide to Programming 32-bit ARM, Thumb, Floating Point and Neon

Bruce Smith
www.brucesmith.info

ARM A32 ASSEMBLY LANGUAGE

© Bruce Smith
ISBN 978-0-9923916-9-0
First edition: May 2017 [0001]

Editor: Alan Ford Edits
Cover: Bruce Smith,
Typeset in 11 on l2pt Garamond by BSB using Serif PagePlus x6

All Trademarks and Registered Trademarks are hereby acknowledged. Within this *Hands On Guide* the term BBC refers to the British Broadcasting Corporation.

ARM A32 ASSEMBLY LANGUAGE is not endorsed by any of the manufacturers mentioned in this book.

All rights reserved. No part of this book (except brief passages quoted for critical purposes) or any of the computer programs to which it relates may be reproduced or translated in any form, by any means mechanical electronic or otherwise without the prior written consent of the copyright holder.

Disclaimer: Whilst every effort has been made to ensure that the information in this publication (and any programs and software) is correct and accurate, the author and publisher can accept no liability for any consequential loss or damage, however caused, arising as a result of the information printed in this book and on any associated websites. Because neither BSB nor the author have any control over the way in which the contents of this book is used, no warranty is given or should be implied as to the suitability of the advice or programs for any given application. No liability can be accepted for any consequential loss or damage, however caused, arising as a result of using the programs or advice printed in this book.

Published by BSB – www.brucesmith.info.

Printed by CreateSpace.

Contents

List of Programs 10
About the Author 12

1: Introduction   13

Architectural Cores 14
Single Board Computers 16
Fully Clothed 18
ARM Board Compatibility 19
Learn By Example 19
What Will You Learn? 20
Notation in Use 21
Companion Website 22
Free Books 23
Acknowledgements 24

2: Starting Out   25

Numbers with Meaning 25
ARM Instructions 26
The Transformation Process 27
Why Machine Code? 28
Language Levels 28
Into Orbit 29
RISC and Instruction Sets 30
Assembler Structure 30
Error Of Your Ways 32

3: First Time Out   33

The Command Line 33
Creating A Source File 34
Come to the Execution 37
Assembler Errors 38
The Components 39
Lack of _start 42
Linking Files 43
Tidying Up 44
A Comment On Comments 45

4: Bits of a RISC Machine — 47

Binary to Decimal 48
Decimal to Binary..........49
Binary to Hex 50
Hex to Decimal and Back..........52
Binary Arithmetic..........52
Addition..........53
Subtraction..........54
Twos Complement Numbers 55
When Twos Don't Add Up..........57

5: ARM Arrangements — 58

Word Lengths..........58
Byte and Word Accessed Memory..........59
Registers..........60
R15: Program Counter..........62
Current Program Status Register..........62
Bits and Flags..........63
Setting Flags..........64
S Suffix..........65
R14: The Link Register..........65
R13: Stack Pointer..........66

6: Data Processing — 67

Arithmetic Instructions..........68
Addition..........68
Subtraction..........72
Multiplication..........73
Move Instructions..........75
Compare Instructions 77

7: Ins and Outs — 78

SWI and SVR Commands..........78
Writing to the Screen..........80
Reading From the Keyboard..........82
Makefiles..........4
eax and Others..........86

8: Logical Operations   87

Logical AND...87
Logical OR..88
Logical EOR..89
Logical Instructions..89
ORR to Convert Character Case..90
Bit Clear with BIC..92
Flag Tests..92
Syscall Registers...96

9: Conditional Execution   97

Single Flag Condition Codes...99
Multiple Flag Condition Code..102
Mixing the S Suffix..104

10: Branch and Compare   105

Branch Instructions...105
The Link Register..105
Using Compare Instructions 106
Compare Forward Thinking...107
Using Conditionals Effectively..108
Branch Exchange...110

11: Shifts and Rotates   111

Logical Shifts..111
Logical Shift Right...113
Arithmetic Shift Right...113
Rotations..114
Extended Rotate..115
Uses of Shifts and Rotates...115
Immediate Constant Range..116

12: Smarter Numbers   119

Long Multiplication..119
Long Accumulation...120
Division and Remainder...122
Smarter Simple Multiplication...122
Saturation and Q Flag...123

13: Program Counter — 124

Pipelining..125
Calculating Branches..126

14: Debugging with GDB — 129

Frozen Cases...129
Assembling for GDB...131
The Disassembler..133
Breakpoints...135
Memory Dump...138

15: Data Transfer — 140

ADR Directive..140
Indirect Addressing...143
ADR and LDR..144
Immediate Constants..144
Pre-Indexed Addressing...145
Accessing Memory Bytes...146
Address Write Back...148
Post-Indexed Addressing...149
Byte Conditions..151
PC Relative Addressing...151

16: Block Transfer — 153

Counting Options...154
Write Back..155
Block Copy Routine..157

17: Stacks — 159

Push and Pull..159
Stack Growth..161
Stack Application..164

18: Directives and Macros — 166

Data Storage Directives...166
ALIGNing Data..169
Macros 169

19: Using libc 173

Using C Functions in Assembler..173
Source File Structure...174
Investigating the Executable...176
Number Input with Scanf...179
Getting This Information...181

20: Writing Functions 184

Function Standards...184
Register Use..186
More Than Three...186
Preserving Links and Flags..189

21: Disassembling C 190

GCC - The Swiss Army Knife..190
A Simple C Framework..192
Getting the Assembler..193
Building Blocks..195
A printf Example...196
Frame Pointer Variables...198
Disassembling Syscalls...199
In Summary..203

22: Floating Point 204

VFP, SIMD and NEON Architecture..205
VFP Types..206
The Register File..208
Managing and Printing...210
Assembling & Compiling FP Code...212
Load, Store and Move...212
Precision Conversion..215
Vector Arithmetic..216
GDB VFP Update...216

23: VFP Control Register 218

Conditional Execution..219
Scalar and Vector Operations...222
Which Type of Operator?...224
Len and Stride..225

24: Neon　　　　　　　　　　　　　　　　　　　230

Neon Instructions..231
Addressing Modes...234
Neon Intrinsics..234
Neon Assembler...235
Neon Arrays..236
Matrix Math...239
VLD and VST In their Stride...244
Load of Others..245

25: Thumb Code　　　　　　　　　　　　　　　246

Differences..247
Assembling Thumb..249
Accessing High Registers..253
Stack Operators..254
Single and Multi-Register..254
Functions in Thumb...255
New ARMv7 Instructions...255

26: Unified Assembler　　　　　　　　　　　　257

Thumb Changes...258
New A32 Instructions..259
Compare by Zero...260
Assembling UAL..261

27: Connectivity　　　　　　　　　　　　　　　263

The GPIO Controller...264
Building the Code..266
Virtual Memory..268
Using and Adapting...271
Other GPIO Functions..274

28: Exception Handing　　　　　　　　　　　275

Modes of Operation...276
Vectors..277
Register Arrangements...279
Exception Handling...281
MRS and MSR..282

Interrupts When?..284
Your Interrupt Decisions...285
Returning From Interrupts 285
The System Control Register...286
Writing Interrupt Routines 286

29: Opcodes, Pipelines, Cycles   286

A Data Processing Example..289
A Thumb Example..292
Pipeline..294
Neon Pipeline...296
Instruction Cycles...296

30: System on a Chip   300

Co-Processors...301
Memory & Caches..302
The GPU..303
Single Board Computers..303

31: ARMv8 Overview   304

Different Compatibility..304
A64 Register Set...305
Syntax Differences..308
Exceptions...309
AArch32 Processor Modes...311
AArch32 State Exceptions..312
AArch32 Exceptions in AArch64...314
Finally..315

APPENDICES

A: Updating GCC..316
B: ASCII Character Set...318
C: Companion Website..320

Index   321

List of Programs

Program 3a. A simple source file..37
Program 3b. Part 1 of the source file...43
Program 3c. Part 2 of the source file...43
Program 6a. Simple 32-bit addition...69
Program 6b. 64-bit addition...70
Program 6c. 32-bit multiplication...74
Program 6d. Using MLA..75
Program 7a. Using Syscall 4 to write a string to the screen....................80
Program 7b. Using Syscall 3 to write a string to the screen....................82
Program 7c. Automate assembly and linking with makefiles................84
Program 8a. Converting character case..91
Program 8b. Printing a number as a binary string..................................93
Program 10a. Using conditional execution to improve program size....109
Program 15a. Use of the ADR directive...141
Program 15b. Use of pre-indexed indirect addressing.............................147
Program 15c. Using post-indexed addressing..150
Program 16a. Moving blocks of memory...157
Program 18a. Use of .byte and .equ directives...167
Program 18b Implementing a simple macro...170
Program 18c Multi-calling a macro..171
Program 19a. GCC source file structure...175
Program 19b. Passing parameters to printf..177
Program 19c. Reading and converting a number with scanf..................180
Program 19d. Combining scanf and printf...182
Program 20a. Passing function values via the stack................................187
Program 21a. A simple C program to print an asterisk..........................192
Program 21b. The final putchar listing. 196
Program 21c. C listing for the 'hello world' program.............................196
Program 21d. A C listing for using the scanf function...........................198
Program 21e. A C program to create a new directory using mkdir.......199
Program 21f. The final mkdir program using Syscall.............................202
Program 22a. Printing a floating point value with printf.......................210
Program 22b. Manipulating and printing two or more fp values...........213
Program 23a. Demonstrating conditional execution based on the
               outcome of a VFP operation..221
Program 23b Using LEN and STRIDE to sum vectors..........................227

Program 24a A simple NEON test..235
Program 24b Rotate a matrix by 90 degrees...237
Program 24c Adding two 4x4 matrix together...240
Program 24d Multiply two 4x4 32-bit floating point arrays....................242
Program 25a. How to invoke Thumb State and run Thumb code.........249
Program 25b. Using external functions by interworking code................252
Program 27a. Setting GPIO 22 to turn on an attached LED.................269
Program 27b. Adapting for GPIO 17..272

Download the source files for all these programs from the author's website at:

www.brucesmith.info

About the Author

Bruce Smith purchased his first computer – an Acorn Atom – in 1980. He was immediately hooked, becoming a regular contributor to the mainstream computer press including 'Computing Today' and 'Personal Computer World'. With the arrival of the BBC Micro, his magazine work expanded into books and his 1982 title 'Interfacing Projects for the BBC Micro' (published by Addison-Wesley) has become regarded as a classic of the time as the first book showing home users how to connect the computer to the outside world. (And now available FREE from his website!) He was one of the first to write about the ARM chip when it was released on the Acorn Archimedes in 1987.

Many books later Bruce has written about all aspects of computer use. His friendly, lucid style of writing caused one reviewer to write, 'This is the first computer book I have read in bed for pleasure rather than to cure insomnia!' Bruce's books have been translated into many languages and sold across the world.

An accomplished sports writer, Bruce has also written books on many major sporting events and compiled numerous record books.

Bruce's publishers have included BBC Books, Virgin Books, Rough Guides, Headline and Mainstream Publishing. He has been a regular contributor to BBC Radio, BBC TV and Channel 4 TV.

Originally from Bethnal Green, London, Bruce now lives in Sydney, Australia. He writes an occasion blog – Alan Turing Rocks – and can be found on Facebook and Twitter.

Facebook: authorbrucesmith

Twitter: @brucefsmith

www.brucesmith.info

1: Introduction

It could be argued that ARM is the most successful company no one has heard of. Unless you are in the computer business of course. Then they are, certainly to my mind, the most innovative of the microprocessor creating juggernauts. I can remember when I first heard about the new RISC processor that Acorn Computers were creating, I was in the Acorn office in Fulbourn Road, Cambridge (UK). Then the design was for the Acorn RISC Machine. I can remember quizzing the team how can a processor with fewer instructions perform better than one with a bigger instruction set? I didn't get it then, but I soon cottoned on as the first ARM-based systems became available.

Acorn has long ceased to exist, and it is now the Advanced RISC Machine. Of course, several of the stalwarts who revolutionised the home computing market with the BBC Micro still serve ARM to this day and help push the capability boundaries of the chip.

Figure 1a. The Odriod C1+ features a Cortex®-A5(ARMv7)microprocessor..

The family of ARM chips has grown phenomenally over the past umpteen years. Each successive generation of the chip has expanded its capability and functionality. Their success has been based on several things but primarily comes down to performance and cost.

Simply, ARM chips outperform all other comparable chips and at a low production cost. It is estimated that almost 80 billion ARM chips have been produced to date. If you have an electronic device, it almost certainly has an ARM chip inside it! The ARM chip offers almost unrivalled backward capability meaning that software written for it today will run on it in the future. This combination of performance, wide offering and low cost, and compatibility make it such that you simply can't ignore ARM.

ARM licences their technology so that other companies – Apple for example, and there are many others – can create their own fit-for-purpose ARM chips.

Figure 1b. The Raspberry Pi Zero might be considered a disposable computer given it's $5 price tag!

Architectural Cores

To most technically-minded PC users, a (micro)processor is the large chip that sits on the computer board and which controls everything that is happening on it. A core, on the other hand, of which there might be two, four, six or eight, is a part of the processor that's responsible for executing instructions. As such you could effectively have several operations running in different cores entirely separately but running concurrently. As you might imagine, this can provide a boost in speed.

With an ARM chip, it is slightly different in that manufacturers can customise the individual cores as part of their chip designs. This allows manufacturers who license the ARM chip to create amazing functionality that is specifically suited to their needs. ARM themselves design cores for their processors and these are generally grouped into named families. By combining these cores with some other function specific chips onto one piece of silicon, you can create what we now know as a System-on-a-Chip or SOC. The fact that these combined systems can share operating space can significantly speed up their performance by another notch.

The other thing to understand when negotiating the ARM world is that there is a difference between architecture and core names. The ARM architecture is based on the ARM instruction set and with each release the instruction set, is often upgraded and expanded, thus bringing even more functionality.

Figure 1c. A BBC Micro Second Processor.

The first ARM hardware application was as an add-on second processor for the BBC Micro. This was a unit, like that shown above, that plugged into the BBC Micro via a port called 'The Tube'. This allowed the users to have access to the ARM and program it for whatever needs via the BBC Micro keyboard. It was a bright idea that never really caught on as the ARM capability merely accelerated past the computers it was being connected too. (In many respects the ARM Second Processor was a proof of concept device that allowed users to access the chip's capabilities in much the same way as single board computers do today.)

This second processor was based on the ARMv2 architecture which contained three separate ARM designed cores including ARM2, ARM250, and ARM3. Note the subtle difference here in that the architecture includes a 'v' or version release letter within the naming mechanism. (Important to understand that ARMv2 has ARM3 as one of its core subsets! This follows in subsequent releases, ARMv6 has ARM11 – so it can be confusing.) Each new architecture release has the number incremented, and this signifies an extension to the instruction set and capability of the ARM chip in question. Figure 1d lists the original ARM 32-bit processors.

As new processors are released they have typically come with an increase of operating speed – often referred to as clock speed. Historically this has been a measure of how fast they execute instructions. However, this is now no longer the case as we shall see when we look at pipelines. The important thing to note here is that the number of cores does not affect clock speed or make an ARM computer necessarily run faster.

Single Board Computers

For a matter of a few dollars, it is now possible to purchase a single board computer (SBC) or development board containing an ARM chip. Once they were the realm of the professional developer and were often custom built for a particular task.

SBC or microprocessor development boards have come a long way. Development boards were used as a proof of concept while the hardware engineers for the project were left to develop the production board that would commercially replace the development board. Additionally, they were used as a means for an engineer to become acquainted with the microprocessor on the board and to learn to program it. It also served users of the microprocessor as a method to prototype applications in products.

Essentially development boards have been a convenience for prototyping the real thing. Typical components of a development system would include:

- power circuit
- programming interface
- basic input; usually buttons
- basic output; usually LEDs
- I/O pins to be used for everything else, motors, temperature sensors, and similar.

ARM A32 Assembly Language

Architecture	Bit width	Cores by ARM Holdings
ARMv1	32	ARM1
ARMv2	32	ARM2, ARM250, ARM3
ARMv3	32	ARM6, ARM7
ARMv4	32	ARM8
ARMv4T	32	ARM7TDMI, ARM9TDMI, SecurCore SC100
ARMv5TF	32	ARM7EJ, ARM9E, ARM10E
ARMv6	32	ARM11
ARMv6-M	32	ARM Cortex-M0, ARM Cortex-M0+, ARM Cortex-M1, SecurCore SC000
ARMv7-M	32	ARM Cortex-M4, ARM Cortex-M7
ARMv7R-M	32	ARM Cortex-M4, ARM Cortex-M7
ARMv8-M	32	ARM Cortex-M23, ARM Cortex-M33
ARMv7-R	32	ARM Cortex-R4, ARM Cortex-R5, ARM Cortex-R7, ARM Cortex-R8
ARMv8-R	32	ARM Cortex-R52
ARMv7-A	32	ARM Cortex-A5, ARM Cortex-A7, ARM Cortex-A8, ARM Cortex-A9, ARM Cortex-A12, ARM Cortex-A15, ARM Cortex-A17
ARMv8-A	32	ARM Cortex-A32
ARMv8-A	32 & 64	ARM Cortex-A35, ARM-Cortex-A53, ARM-Cortex-A57, ARM-Cortex-A72 ARM-Coretx-A73

Figure 1d. ARM 32-bit processors.

That was then. Today what used to be a mishmash of breadboards, wires, and connectors can be fitted with a single specialised microchip. Indeed ten-fold so. Mass produced to meet demand; individual component cost came crashing down to a matter of cents.

By increasing the density of theses integrated circuits the system's overall cost is greatly reduced. Almost overnight, multi-purpose development boards became a commercial reality. Boards with more computing sophistication than a room full of computers ten years ago were available for a handful of dollars. Indeed, boards are available for as little as $5, so we could say the day of the disposable computer has arrived!

The increased on-board complexity also meant that they could support and run industry standard operating systems, such as Linux, and more recently

Windows. Whereas before the programmer had to provide the entire infrastructure, which included all the input/output processing for keyboard and video – this was now available via the OS provided software. The former is known as bare-metal programming because you are programming the hardware or bare-metal directly.

Fully Clothed

This is an introductory text to programming ARM 32-bit assembly language and as such will assume the intermediary use of an operating system. We'll also look at other programmable components of the modern-day ARM chips such as Thumb and Floating Point code. This book doesn't cover bare-metal programming, which is processor specific and is best achieved via the C programming language (there are some excellent on-line tutorials which I have included links to on my website at www.brucesmith.info).

The operating system you select to use on your computer or development board may well be the official one recommended for your development board. A part of one of the tools available in your chosen operating system will be an assembler. The most common assembler supplied with 'free' operating systems such as Debian and Linux is GCC, the GNU Compiler Collection.

The original author of the GNU C Compiler (GCC) was Richard Stallman, the founder of the GNU Project. The GNU project was started in 1984 to create a complete operating system as free software, to promote freedom and cooperation among computer users and programmers. Every operating system needs a C compiler, and as there were no free compilers in existence at that time, the GNU Project had to develop one from scratch.

You may be aware that C is a very popular programming language; it is also one that is very closely tied to programming the ARM microprocessor. You do not need to know C to write assembly language programs, so don't be too concerned about that (although we will look at the integration of C and ARM assembly language later in this book).

GCC is an ingenious piece of software and is used in many ways. One of its primary components is an assembler, and this is the part of GCC we are primarily interested in.

The first release of GCC came in 1987. Since that time GCC has become one of the most important tools in the development of free software and is available on almost every operating system platform in existence.

GCC is free software, distributed under the GNU General Public License (GNU GPL). Therefore you have the freedom to use and to modify GCC, as with all GNU software. If you need support for a new type of CPU, a new language, or a new feature you can add it yourself, or get someone to do it for you.

GCC is not the only assembler available. Your OS may provide a different one as standard. It is impossible to cover all the available compilers in these pages, so programs as such are provided in GCC format. It will be necessary to translate these to your format if required. Regardless, GCC is probably available for you to download and use even if it is not part of your installation software.

ARM Board Compatibility

If your chosen board has an ARM microprocessor at its heart, the contents of this book should be applicable. There is a wide variety of ARM chips available, and they will not doubt continue to appear long after this book is published. However, their fundamental operation remains the same, and the introductory text herein will apply to the chip in your possession.

This book is specific to 32-bit ARM – A32. It is compatible with all the 32-bit processors listed in Figure 1d, including the ARM v8-A operating in 32-bit mode also known as the AArch32 state. Some of the newer ARM processors, such as the ARMv8-A, also support a 64-bit state (AArch64) and provide a 64-bit instruction set – A64. This instruction set is very different to the A32 instruction set and the two are not compatible. In general, it should be possible to run a 64-bit ARM processor in the A32 state and therefore run A32 code. The reverse is not true.

Learn By Example

For the practical examples, herein a Linux-based operating system has been assumed. If you are not using a Linux based OS you may need to reference your own operating system support site, or forums, to extract the correct information to be substituted.

The programs presented in this book are provided to illustrate concepts with a simple and – where possible – practical application. I will not try to baffle you with long and complicated listings; there is no need. I will leave it to you to take the examples and information and combine them two, three, four and more at a time to create a useful outcome, learning a great deal along the way.

Some degree of 'chicken and egg' syndrome has been unavoidable, but I have tried to keep it to a minimum. Concepts are introduced in an order that goes with knowledge so far acquired. However, sometimes this is not always possible; in such cases, I will highlight the fact. In such situations, you need to accept that it works and you will understand the how and why later in the day!

Programming is fun. I have written many books on the subject and a good percentage of them have been about home computers – how to program and use them. I have never had a computer lesson in my life. If I can do it, so can anyone. It is also frustrating! There is not a programmer who ever lived, novice or expert, who has not spent an inordinate amount of time trying to solve a programming problem, just to realise later that the issue was right there in front of them all along. I would go so far as to say the real satisfaction comes when you solve problems for yourself.

One word of advice: If you can't solve something, walk away and do something else for a while. It's amazing how often the solution comes to you when you are doing something else.

What Will You Learn?

In a nutshell, you will learn to become a proficient ARM chip programmer. Specifically, you will learn the fundaments of programming the 32-bit (A32) version of ARM's Universal Assembly Language. UAL is the standard defined by ARM for programming its microprocessor. It includes 'Thumb' which is a 'lite' version of the ARM assembly language. Also, we'll look at advanced operation such as floating point and vector programming.

This book is not a guide to every single ARM instruction. The ARM Reference Guide provide comprehensive details of all instructions. These manuals are available on-line or in PDF format and can be accessed free of charge. Some number several thousand pages in length. Links to these various manuals are on the website support pages of this book. Go to www.brucesmith.info and click on the cover image of this book, or select the Book Resource Pages option from the ARM menu, to access the programs in this book and other resources.

By the end of this book, provided you have worked through and applied the example programs and small snippets of programs in the text, you will be able to design, write and produce machine code programs to undertake any number of tasks. You will also have the grounding to allow you to delve into the more generic texts relating to the ARM chip and system programming,

You will also become familiar with using GCC in a whole variety of ways including writing programs for your Operating System and also by combining your assembled programs with libraries of standalone functions.

You will learn how to interpret and manipulate what your development board is doing at its most fundamental level. You will be right in there programming, deep inside the ARM chip!

Problem-solving is something you will also need to learn. When a machine code program will not work as you intended it is often a simple logical flaw that is the cause. GCC comes with debugging tools, and we'll see how to use these to good effect. I'll also provide some useful tips on the best way you can narrow down your search area to the source of the problem.

Notation in Use

A standard notation has been adopted throughout this book. Number types and certain operations on numbers are common place in programming books such as this, and it is important to distinguish among them. The short list here is for reference. Their exact meaning will be described as we encounter them within the text of the book.

% or 0b	Denotes that the number that follows it is in binary or base 2. For example: %11110000 or 0b11110000.
0x	Denotes that the number that follows it is hexadecimal or base 16. For example: 0xCAFE
< >	Angle brackets or chevrons are used extensively to enclose a word that should not be taken literarily, but read as the object to use with the command. For example, <Register> means a register name, R0 for example, should be used in the angled brackets and not the word 'Register' itself.
Dest	Short for destination.
Operand1	The commentary in the text often talks about Operand1 and its use. The relevant values for Operand1 as defined at that point should be used. For Operand1, this is normally a register.
Operand2	The commentary in the text often talks about Operand2 and its use. The relevant values for Operand2 as defined at that

point should be used. For Operand2, this is normally either a register or an immediate value.

Op1   Shorthand format for <Operand1> when space is tight.

Op2   Shorthand format for <Operand2> when space is tight.

( )   Brackets show that the item within is optional and may be omitted if not needed. For example, ADD (S) means that S may or may not be included.

Companion Website

Go to **www.brucesmith.info** and follow the directions to the book companion pages. From the site, you can download all the programs and access updates to the book and additional information and features. In addition, links to other support websites and useful downloads can be found, along with details of forthcoming Bruce Smith Books publications. See Appendix C for more details.

Follow me on Twitter: **@brucesmith** Facebook: **authorbrucesmith** and check out my occasional blog **Alan Turing Rocks** which can be found on my website.

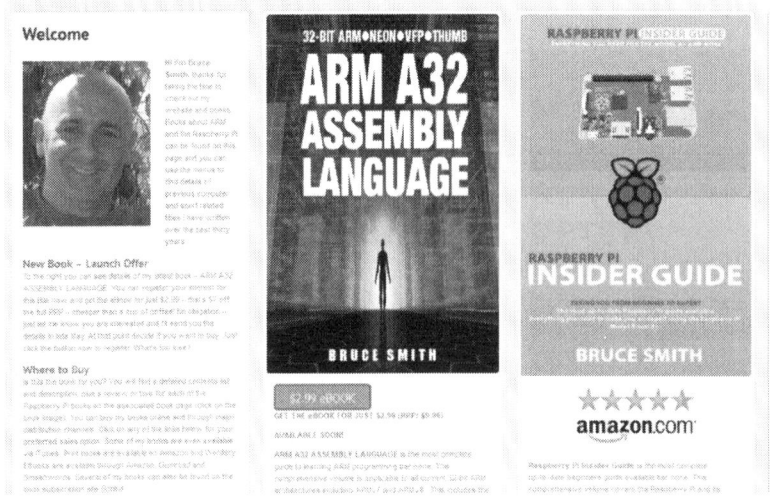

Figure 1e. The author website contains book support pages.

Free Books

Recently I managed to organise myself to do something that has been in my head for a couple of years. No not a sanity check, although that might still be on the cards – but getting the text and substance of some of my pre-Print-On-Demand books into an electronic format.

These are books that were published prior to 2004 before the whole eBook and self-publishing era got full on. Whilst I did author many of them (all but two in fact) using a wordprocessor the original text has long since washed away (the first two were written long-hand – blue ink on A4 ruled pages!).

I found a local company here in Sydney to do the first ten books of my choice and I now have these as both PDF and text files. I had hoped to use the text files to create eBook versions however, the technology (and also some of the fonts used in those original books) does not allow for a perfectly clean and accurate file to be produced. There is no regular consistency to the 'errors' so all the files require a lot of editing. I am not sure they will appear as eBooks anytime soon. However, the PDFs are very usable so these are available via my website, free of charge.

Figure 1f. PDFs for a number of my original books can be found to download free-of-charge via my website.

Acknowledgements

Extra special thanks go to **Richard Khoury** for his help with the C segments within this book and the finer art of using GCC and GDB. His assistance with programming the GPIO is also very much appreciated.

Thanks to **Mike Ginns** for the concepts of several programs listed here. Some listings originate from his book Archimedes Assembly Language which was first published by Dabs Press in 1988. (A key to how old the ARM actually is!)

Thank you also to my Beta Readers who gallantly read through the page proofs and marked up errors, typos and made suggestions to further improve the book. They are, in first name order only:

Richard Costello

Robin Karpeta

Tony Palmer

Any remaining errors are entirely my fault, and if you find them please be kind enough to let me know via my website or at feedback@brucesmith.info.

Reviews

I am an independent publisher. I write and publish my own books. This means I can write about subjects other 'mainstream' publishers would not normally take on. As such reviews are very important to me. Please take the time to write an honest review of this book if you are able. If you have a concern or issue please write to me at feedback@brucesmith.info. I do my best to respond to every email I get. Your sale is important to me to ensure I can continue to write and publish books like this. Thank you.

Bruce Smith
Sydney, May 2017.

Dedication

Baby Léa, Alice and Oliver

2: Starting Out

Assembly language gives you access to the native language of your microprocessor – machine code. This is the tongue of the ARM chip which is the heart and brain of your computer system. ARM stands for Advanced RISC Machine, and it ultimately controls everything that takes place on your computer.

Microprocessors such as the ARM control the use and flow of data. The processor is also often called the CPU – Central Processing Unit – and data the CPU processes are digested as a continuous, almost never ending stream of 1s and 0s. The order of these 1s and 0s has meaning to the ARM, and a particular sequence of them will be translated into a series of actions. Just like Morse Code where a series of dots and dashes in the correct order has meaning if you know how each letter is represented.

Numbers with Meaning

A machine code program is a sequence of numbers which are a form of code and represent actions the microprocessor chip must take. In their basic form these numbers are endless strings of 1s and 0s. For example:

```
11010111011011100101010100001011
01010001011100100110100011111010
01010100011001111110010100101000
10011000011101010100011001010001
```

It would be almost impossible — or at the very least extremely time-consuming — to interpret what these numbers mean. Assembly language helps to overcome these issues.

Assembly language is a form of shorthand that allows machine code programs to be written using an English style lexicon. An assembler is a program which translates the assembly language program into the machine code, thereby taking away what would otherwise be a laborious process. The assembly language program is often just a text file and this is read by the assembler before being converted into its binary (1s and 0s) equivalent. The assembly language program is called the input or source file, and the machine code program the object file. The assembler translates (or compiles) the source file into an object file.

Assembly language is written using *mnemonics*. A mnemonic is a device that aids learning or acts as a reminder. This relies upon associations among easy-to-remember letter sequences that can be related back to the information to be remembered. You've probably encountered these at some point as acronyms. For example, to remember the colours of the rainbow you could take the phrase:

'Richard Of York Gave Battle In Vain'

And use the first letter of each word. Or use the fictitious name:

'Roy G. Biv'

A mnemonic language has developed around SMS messages sent on mobile phones. These enable text messages to be shorter and more compact. For example, 'L8R' for later', 'GR8' for Great and '2mrw' for 'tomorrow'.

ARM Instructions

The ARM chip has a specific set of machine code instructions that it understands. These operation codes or *opcodes* and their use are really what this book is about. The ARM is just one type of microprocessor; there are many different types and each has its own unique set of instructions.

You cannot take a machine code program written for ARM and run it successfully on a different microprocessor. It simply would not work as expected, if at all. That said, the concepts introduced here can be applied with a broad brush to most other microprocessors available and are pretty consistent in application. If you learn to program in one, you are well on your way to programming others. Essentially you just need to learn a new set of mnemonics, and most likely many will be similar to the ones you are about to learn.

Microprocessors move and manipulate data, so not surprisingly many of the machine code commands deal with this control, and most instruction sets (the collective term for these *mnemonics*), include commands to add and subtract numbers. The assembly language mnemonics used to represent these tasks are typically in the form:

```
ADD
SUB
```

ARM A32 Assembly Language

These examples are pretty straightforward as are many other ARM mnemonics, However, they can also appear complex when combined in a single line sequence. By breaking them down into their component parts their action can be determined without any real difficulty.

An assembly language mnemonic is normally three characters in length, but there are occasions when it may be longer. Like anything new, this may take a bit of 'getting used to', but if you work through the examples given in this book, and apply them in your own examples you should not have too much trouble.

MOV is the mnemonic for the MOVe command. It takes information from one place and moves it to another place. How hard was that?

The Transformation Process

Once you have developed your assembly language program you have to convert it into machine code. This is done using an application called an *assembler*. For example, when the assembler encounters the MOV mnemonic it will generate the correct number that represents the instruction. It stores the assembled machine code as a sequential file in memory and then allows you to run or *execute* it. In the process of assembling the program, the assembler also checks its syntax to ensure it is correct. If it spots an error, it will identify it to you and allow you to correct it. You can then try and assemble the program again. Note that this syntax check will only ensure that you have used the assembler instructions correctly. It cannot check their logic so if you have written something that has used instructions correctly, but not in the way that achieves what you wanted, it will assemble without error but will produce an unwanted result.

There are various ways to write an assembly language program. The first ARM chips were designed by Acorn and so not surprisingly appeared on a range of Acorn-based computers running RISC OS. This included the Archimedes and RISC PC. These machines ran BBC BASIC, which was innovative in that it allowed you to write assembly language programs as an extension of BBC BASIC.

As we have already identified, this book assumes you are using a suitable operating system (I would suggest the official (or unofficial) OS recommended for your board with a suitable compiler)– in this the GNU GCC software is recommended. Other assembler software does exist — much of it free — and a quick search on the internet will reveal what the

27

offerings are. A major advantage of GCC is that it can also assemble programs written in the C programming language.

Although this book is not about programming C, there are reasons why some familiarity with the infrastructure it employs is advantageous, and with just a bit of knowledge this can help make programming easier. We'll discuss this with examples later in the book.

The bottom line is that there is nothing to stop you trying any or all of these other assemblers, and certainly what you learn here will be beneficial in that process.

Why Machine Code?

This is an easy question to answer. Essentially everything your development board does is done using machine code. By programming in machine code you are working at the most fundamental level of the board's operation.

If you are using a 'high level' language such as Python then ultimately all its operations have to be converted into machine code every time you run the program. This takes a finite amount of time – in human terms lightning fast – but still time. This conversion or interpretation process does therefore slow the operation of the software down. In fact, even the most efficient languages can be over 30 times slower than their machine code equivalent, and that's on a good day!

If you program in machine code, your programs will run much faster as there is no conversion being undertaken. There is a conversion process when you run the assembler, but once you have created the machine code you can execute this directly — it is a one-off process. You do not have to run the assembler every time. Once you are happy with your program you can save the machine code and use it directly. You can also keep the assembly language source program and use it again, or perhaps make changes at some later point.

Language Levels

Languages such as C, BASIC or Python are called high-level languages. High level languages are often easier to write as they have a more English-like syntax and also include commands that do a complex sequence of actions using one command that would otherwise take a long list of machine code instructions to perform. Machine code is a *low level* language as it is working amongst the 'nuts and bolts' of the computer: it spells out every technical step and detail and as a result is harder to understand.

This is the advantage of a high level language as opposed to a low-level one. That said, as you become more proficient in assembly language, there is nothing stopping you from building libraries of routines to do a specific task and just adding them to your programs as you write them. As you dig deeper into the world of the ARM, you will find that such libraries already exist out there in cyberspace.

By writing in assembler you can also transport your assembly language programs onto other computers or systems that use the ARM chip. You simply load the assembly language file into an assembler at the new destination, assemble it and run the machine code program.

The GNU GCC compiler is available for just about all flavours of microprocessor, so being familiar with the use of GCC will allow you to transport your new-found skill onto other systems should you so desire.

Provided you take full advantage of the ARM chip's facilities you can even transfer and run the machine code directly. This has exciting possibilities when you consider that just about every Smart Phone and Tablet device available these days utilises ARM chips!

Into Orbit

Just to underline the power of the ARM chip and indeed smart phones in general, a whole new generation of satellites called CubeSats, are being placed into orbit around the Earth.

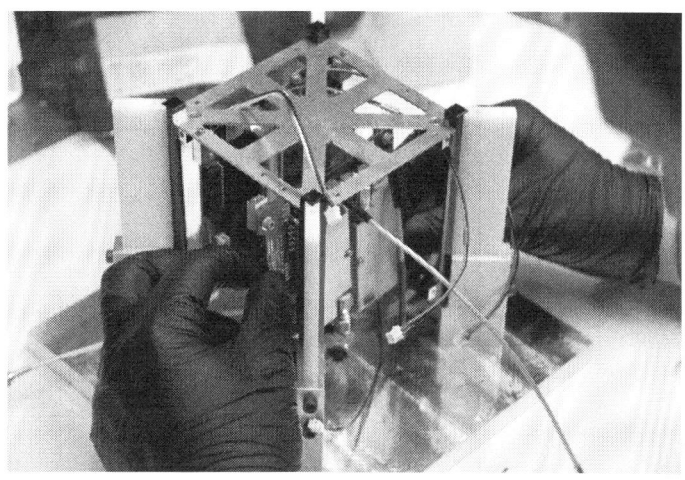

Figure 2a. A Cubesat under construction.

They are small (about 10cms square) and have very specific tasks. The Surrey Space Centre in the south of England has designed several CubeSats that are powered by Android phones. At around $100,000 each, these satellites are a fraction of the cost of previous machines. At the same time, the computing power of a single smart phone is perhaps tens of thousands of times more than could be found in the computers on all the Apollo moon missions put together! This is all at your disposal on your ARM-based development board.

The world is not all rosy! There are differences in the CPU releases. As with software, the ARM chip has gone through continual development and has had new version issues. But the base instruction set remains the same so 'porting' is not as hard as it might seem. It only becomes an issue if you are using more advanced features of the microprocessor. For this introductory guide, these changes are not relevant. Everything in these pages should be applicable to your ARM development board.

RISC and Instruction Sets

The R in ARM stands for RISC. This is an acronym for Reduced Instruction Set Computing. All CPUs operate using machine code and each of these machine code instructions or opcodes has a specific task. Together these instructions form the instruction set.

The philosophy behind RISC has been to create a small, highly-optimised set of instructions. This has several advantages — fewer instructions to learn for one — but obviously greater variation in their use. A lot of this will become apparent as we progress, and as you start to look at the instruction sets of other microprocessors.

Assembler Structure

Programming in any language, just like speaking in any language, requires us to follow a set of rules. These rules are defined by the structure and syntax of the language we are using. To program effectively, we need to know the syntax of the language, and the rules that structure the language.

The simplest way to design a program is simply to create a simple list of things you want it to do. It starts at the beginning and executes linearly until it gets to the end. In other words, each command is executed in turn until there are no more commands left. This works, but is very inefficient.

Program languages today are structured and allow you to build them as a set of independently executable procedures or subroutines. These subroutines are then called from a main program as and when they are required. The main program, therefore, controls the flow of control and also executes anything that may not be available as a subroutine. Programs are smaller and more manageable when they are created using subroutines. In a linear program concept, we would have probably had to repeat large sections of code several times to have achieved its goal.

Figure 2b illustrates some pseudo-program language to show how such a structured program might look.

In the example, program *commands* are listed in capitals – uppercase letters. Sections of subroutine code are given names – in lowercase – and are identified with a full-stop at their start. The entire flow of the program is contained in the six lines starting with '.main' and finishing with 'END'. Admittedly it is short, but it is clear to read, and you can understand just with a glance, what is happening. Each subroutine name is meaningful.

```
.main
     DO getkeyboardinput
     DO displayresult
     DO getkeyboardinput
     DO displayresult
END

.getkeyboardinput
     ; Instructions to read input from keyboard
RETURN

.displayresult
     ; print the result on the screen
RETURN
```

Figure 2b. Pseudo code illustrating a structured approach to programming.

In this example, the main program just calls subroutines. In a perfect world, this would always be our aim because it also makes it easier to test individual subroutines separately before they are included in the main program. This helps to ensure our program works as we put it together.

Error Of Your Ways

One big challenge you face when learning any new program is locating errors. This process is known as *debugging*. I guarantee (and I have proven this many times) you will first write a program that does not work as expected. You will look at it until the cows come home and not see the error of your ways. You will insist you are right and the computer is the issue. Then like a bolt out of the blue, you will see the error right there staring at you — and this does not always happen when you are sitting in front of the keyboard.

By building a subroutine and then testing it separately, ensuring that it works, you will know when you come to use it as part of your larger program that your hair is safe for another day (by the way, mine is all gone...).

3: First Time Out

In this chapter we'll go step-by-step through creating and running a machine code program. This program will not do anything spectacular. In fact you won't see anything other than the prompt symbol return, but the process contains every single step you need to know and implement when entering and running the other programs in this book.

If your operating system displays a 'Desktop' environment on the screen then select a 'Terminal' program. You might find this under a 'System' or 'Accessories' menu. This should open a window inside which will be a command prompt and cursor. This is the 'Command Line' interface.

If your screen does not show a 'Desktop' environment and only provides a command prompt and a cursor then you are already at the command line.

The Command Line

The term 'command line' is pretty self-explanatory. It is a line onto which you enter commands to be executed by your computers operating system. The command line starts where you see the cursor (this is often a small line or a square block which may be flashing). Anything you type in now, is expected to be a command, so the Operating System will attempt to execute it when you press the <Return> key. Try typing this:

```
dir
```

Type it exactly as it is above. When you press the <Return> key you will get a list of any directories or files that are stored in the current directory (in a Linux-based system). (I will omit the <Return> key detail from now on but please take it as read that when I suggest entering something at the keyboard-especially the command line, you should finish by pressing the <Return> key.)

Now type:

```
Dir
```

You will get a message similar to this:

33

```
Dir: command not found
```

This is an error message. The command line (in almost all instances) is case sensitive, thus:

```
dir
```

and:

```
Dir
```

are not identical in the system's eyes which are case sensitive. This is also the case with program file names so:

```
program1
```

and:

```
Program1
```

are seen as being different files. This can be a blessing but also a source of annoyance!

Command line convention is always to work in lowercase characters. File names may have a mixed bag of character cases as long as you are aware of the difference. It's best always to use lowercase characters so as a matter of course you should ensure that the Caps Lock light is always off!

Creating A Source File

To create a machine code program we need to go through a *write – assemble – link* process before we can end up with a file that can be executed. The first step is to write the assembly language program. Because this is the source from which everything flows, this file is called the *source file*. It is also signified by having an '.s' appended to its name. For example:

```
program1.s
```

The source files can be created in any suitable text editor. There are plenty of excellent ones around to be had at no cost, so it is worth spending time reading reviews and checking the options out for yourself. A very good text editor that comes with most installations is called *Vim*.

If you don't have Vim then you can install it from the command line on most Linux systems by typing the following command at the prompt:

```
sudo apt-get install vim
```

```
Cursor Movement Commands
Letter  Action
  ←     move left
  ↓     move down
  ↑     move up
  →     move right
  w     jump by to start of words
  W     jump by words (spaces separate words)
  e     jump to end of words
  E     jump to end of words (no punctuation)
  b     jump backward by words
  B     jump backward by words (no punctuation)
  0     (zero) start of line
  ^     first non-blank character of line
  $     end of line
  G     Go To command (ie, 5G goes to line 5)
Note: Prefix a cursor movement command with a number
to repeat it. For example, 4j moves down 4 lines.

Insert Mode - Inserting/Appending text
Letter  Action
  i     start insert mode at cursor
  I     insert at the beginning of the line
  a     append after the cursor
  A     append at the end of the line
  o     open (append) blank line below current line
        (no need to press return)
  O     open blank line above current line
  Esc   exit insert mode

Command mode
Letter  Action
  :w    write (save) file but do no exit
  :wq   write file (save) and quit Vim
  :Q    quit (fails if anything has changed)
  :Q!   quit and lose any changes made
  :set number - use line numbering
```

Figure 3a: Important Vim commands

Reply to any prompts – one might ask you about adding extra functionality. It should be safe to respond 'Y'. Installation takes a few minutes and the Vim website has a lot of useful hints and tips.

As you will spend a lot of your programming time developing assembler it makes sense to spend time getting to learn the ins and outs of Vim.

You can use any text editor you like and chances are you will have several to select from already installed as part of your chosen operating system - Nano is another popular editor. You are not restricted to Vim.

Because this version of Vim is used from the command line (there is a version called **gvim** and has a GUI – Graphical User Interface), the commands it uses are all key combinations typed at the keyboard. Figure 3a on the previous page lists some commands you need to know. The table is not exhaustive by any means and you will find a complete set on the Vim website.

If you wish to work from the Desktop then you can install the GUI version of Vim using:

```
sudo apt-get install vim-gnome
```

When you start Vim from the command line you can also specify the file name you want to create. If the file already exists it will load the file into the editor window and you can use it as you please. If the file does not exist then Vim creates a new blank file of that name for you. Type this at the command line prompt:

```
vim prog3a.s
```

Note that there is a space between 'vim' and 'prog3.s' and also note that there is an '.s' at the end of the name 'prog3' to denote a source file. Convention dictates that 's' represents an assembly language source file.

The screen will now be largely blank apart from a column of tildes running down the left hand edge and the file's name at the bottom – plus words to denote that it is a new file.

Press the 'i' key. Note how the text:

```
--INSERT --
```

has appeared at the bottom left of the screen. This signifies we are in *insert mode*. Press the <Esc> key. The '--INSERT--' has disappeared. We are now in Vim *command mode*.

Pressing 'i' and 'Esc' will become second nature to you. When insert mode is enabled it's a simple matter to key in the assembly language program, and

ARM A32 Assembly Language

edit until your heart is content. In command mode, key presses are interpreted as direct commands to Vim, giving it commands to perform.

The file name for this program, here prog3a.s, is not particularly special. I name all the programs in this book by chapter name. So prog3a.s signifies that the program source file is from Chapter 3 in the book. A file called 'prog4b.s' would signify the program is from Chapter 4 and listed as Program 4b and it is the second one in the chapter. This is just for your ease of reference. You can use whatever name you want.

Move back into insert mode (i) and note the flashing cursor at the top left of the screen. Anything you type now will appear where the cursor is. Enter the listing given below in Program 3a. Page 10 has a complete list of programs presented in this book.

Program 3a. A simple source file.

```
    .global   _start
_start:
    MOV R0, #65
    MOV R7, #1
    SWI 0
```

You can create the indent by pressing the <Tab> key. Other keys behave as you would expect them to, such as arrow keys to move around and the <Delete> and <Backspace> keys to move and edit text. Note that there is a space between the words 'global' and '_start'. The amount of indent you add, or even where you place indents do not really matter; they are simply to make it easier to read the program, and see where the different layers of the program are. We'll look at what the listing all means shortly.

Press <Esc> and then type:

    :wq

This will save your file and in turn also quit Vim. You will now be back at the command prompt. The source file is now complete!

Come to the Execution

The next step is to convert the source file into an executable file of machine code. We do this with two commands entered at the command line. Enter the following two lines, one after the other, at the command line prompt:

```
as -o prog3a.o prog3a.s
ld -o prog3a prog3a.o
```

These two lines first *assemble* and then *link* the assembly language program. On completion the machine code can be executed and the syntax for this is:

```
./<filename>
```

The './' Indicates the file is in the currently selected directory and the file to be run is named immediately afterward – no spaces. Thus:

```
./prog3a
```

When the prompt reappears, the machine code program has completed. Easy as that!

So we have just written, compiled and executed a machine code program – all the basic steps needed were involved in the process above. Of course, as the programs get more complex and we seek to make more use of the tools available in the Operating System then the process will itself become more involved, as we shall see.

Assembler Errors

If at any time during the above process you receive an error message – or any message at all, then look carefully at what you have typed. First look carefully at the assembly language program and then the individual lines of code to assemble, link and finally run the program. If there was an error and you found it, congratulations, you have just debugged your first assembly language program.

If you get an error message from the assembler (this will be after you have pressed <Return> at the end of the first line) it will normally provide you with a line number as a guide. Even if you do not know what the message means note the line number and then reload the source file back into Vim. For example:

```
prog3a.s:5: Error bad expression
```

would indicate there is an error in line 5 of the source file.

With a small file such as this you can count down the lines and locate the one containing the error. Vim also has a line numbering ability. When in Vim command mode type:

```
:set number
```

ARM A32 Assembly Language

Notice how line numbers appear down the left of the screen. These line numbers do not get saved as part of your source file – they are here as a guide only. Figure 3b shows all this in action using 'gvim'. Notice the line numbers down the side of the screen and also how Vim is operating in Insert mode. If you use gvim you will also notice how the various items of syntax are highlighted by different colours. This makes it easy to identify the different components of the listing which will describe below.

You can run gvim from the command line using:

```
gvim <filename>
```

So to create or edit Prog3a you might use:

```
gvim prog3a.s
```

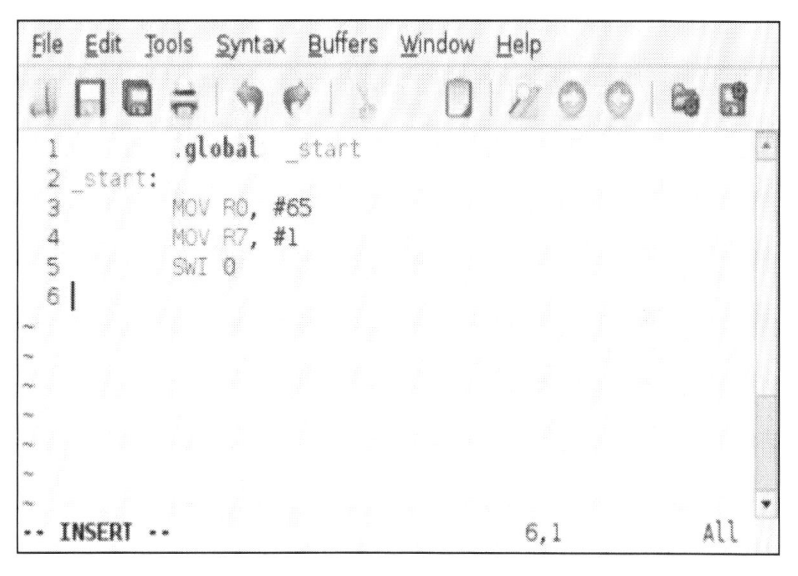

Figure 3b. How line numbers appear in gvim.

The Components

Let's now look at the above process and understand a bit more the anatomy of the source file and what we did to make it all come together. Look at prog3a.s again. It consists of just five lines.

Each assembler source file must have a starting point, and by default in the GCC assembler this is the label:

39

```
_start:
```

So the first line of this program defines '_start' as a global name and available to the whole program. We'll see later why making it a global name is important. The second line defines where '_start:' is in the program. Note the use of the ':' at the end to define it as a label. We've defined _start as global and now marked where _start is.

The next three lines are actually assembly language mnemonics, and two of the lines are similar, and use the MOV instruction. When the hash symbol is used in assembly language it is used to denote an immediate value. In other words, the value after the hash is the value to be used. In the first case, the value 65 is to be moved into Register 0. Here 'R' stands for register which is a special location in the ARM chip, more on which shortly. In the second line, the value 1 is moved into R7 or Register 7.

The final instruction is SWI 0. This is a special instruction that is used to call the Operating System itself. In this instance it is being used to exit the machine code program and return control back to the command line prompt (when the program is run of course).

Just a note on the character case used for the assembly language commands in these source files. I am using uppercase letters for mnemonics and registers, I could have just as easily used lower case – inside the source files the character case does not matter, thus:

```
MOV R0, #65
```

and:

```
mov r0, #65
```

are seen as being one and the same thing. I will be using uppercase characters during this book. This makes the commands easier to identify in the text of the book, and also makes the commands stand out from labels – which I will continue to place in lower case.

Run the program again:

```
./prog3a
```

At the prompt type:

```
echo $?
```

The following will be printed on the screen:

```
65
```

This was the immediate value loaded into R0. Try editing the 65 to another number, say 49. Now save, re-assemble and re-link. If you now type:

```
echo $?
```

You should get 49 printed out. The OS has a limited way of returning information from machine code programs and we'll look at this later.

If you look at prog3a.s again you can see that it consists of two clear sections. At the top (start), are some definitions, and in the lower half, the actual assembly language instructions. Assembly language source files always consist of a sequence of statements, one per line. Each statement has the following format, each part of which is optional:

```
<label:>   <instruction>      @ comment
```

All three of these components can be entered on the same line, or they can be split across lines. It's up to you. However, they must be in the order shown. For example an instruction cannot come before a label.

The 'comment' component is new. When the assembler encounters the '@' it ignores everything after it until the end of the line. This means you can use it to annotate your program. For example go back and edit prog3a.s by typing:

```
vim prog3a.s
```

The editor window will display your original source file. The cursor will be at the top of the file. Enter insert mode, create a new line and enter the following:

```
@ prog3a.s - a simple assembler file
```

The comment line, marked by the '@' at the start, is totally ignored by the compiler. Of course, it does make the source file bigger, but this does not affect the executable's performance in any way.

You can also add comments using '/*' and '*/' to enclose the comment at the start and end respectively. For example:

```
/* This comment will be ignored by the assembler */
```

Both methods are acceptable and it is simply a matter of taste — whichever you prefer.

To convert the source file into an executable file we needed two steps. The first was:

```
as -o prog3a.o prog3a.s
```

The 'as' at the start invokes the assembler program itself which expects several arguments after the command to define the files it will be working with and what it will be doing with them. The first of these is '-o' and this tells the assembler that we want to produce an object file, here called 'prog3a.o' from the source file 'prog3a.s' You can choose another name if you wish; the body of the name does not have to be the same, although making it the same makes it easier to keep track of your files. Of course, the suffix is *not* the same!

The second and final step is to 'link' the file object file and convert it into an executable file using the 'ld' command as follows:

```
ld -o prog3 prog3.o
```

You can think of linking as the final bit of binding that makes the machine code work. We will look more at what it does in a later chapter. What it produces is an executable file (called an elf file) from the .o (object) file created in the assembly process. It is this ld command that uses the _start: label to define where the program is to be run from. (This may sound crazy, but sometimes the start point of a file may not be at the very front of it, as we shall see!)

Lack of _start

You can learn a lot about the workings of the GCC assembler and linker simply by experimenting. What do you think would happen if we omitted the _start: label from the source file?

Open the prog3a.s file in Vim and delete the line '_start:' thereby erasing the label.

Exit Vim and then assemble the program:

```
as -o prog3a.o prog3a.s
```

and now link the program:

```
ld -o prog3a prog3a.o
```

The following error message (or similar) will be produced:

```
ld: warning: cannot find entry symbol _start; defaulting to 00008054
```

The error message is clear enough. Because it can't find a pointer to where the program starts, the linker is assuming that the program start point is right at the beginning, and the location of this in memory is at the address

00008054. This is a safety net, but not a fail-safe. Always use the _start: in your files to define the start of execution. This program will run perfectly well — others might not and probably won't!

Linking Files

The letters ld stand for link dynamic and the linking command is capable of linking or daisy- chaining several files together into one long executable program. In such cases only one '_start:' label should be defined across all these files, as there should be only the one start point, and this defines it. This is easy to demonstrate using our sample program.

Create a new file in Vim and call it:

```
part1.s
```

In this file enter the listing shown below as Program 3b:

Program 3b. Part 1 of the source file.

```
/* part1.s file             */
    .global _start

_start:
    MOV R0, #65
    BAL _part2
```

Save the file. Now create a new file called:

```
part2.s
```

and it should contain these lines in the listing below as Program 3c:

Program 3c. Part 2 of the source file.

```
/* part2.s file             */

    .global _part2
_part2:
    MOV R7, #1
    SWI 0
```

Save and exit this. We have written two source files that we will now compile and link to create a single file. At the end of the part1.s file we added a new instruction:

```
BAL _part2
```

BAL means branch always, and here branch always to the point in the program marked with the label 'part2:' In the second file we have defined a global variable called part2 and also marked the point where part2 begins. Because we have used the global definition, the location of the address made known by the global definition will be available to all the program parts.

The next step is to compile both new source files:

```
as -o part1.o part1.s
as -o part2.o part2.s
```

Now the labels must be identified and linked using the linker thus:

```
ld -o allparts part1.o part2.o
```

Here the linker will create an executable file called 'allparts' from the files part1.o and part2.o. You can try running the file with:

```
./allparts
```

The order of part1.o and part2.o could have been swapped — it would not have mattered as the linker resolves such issues. The key here is that each source file is independently written, created but then joined (we might say tethered) together by linking. If you tried to link just one file on its own, you would get an error message because when linking each part references the other. So in this case the linker is also a safety check.

What this small demonstration shows is that if you start to think carefully about your source files, you can start to develop a library of files that you can dip into each time you need a particular function. If you think back to the last chapter and the concept of a pseudo-program, this could be created using such functions. We'll look at function creation later on.

Tidying Up

If you catalogue the root directory by typing;

```
dir
```

you will see that amongst other things there are three prog3 files as follows:

```
prog3a.s              the source file
prog3a.o              the object file
prog3a                the executable file
```

Ultimately you only need the source file as you can create your executable file from this at any time. At the very least you can get rid of the object file using the rm command (rm=remove):

```
rm prog3a.o
```

To keep things tidy it is worth creating a separate directory for all your assembler files, and you can do this using the mkdir command. To create a directory called aal (arm assembly language) use:

```
mkdir aal
```

Now you can make that directory your current directory by typing:

```
cd  aal
```

Notice that the command line prompt has been extended to include:

```
/aal $
```

Anything you now create or do will be done so in the aal directory. To move back up to the root directory type:

```
cd
```

Note how the prompt on the command line always reflects where you currently 'are' within the hierarchy of the filing system.

A Comment On Comments

Not everyone will agree, but I think it is imperative you comment your assembly language programs. What you write today will be fresh in your mind, but if you need to upgrade or adapt it later you will almost certainly be struggling to remember exactly what each segment does, and another programmer looking at or trying to improve your work will be completely at sea. To my mind commenting – that is good commenting – is an essential part of writing assembly language programs. All assemblers allow you to place comments in your source file. Comments do not make the final machine code file any longer or any slower in execution. The only overhead is that they affect the size of your source program.

So comments are a good thing but don't comment for comment's sake. If every line of your assembly language program had a comment it would

45

become ungainly and would detract from the important comments. For example, look at this simple line and comment relative to the ADD instruction:

```
ADD R0, R1, R2          @   R0=R1+R2
```

The comment here is really pointless from a program documentation perspective, as we already know – or we should know – from the program line itself what the operation does. What would be relevant here is detailing the significance of the values stored at locations R1 and R2. This might be a better comment then:

```
ADD R0, R1, R2          @ Balance of act1 + act2
```

If you break your assembly program into segments using the format shown in Chapter 1, then for a lot of the time a pertinent comment or two at the start of the section is often also enough. Some things to keep in mind as guidelines:

- Comment all key points in your program.
- Use plain English; don't invent shorthand that someone (including you later!) may not understand.
- If it is worth commenting, then comment properly.
- Make comments neat, readable and consistent.
- Comment all definitions

If you keep these key points in mind you shouldn't go wrong, and I mention them at the start so you'll hopefully take the point and get into good habits that will last a programming lifetime.

If you are planning to write a lot of machine code, you might want to consider documenting your files externally, creating a database or perhaps a workbook where you keep their details.

4: Bits of a RISC Machine

There are 10 types of people in the world – those that understand binary notation and those that don't.

If that statement leaves you confused then don't worry. After reading this section of the book you'll 'get' the joke. If you have already had a smile at it then you're well on your way to racing through this section. What I will say at the onset though is that a thorough understanding of the way binary notation is presented and how it can be manipulated is absolutely fundamental to effective, efficient machine code programming.

When you create machine code programs you are working at the most basic level of the computer. There is nothing below it. In the opening chapters we touched on binary and hexadecimal numbers. Hex numbers are actually a compact way of writing numbers which in binary would be long strings of 1s and 0s. Because of its design as a reduced instruction set computer, the ARM can do many different things using a base set of instructions, and does so by getting the absolute maximum meaning out of every single one of these 1s and 0s. To understand fully how a RISC machine works we need to understand how binary and hex are constructed and how they are utilised by the ARM chip.

To recap from the opening chapters: The instructions the ARM CPU operates with consist of sequences of numbers. Each number represents either an instruction (opcode) or data (operand) for the machine code to execute or manipulate. Internally these numbers are represented as binary numbers. A binary number is simply a number constructed of 1s or 0s. Binary is important as internally these 1s and 0s are represented as 'on' or 'off' conditions (electronically usually +3.3V and 0V) within the microprocessor, and as an assembly language programmer we will often want to know the condition of individual binary digits or bits.

Opcodes and operands are built by combining sets of eight bits, which are collectively termed a byte. Convention dictates the bits in these bytes are numbered as illustrated in Figure 4a.

The number of the bit increases from right to left, but this is not as odd as it may first seem.

ARM A32 Assembly Language

Consider the decimal number 2934, we read this as two thousand, nine hundred and thirty four. The highest numerical value, two thousand is on the left, while the lowest, four, is on the right. We can see from this that the position of the digit in the number is very important as it will affect its weight.

| 7 | 6 | 5 | 4 | 3 | 2 | 1 | 0 |

Figure 4a. Numbering of the bits in a byte.

The second row of Figure 4b introduces a new numerical representation. Each base value is suffixed with a small number or power, which corresponds to its overall position in the number. Thus, 10^3 is 10 x 10 x 10 = 1000. The number in our example consists of two thousands plus nine hundreds plus three tens and four units.

Value	1000s	100s	10s	1s
Representation	10^3	10^2	10^1	10^0
Digit	2	9	3	4

Figure 4b. Decimal weights of ordinary numbers.

In binary representation, the weight of each bit is calculated by raising the base value, two, to the bit position (see table below). For example, bit number 7 (b7) has a notational representation of 2^7 which expands to: 2 x 2 x 2 x 2 x 2 x 2 x 2= 128. The weight or value of each bit is shown in Figure 4c.

Bit Number	b7	b6	b5	b4	b3	b2	b1	b0
Representation	2^7	2^6	2^5	2^4	2^3	2^2	2^1	2^0
Weight	128	64	32	16	8	4	2	1

Figure 4c. The binary weights of numbers.

Binary to Decimal

As it is possible to calculate the weight of individual bits, it is a simple matter to convert binary numbers into decimal. The two rules for conversion are:

1. If the bit is set, add its weight
2. If the bit is clear, ignore its weight

Let's try an example and convert the binary number 10101010 into its equivalent decimal value.

Bit	Weight	Value
1	128	128
0	64	0
1	32	32
0	16	0
1	8	8
0	4	0
1	2	2
0	1	0

Figure 4d. Converting binary numbers to decimal numbers.

In Figure 4d, we add the value column to get 170. Therefore, 10101010 binary is 170 decimal (128+0+32+0+8+0+2+0). Similarly, the binary value 11101110 represents 238 in decimal as shown in Figure 4e.

Bit	Weight	Value
1	128	128
1	64	64
1	32	32
0	16	0
1	8	8
1	4	4
1	2	2
0	1	0

Figure 4e. Converting binary numbers to decimal numbers.

Decimal to Binary

To convert a decimal number into a binary number, the procedure is reversed — each binary weight is, in turn, subtracted. If the subtraction is possible, a 1 is placed into the binary column, and the remainder carried down to the next row. If the subtraction is not possible, a 0 is placed in the binary column, and the number moved down to the next row. For example, the decimal number 141 is converted into binary as shown in Figure 4f.

Decimal	Weight	Remainder	Binary
141	128	13	1
13	64	13	0
13	32	13	0
13	16	13	0
13	8	5	1
5	4	1	1
1	2	1	0
1	1	0	1

Figure 4f. Converting a decimal number to its binary equivalent.

Therefore, 141 decimal is 10001101 binary.

Binary to Hex

Although binary notation is probably as close as we can come to representing the way numbers are stored within the computer they are rather unwieldy to deal with. And row after row of 1s and 0s simply get lost as your eyes start to rebel and make funny patterns. When dealing with binary numbers we more commonly use an alternative form to represent them – hexadecimal or 'hex' for short. Hexadecimal numbers are numbers to the base of 16. This at first sight may seem singularly awkward; however, it really isn't and presents many advantages.

Base 16 requires sixteen different characters to represent all possible digits in a hex number. To produce them, the numbers 0 to 9 are retained and then we use the letters A, B, C, D, E, F to represent values from 10 to 15. The binary and decimal values for each hex number are shown in Figure 4g. If you have followed the previous section on binary numbers something interesting may stand out when you look at Figure 4g.

Notice how four bits of a binary number can be represented in one hex number. Thus, a full byte (8 binary bits) can be depicted with just two hex characters. Using decimal notation a byte would require three characters. Hex is a very compact and easy way of representing binary.

To convert a binary number into hex, the byte must be separated into two sets of four bits, termed nibbles, and the corresponding hex value of each nibble extracted from the table above:

Convert 01101001 to hex:

```
0110 = 6
1001 = 9
```

The answer is 69.

Decimal	Hex	Binary
0	0	0000
1	1	0001
2	2	0010
3	3	0011
4	4	0100
5	5	0101
6	6	0110
7	7	0111
8	8	1000
9	9	1001
10	A	1010
11	B	1011
12	C	1100
13	D	1101
14	E	1110
15	F	1111

Figure 4g. Decimal, hexadecimal and binary numbers.

Because it is not always apparent whether a number is hex or decimal (69 could be decimal), hex numbers are usually preceded by a unique symbol such as 0x (which is the notation used in this book):

```
0x69
```

By reversing the process hex numbers can be converted into binary.

Hex to Decimal and Back

To transform a hex number into decimal, the decimal weight of each digit should be summed,

Convert 0x31A to decimal:

    3 has a value of $3 \times 16^2 = 3 \times 16 * 16 \quad = 768$

    1 has a value of $1 \times 16^1 = 1 \times 16 \quad = 16$

    A has a value of $1 \times 16^0 = 10 \times 1 \quad = 10$

Add these together to give 794 decimal.

Converting decimal to hex is a bit more involved and requires the number to be repeatedly divided by 16 until a value less than 16 is obtained. This hex value is noted, and the remainder carried forward for further division. This process is continued until the remainder itself is less than 16.

Example: convert 4072 to hex:

    4072/16/16   =15   = F   Remainder: 4072-(15*16*16)=232

    232/16   =14 = E   Remainder: 232-(14*16)=8

    Remainder =8 = 8

Therefore, 4072 decimal is 0xFE8.

Both of these conversions are a little long winded, and you can probably see why it is so much easier to work in hex and forget about decimal equivalents. In truth, this is what you will get used to doing. Although it may seem alien at present, it will become second nature as you develop your assembly language expertise.

Binary Arithmetic

It is easy to add and subtract binary numbers. In fact, if you can count to two you will have no problems whatsoever. Although it is not vital to be able to add and subtract 1s and 0s 'by hand', this chapter introduces several concepts which are important, and will help you in your understanding of the next chapters and ultimately in programming the ARM.

Addition

There are just four simple straightforward rules when it comes to adding binary numbers. They are:

    0+0=0   [nought plus nought equals nought]

    1+0=1   [one plus nought equals one]

    0+1=1   [nought plus one equals one]

    1+1=0(1) [one plus one equals nought, carry one]

Note in the last rule, *one plus one equals nought, carry one*. The '1' in brackets is called a carry bit, and its function is to denote an overflow from one column to another, remember, 10 binary is 2 decimal (and thus the opening funny!). The binary carry bit is like the carry that may occur when adding two decimal numbers together whose result is greater than 9. For example, adding together 9+1 we obtain a result of 10 (ten), this was obtained by placing a zero in the units column and carrying the 'overflow' across to the next column to give: 9+1=10. Similarly, in binary addition when the result is greater than 1, we take the carry bit across to add to the next column (the twos column). Let's try to apply these principles to add the two 4-bit binary numbers, 0101 and 0100.

```
    0101      0x5
+   0100      0x4
=   1001      0x9
```

Going from right to left we have:

```
    1+0         =1
    0+0         =0
    1+1         =0(1)
    0+0+(1)     =1
```

In the example, a carry bit was generated in the third column, and this is carried to the fourth column where it is added to two nought's. Adding 8-bit numbers is accomplished in a similar manner:

```
    01010101    0x55
+   01110010    0x72
=   11000111    0xC7
```

If the eighth bit, also called the most significant bit, creates a carry then this can be carried over into a second byte. However, within the CPU of most chips there is another way to handle this using something called a *Carry flag*.

Subtraction

So far we have dealt exclusively with positive numbers, however, in the subtraction of binary numbers we need to be able to represent negative numbers as well. In binary subtraction though, a slightly different technique from everyday subtraction is used, in fact we don't really perform a subtraction at all – we add the negative value of the number to be subtracted. For example, instead of executing 4-3 (four minus three) we actually execute 4 + (-3) (four, plus minus three).

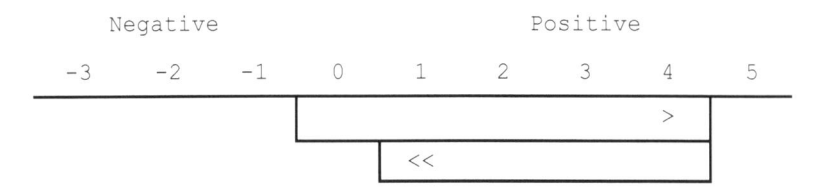

Figure 4h. Subtracting numbers.

We can use the scale in Figure 4h to perform the example 4+(-3). The starting point is zero. First move to point 4 (four points in a positive direction) signified by the '>' and add to this -3 (move three points in a negative direction). We are now positioned at point 1 which is indicated by '<<'. Try using this method to subtract 8 from 12, to get the principle clear in your mind.

To do this in binary we must first have a way of representing a negative number. We use a system known as signed binary. In signed binary, bit 7 is used to denote the sign of the number. Traditionally a '0' in bit 7 denotes a positive number and a '1' a negative number.

Sign Bit	Bits 0-6 give value	
1	0 0 0 0 0 0 1	

Figure 4i. Signed binary representation of -1

Figure 4i shows how a signed binary number is constructed. Here, bits 0-6 give the value, in this case '1'. The sign bit is set so denoting a negative value, so the value represented in signed binary is -1.

ARM A32 Assembly Language

Sign Bit	Bits 0-6 give value						
0	1	1	1	1	1	1	1

Figure 4j. Signed binary representation of 127.

The value 01111111 would represent 127 in signed binary. Bits 0-6 give 127, and the sign bit is clear. This is illustrated in Figure 4j.

Twos Complement Numbers

Just adjusting the value of bit 7 in this way is not an accurate way of representing negative numbers. Adding -1+1 should equal 0, but ordinary addition gives the result of 2 or -2 unless the operation takes special notice of the sign bit and performs a subtraction instead. Twos complement representation provides a means to encode negative numbers in ordinary binary, such that addition still works, without having to take the additional sign adjusting step.

So to convert a number into its negative counterpart, we must obtain its twos complement value. This is done by inverting each bit and then adding one. To represent -3 in binary, first write the binary for 3:

```
00000011
```

Now invert each bit by flipping its value so that 0s become 1s and 1s become 0s. This is known as its ones complement value:

```
11111100
```

Now add 1:

```
    11111100
+   00000001
=   11111101
```

Thus, the twos complement value of 3 = 1111101. Now apply this to the original sum 4+(-3):

```
      00000100    4
      11111101   -3
=(1)  00000001    1
```

We can see that the result is 1 as we would expect, but we have also generated a carry due to an overflow from bit 7 (this is the value in brackets above). This carry bit can be ignored for our purposes at present, though it does

55

have a certain importance as we shall see later on when performing subtraction in assembly language.

Here's another example that performs 32-16, or: 32+(-16).

32 in binary is:
```
00100000
```
16 in binary is:
```
00010000
```
The twos complement of 16 is:
```
11110000
```
Now add 32 and -16 together:
```
      00100000    32
+     11110000   -16
=(1)  00010000    16
```
Ignoring the carry, we have the result, 16.

We can see from these examples that, using the rules of binary addition, it is possible to add or subtract signed numbers. If the carry is ignored, the result including the sign is correct. Thus, it is also possible to add two negative values together and still obtain a correct (negative) result. Using twos complement signed binary let's perform -2+-2

2 in binary is:
```
00000010
```
The twos complement value of 2 is:
```
11111110
```
We can add this value twice to perform the addition:
```
      11111110    -2
+     11111110    -2
=(1)  11111100    -4
```
Ignoring the carry, the result is -4. You might like to confirm this by obtaining the twos complement value of -4 in the usual manner.

Understanding twos complement isn't strictly necessary for most applications, but it can come in handy as you can discover the value of every bit in a number whether it is positive or negative.

When Twos Don't Add Up

There are a couple of occasions when twos complement doesn't add up and interestingly they are based around representing 0 and -0.

The first is when dealing with 0 (zero). Working with 8-bits for simplicity, the twos complement of 00000000 is 10000000. When you drop the most significant bit, you get 00000000, which is what you started with. This works as it means that you can't really have -0 and also that you can only have one value of 0 in twos complement.

The second situation arises with 10000000 because it can have no negative value. The inverse of 10000000 is 01111111, and now add one to obtain its twos complement and you get 10000000, which is what you started with.

Because the most significant bit in 10000000 is 1, the value is negative. When you invert it and add 1, you get 10000000 which is the binary representation of 128 so the original value must, therefore represent -128.

This anomaly is the reason why integer and long value variables in many forms of BASIC are asymmetrical. In 8-bits, the values range from -128 to +127 and in 32-bits values range from -2,147,483,648 to +2,147,483,647.

5: ARM Arrangements

The ARM has a very specific and special design. This is known as its *architecture* because it refers to how it is constructed and how it looks from the user's point of view. Having an understanding of this architecture is an important aspect of learning to program the chip. You need to appreciate how it all fits together and how the various elements interact. In fact, the purpose of much of the machine code we will be creating is to gain access and manipulate the various parts in the ARM itself.

Because of its design as a reduced instruction set computer it can do many different things using a small set of instructions. The way it operates is determined by the mode. This means that once you have understood the basic layout of the ARM chip you only then have to understand what its different operational modes are. That said, for almost all situations that you encounter when learning to program the ARM you will be operating in User Mode.

Word Lengths

In the binary examples we looked at in the previous chapters we have used single byte values. Indeed all the early popular computers worked at this level with machine code. The design of these circuit boards reflected this in that they had eight data lines. In broad terms, these lines were directly related to the bits in the CPU byte. Thus, the CPU could move data around the board by toggling the logical condition on each line by making it a 1 or 0. It did this by changing the voltage on the line between 5V and 0V.

An ARM chip is more sophisticated and is able to operate much faster by manipulating larger amounts of information. It does this by being designed as a 32-bit CPU. This equates to four bytes of information. So instead of manipulating eight lines of information there are 32 lines. Collectively these four bytes are called a word. The ARM word length is said to be four bytes. However, it is more than capable of working with single byte lengths, and it does this just as effectively. Keep in mind that other computer systems may define their word length as something different, but on the ARM a word is four bytes or 32-bits in length.

The most significant bit (msb) in an ARM word is located at bit 31 (b31), and the carry bit in an operation is generated if there is an overflow out of bit 31. If a carry occurred from bit 7 it would be carried into bit 8, or from the first byte in the second byte.

Byte and Word Accessed Memory

The early ARM chips only used 26-bits of the 32-bits for addressing memory. This placed certain restrictions on the processor — and of course, the amount of memory it could directly address — so later ARM chips had full 32-bit addressing. The lowest address in this range is accessed by placing 0s on all the lines, and the highest by placing 1s on all the lines. The first is addressed as 0x00000000 and the highest as 0xFFFFFFFF (or 0x3FFFFFF on original ARM architectures with 26-bit address buses).

Memory control devices for the ARM allowed for 32-bit addressing. Figure 5a illustrates schematically how this memory is arranged as word blocks composed of four bytes a piece, so the minimum and maximum memory addresses are extended to 0x00000000 and 0xFFFFFFFF.

	bit31			bit 00
(Word 0)	b03	b02	b01	b00
(Word 1)	b07	b06	b05	b04
(Word 2)	b0B	b0A	b09	b08
(Word 3)	b0F	b0E	b0D	b0C

Figure 5a. Memory word blocks on the ARM.

The ARM 'sees' memory in these word blocks, but can also address the individual bytes within each word. From an operation point of view, all memory is arranged as word-aligned blocks. As illustrated in Figure 5a above the word-aligned blocks correspond with Word 00, Word 01, Word 02 and Word 03. Note how Word 00 has the byte numbers b00, b01, b02 and b03 within it. Word 01 has bytes b04, b05, b06 and b07 in it, and so on. Word blocks are aligned in this fashion and cannot be changed. You cannot have a word-aligned block that consists of the bytes, b02, b03, b04 and b05. (Note that 'b' here relates to byte and not bit, as used in some previous examples.)

Addresses in memory are given in hexadecimal numbers. A memory address that corresponds to the start of a word is called a word boundary and is said

ARM A32 Assembly Language

to be word-aligned. A memory address is word-aligned if it is directly divisible by 4. The following addresses are all word-aligned:

```
0x00009030
0x00009034
0x00009038
0x0000903C
```

Word-aligned addresses are especially significant to the ARM as they are fundamental to the way the ARM chip fetches and executes machine code.

For example, the address 0x00009032 is not word-aligned. You cannot store an ARM machine code instruction on a non-word-aligned address.

The GCC assembler provides a few tools to help ensure word boundaries are correctly managed. At the very least trying to assemble something that is not correctly addressed will generate an error message to that effect.

Registers

The ARM has several internal areas where it stores, tracks and processes information. This speeds things up and makes operations quicker as there is no external memory access required. These internal areas are called registers. In User Mode (the standard operating configuration) there are 16 registers available and each is capable of holding a word (four bytes) of information. You can think of these registers as single word locations within the ARM. Figure 5b shows how this comes together and includes an extra register – the Status Register.

As you can see from this programmer's model, registers R0-R12 are available for use at any time. R13-R15 have defined uses, however R13 and R14 are only used occasionally and are manipulated by just a few instructions. As the programmer will be controlling these operations we can also use them if required. Only R15 should not be used. I don't say cannot because it can be used, but you should be very clear what you are doing with it, and the complications it can bring if you do. ARM instructions can access R0 to R14 directly while most instructions can access R15.

As each register is one word wide, this means that each register is capable of holding an address location in a single register. In other words, a register can hold a number which points to a location anywhere in the memory map. A key function of registers is to hold such addresses.

The GCC Assembler allows us to use the labels listed above to refer to these registers, for example, R0 and R10.

Handwritten annotations at top:
1 LDR Load a Register
2 STR STORE TO MEMORY

ARM A32 Assembly Language

The LDR and STM instructions are used to LoaD a Register and STore to Memory in a variety of ways. Here are a couple of examples:

```
LDR R1,[R5] @ Load R1 with contents of loc in R5
STR R1,[R6] @ Store R1 content at location in R6
```

In both of these examples, one register is expected to have a memory address in it. The registers are enclosed in square brackets in these examples, and this tells the assembler that they contain addresses. This type of specification is called an addressing mode and the ARM instructions have several addressing modes. We'll examine these in later chapters.

Register Bank	
R0	Available
R1	Available
R2	Available
R3	Available
R4	Available
R5	Available
R6	Available
R7	Available
R8	Available
R9	Available
R10	Available
R11	Available
R12	Available
R13	Stack Pointer
R14	Link Register
R15	Program Counter
Current Program Status Register	

Figure 5b. The ARM User Mode register bank.

R15 - Program Counter

The Program Counter R15 is important. If you don't treat it with respect, your whole program can crash. Its function is simple — to keep track of where your program is in its execution of machine code. In fact, the PC

61

holds the address of the instruction to be fetched next. We will look at this register in more detail later in the book, Chapter 13 is dedicated to it.

The GCC Assembler allows you to use PC as well as R15 when referring to the Program Counter. For example:

```
MOV PC, R0 @ Move R0 into R15, Program Counter
```

The PC in the instruction will resolve correctly as if you had used R15.

Current Program Status Register

The CPSR – or just plain Status Register – is used to store significant information about the current program and the results of operations it is carrying out and has carried out. Specific bits within the register are used to denote pre-assigned conditions and whether they have occurred or not. So how does the information get flagged inside the one register? It does this by manipulating the values of individual bits within the register. Figure 5c illustrates how this is configured.

31	30	29	28	27...8	7	6	5	4	3	2	1	0
N	Z	C	V		I	F	T	MODE			

Figure 5c. The Status Register configuration.

The four most significant bits hold what are known as flags, called as such as they are designed to flag a certain condition when it happens. These flags are:

N = Negative flag

Z = Zero flag

C = Carry flag

V = Overflow flag

When an instruction executes, if it has been requested to, the ARM updates the Status Register. If the condition under test occurred then a 1 is placed in the relative flag bit: it is set. If the condition has not occurred then the flag bit is cleared: a 0 is placed in it.

Bits and Flags

If you followed the previous sections on binary arithmetic, then some of the concepts here will be familiar to you. We have discussed negative numbers, and the Negative flag is used to signify a potential negative number. The Carry flag represents the carry bit — we discussed this in 8-bit operations, but the addition of 32-bit numbers works the same. The Zero flag is straightforward; it's set if the result is zero. Finally, the Overflow flag is new, but simply sets if the operation caused a carry from bit 30 into the top bit at bit 31. If this occurred using signed numbers, it could indicate a negative result, even if a negative number was not generated. (Remember, bits start numbering at zero so, the 32nd bit is, in fact, numbered bit 31, or b31.)

For example, if the result of an operation gave 0, the Zero flag would be set. This is the Z bit in Figure 5c. If an addition instruction generated a carry bit then the Carry flag would be set to 1. If a carry was not generated then the Carry flag would be cleared (C=0).

Assembly language has mnemonics that allow us to test these Status Register flags and take action based on their condition. Here are a couple of examples:

```
BEQ zeroset         @ jump to zeroset if Z=1
BNE zeroclear       @ jump to zeroclear if Z=0
```

BEQ is Branch if EQual and this instruction will cause a 'jump' to a named label if the Zero flag is set. BNE is Branch if Not Equal and this instruction will cause a jump to the named label if the Zero flag is clear.

There are instructions to test the other flags in a like manner. The BNE instruction is often used to make sections of program repeat or loop a predetermined number of times until counter decrements to 0 at which point the Zero flag will be set.

In Figure 5c, the I and F bits are called interrupt disable bits and we'll discuss these in Chapter 27. The T bit is to do with processor states. At this point we'll assume that it is always set to 0 to signify ARM state (we will come back to this in Chapter 24). The final five bits are used to signify the processor mode — we will be largely using User Mode (but this will be touched on again in Chapter 26 as well).

Interestingly there is no one single instruction that you can use to gain access to the Status Register. You can only manipulate its contents at bit level by carrying out an associated action. Things like flags and program counters will become second nature to you as you begin to master assembly language.

Setting Flags

There are two instructions that have a direct effect on the Status Register flags. They are CMP (CoMPare) and CMN (CoMpare Negative). Of these the first is the more common in use and it takes the form:

```
CMP <Operand1> <Operand2>
```

CMP performs a notional subtraction, taking Operand2 away from Operand1. The physical result of the subtraction is ignored, but it updates the Status Register flags according to the outcome of the subtraction, which will be positive, zero or negative (there can never be a carry). If the result of the subtraction was 0 the Zero flag would be set.

Operand1 is always a register, but Operand2 can be a register or a specific or immediate value. For example:

```
CMP R0, R1    @ Compare R0 with R1. R0 minus R1
CMP R0, #1    @ Compare R0 with 1.  R0 minus 1
```

The CMP instruction is often used in combination with the BEQ instruction, to create a branch or jump to a new part of the program:

```
CMP R0, R1
BEQ zeroflagset
```

Here control will be transferred to the part of the program marked by the label 'zeroflagset' if the comparison between R0 and R1 is zero. If the branch does not take place then it would show that the result of the CMP was not zero – there would be no need to perform a BNE function. The code following could handle that situation.

CMP and CMN are the only instructions that directly affect the condition of the Status Register. By default, the rest of the ARM instruction set does not update the Status Register. For example, if R0 and R1 both contained 1 and we performed:

```
SUB R0, R0, R1
```

The result would be 0. But none of the flags in the Status Register would be altered in any way. They would retain the status they had before the instruction was performed.

S Suffix

SUBS (handwritten)

However, the ARM does provide a method of allowing an operation such as SUB to update the Status Register. This is done by using the Set suffix. All we have to do is append an 'S' to the end of the mnemonic we want to use to modify the flags:

```
SUBS R0, R0, R1
```

This subtracts the contents of R1 from R0, leaving the result in R0 and at the same time updating the flags in the Status Register.

This S suffix effectively allows you as the programmer to use one less set of instructions. Without it we might use:

```
SUB R0, R0, R1
CMP R0, #0
BEQ iszero
```

But with it we can remove the CMP line thus:

```
SUBS R0, R0, R1
BEQ iszero
```

The GCC Assembler recognises the use of the S suffix. It is also tolerant of spaces between the instruction and the S, so these two examples will assemble perfectly:

```
SUBS R0, R0, R1
SUB S R0, R0, R1
```

The Set suffix is one of many that exist, and we'll have a look at more of these in Chapter 9.

R14: The Link Register

The BEQ and BNE instructions illustrated above are examples of conditional branch instructions. These are absolute in that they offer a definitive change of direction — branch if equal or branch if negative. There is a second style of branch instructions known as Branch (B) and Branch with Link (BL). The BL implements a subroutine operation; effectively it jumps to somewhere else in the program and allows you to come back to the point right after the BL instruction in the program.

When the BL instruction has executed, this return address (the address of the next instruction) is loaded into R14, the Link Register (LR). When the subroutine has completed, the Link Register is copied into the Program

Counter, R15, and the program continues operating where it left off before the call was made.

One way of copying the Link Register into the Program Counter would be thus:

```
MOV R15, R14
```

The following is also accepted by the assembler:

```
MOV PC, LR
```

If you are familiar with any form of BASIC you can think of BEQ and BNE as being the equivalent of GOTO commands and BL as being a GOSUB command.

R13: Stack Pointer

The Stack Pointer contains an address that points to an area of memory which we can use to save information. This area of memory is called a stack and it has some special properties that we will look at in Chapter 17. It is worth noting at this point that you can have as many stacks as you like, you are not limited to just one.

6: Data Processing

In this chapter we'll look at some of the data processing instructions. This is the largest group of instructions, 18 in all, which manipulate information. They can be divided further into sub-groups as follows:

ADD, ADC, SUB, SBC, RSB, RSC

MOV, MVN, CMP, CMN

AND, ORR, EOR

BIC, TST, TEQ

MUL, MLA

The AND, ORR, EOR, BIC, TST and TEQ instructions are examined in the next chapter.

Each of these instructions expect information to be supplied to them in the following configuration:

```
<Instruction> <Dest>, <Operand1>, <Operand2>
```

Let's look at each field in more detail.

<Instruction>
This is the assembly language mnemonic to be assembled. It can be used in its raw form as listed above, or with the additions of suffixes, such as S.

<Dest>
This is the destination where the result is to be stored, and the destination is always an ARM Register, in the range R0-R15.

<Operand 1>
This is the first item of information to be manipulated and, again, will always be an ARM Register in the range R0-R15. Operand1 may be the same as the Destination register.

<Operand 2>
Operand2 has more flexibility than Operand1 in that it can be specified in three different ways. As with Operand1, it may be an ARM Register in the range R0-R15. It may also be a specified value or constant — a number for example. For a constant, the exact number to be used is quoted in the

assembler listing. The hash – '#' – is used to signify an immediate constant. Operand2 may also be what is called a shifted operand and we will look at this instance in Chapter 11 when we have looked at the arithmetic shifting of numbers.

Here are some examples of data processing instructions in use:

```
ADD R0, R1, R2         @ R0=R1+R2
ADDS R2, R3, #1        @ R2=R3+1 and set flags
MOV R7, #128           @ R7=128
```

Some instructions do not require both operands. For instance, the MOV instruction does not use Operand1; it only requires Operand2. The reason for Operand2 rather than Operand1 is that it is able to use a Register definition or a constant value (or shifted, as we shall see).

Arithmetic Instructions

In this section we'll look at the ADD and SUB commands in a little more detail, and we'll also start looking at what is happening in the registers themselves, including the Status Register and its flags.

Addition

There are two instructions that handle addition. They are ADD and ADC. The latter is ADd with Carry. They both take a similar form:

```
ADD (<suffix>) <dest>, <Operand1>, <Operand2>
ADC (<suffix>) <dest>, <Operand1>, <Operand2>
```

Here's some code that uses the ADDS instruction. This program clears R0, places 1 in R1 and sets all 32-bits of R2. This is the largest number we can store in a four-byte register. So what will happen if we were to run this program?

```
MOV R0, #0
MOV R1, #1
MOV R2, #0xFFFFFFFF
ADDS R0, R1, R2
```

On completion the registers will show:

```
R1:   0x00000001
R2:   0xFFFFFFFF
R0:   0x00000000
```

Nothing seems to have happened! The values have all been loaded, but no addition seems to have taken place as R0 still has 0 in it. In fact it has, but by adding the 1, we created a carry bit (remember the binary additions we did in the earlier chapters?). So if we were to look at the Status Register we would see:

```
NZCV
0110
```

If we had run this program using only ADD and not ADDS then the Carry flag would not have been updated and would merely reflect the condition they were in when they were last updated via an appropriate instruction. Of course, the Carry flag may have been set by a previous instruction, so we might have received a correct answer, but only by good fortune. The good fortune method is not an efficient way to program in any language. It pays to double check.

Program 6a shows how simply two numbers can be added together in machine code. Enter this in Vim using:

```
vim prog6a.s
```

Program 6a. Simple 32-bit addition.

```
/* Perform R0=R1+R2          */

    .global _start
_start:
    MOV R1, #50             @ Get 50 into R1
    MOV R2, #60             @ Get 60 into R2
    ADDS R0, R1, R2         @ Add the two, result in R0

    MOV R7, #1              @ exit through syscall
    SWI 0
```

You can assemble, link and run this using the following:

```
as -o prog6a.o prog6a.s
ld -o prog6a prog6a.o
./prog6a
```

Now print the result with:

```
echo $?
```

The result will be 110.

ARM A32 Assembly Language

(Remember, to be able to print a result from the machine code using bash, we need to ensure that the result is held in R0 and that the system exit SWI is used.)

Whenever we add two values, unless we are 100% sure that there will have been no carry, or the significance of that fact is not important to us, a check for the carry should always be made.

Program 6b below adds two 64-bit numbers. This relates to two words, so two registers are needed to hold the number, with one holding the low bytes and the other the high bytes. Because we have a potential carry situation from low-word to high-word when we add the two it is imperative we take the Carry flag into consideration. For this we need to use the ADC instruction.

The code assumes that the first number is in R2 and R3 and the second is in R4 and R5. The result is placed in R0 and R1. By convention, the lower register always holds the lower-half of the number:

Program 6b. 64-bit addition.

```
/* Add two 64-bit numbers together      */

    .global _start
_start:

    MOV R2, #0xFFFFFFFF     @ low half number 1
    MOV R3, #0x1            @ hi half number 1
    MOV R4, #0xFFFFFFFF     @ low half number 2
    MOV R5, #0xFF           @ hi half number 2
    ADDS R0, R2, R4         @ add low and set flags
    ADCS R1, R3, R5         @ add hi with carry

    MOV R7, #1              @ exit through syscall
    SWI 0
```

You can assemble, link and run this using the following:

```
as -o prog6b.o prog6b.s
ld -o prog6b prog6b.o
./prog6b
```

Now print the result with:

```
echo $?
```

The result will be 254. Why?

On completion, registers R0 and R1 will contain 0xFFFFFFFE and 0x101 respectively. So the result was:

0x101FFFFFFFE

In the first ADDS instruction, the addition caused the Carry flag to be set, and this was picked up in the ADCS operation. If we substitute the ADCS with another ADDS the result is:

0x100FFFFFFFE

In decimal terms the result is starker, out by 4,294,967,296!

You may be wondering why the ADCS instruction was not used in both parts of the addition. Generally if you set out doing any addition you would want to ensure the Carry flag is clear before starting. If not and you used ADCS and it was set from a previous operation you would get an erroneous result. Use of ADDS ensures that the carry is ignored but gets updated at the end of the addition.

In answer to the question earlier about why the echo command returned 254, this is 0xFE in hex, which is the least significant byte of the value stored in R0. So in reality the echo command does not return what is stored in R0 but what is in the least significant byte of R0.

How would you modify this segment to add two three-word values? The temptation might be to repeat the ADDS and ADCS sequence. This would be wrong. You should continue using the ADCS instruction until all the words have been added. You only use ADDS on the first word to define the Carry condition in the first instance. From then on it is ADCS.

If you are writing a program that does not produce the correct result and the values it is returning are wildly out, it is always worth checking that you have used the correct sequence of addition instructions. Chances are that is where the 'bug' sits.

If the three word numbers were held in R4, R5, R6 and R7, R8, R9 we could sum the result in R1, R2, R3 as follows:

```
ADDS R1, R4, R7 @ Add low words & check for carry
ADCS R2, R5, R8 @ Add middle words with carry
ADCS R3, R6, R9 @ Add high words with carry
```

It should go without saying that you need to check to see if the Carry flag is set as it is the most significant bit in your result.

Subtraction

While there are two instructions that deal with addition, there are four for subtraction.

```
SUB (<suffix>) <dest>, <Operand1>, <Operand2>
SBC (<suffix>) <dest>, <Operand1>, <Operand2>
RSB (<suffix>) <dest>, <Operand1>, <Operand2>
RSC (<suffix>) <dest>, <Operand1>, <Operand2>
```

You can see that there are complementary instructions to addition: a straightforward subtraction that ignores the flags and then one that takes into account the Carry flag (SBC). The second set of subtraction instructions works in an identical fashion, but uses the operands in the reverse order. For example:

```
SUB R0, R1, R2
```

subtracts the contents of R2 from R1 and puts the result in R0. However,

```
RSB R0, R1, R2
```

subtracts the contents of R1 from R2 and puts the result in R0. As with the previous examples the S suffix can be used with the instructions:

```
SUBS R0, R1, R2
```

If R0=0, R1=0xFF and R2=0xFE, the SUBS instruction is performing 0xFF-0xFE which is 255-254. The result should be 1, and this is indeed so. However on investigation the Status Register would show that the Carry flag has been set. Why?

If we change SUBS to RSB so that:

```
RSBS R0, R1, R2
```

Then by loading the same values into the registers the result in R0 is 0xFFFFFFFF and the Carry flag is clear! In subtraction, the Carry flag is used the 'wrong' way round so that if a borrow is required the flag is unset or clear. It acts like a NOT Carry flag! (A logical NOT is an operation which flips the value of each binary digit in a number – this is explained in Chapter 8.) This is useful when dealing with numbers over 32-bits and ensures the correct result. The result in this last instance also sets the Negative flag as 0xFFFFFFFF represents a negative value in signed numbers. The above example illustrates this perfectly and is because of the use of twos complement numbers.

When a section of code is not giving you the result you expect it always makes good sense to check the condition of the Status Register flags.

The two rules here to remember then are:

- If a borrow is generated, then the Carry flag is clear, C=0
- If a borrow is not generated, then the Carry flag is set, C=1

When we perform a multi-word subtraction, borrowing from one word means we need to subtract an extra one from the next word. However, as we have seen, a borrow results in the Carry flag being zero, not one as we would have liked. To compensate for this, the ARM actually inverts the Carry flag before using it in the SBC operation. This system can be extended to subtract operands which require any number of words to represent them — simply repeat the SBC instruction as many times as required.

You may be wondering why the ARM instruction set has reverse subtract instructions. Again, this ties in with the overall philosophy of speed. By being able to specify which operand is subtracted from which, we effectively remove the necessity of having to go through a data swapping process to get the operands in the right order.

Multiplication

The ARM has a couple of instructions that will perform 32-bit multiplication. The first of these, MUL provides a direct multiplication and takes the form:

```
MUL (<suffix>) <dest>, <Operand1>, <Operand2>
```

MUL is a bit different to instructions such as ADD and SUB in that it has certain restrictions on how its operands can be specified. The rules are:

Dest: Must be a register and cannot be the same as Operand1. R15 may not be used as the destination of a result.

Operand1: Must be a register and cannot be the destination register.

Operand2: Must be a register, and cannot be an immediate constant or shifted operation.

In summary, you can only use registers with MUL, cannot use R15 as the destination, and the destination register cannot be used as an operand. Here's an example:

```
MUL S R0,R4,R5   ; R0=R4*R5 and set status
```

Program 6c demonstrates MUL in action. Two numbers are placed in R1 and R2 and the multiplied result into R0.

ARM A32 Assembly Language

Program 6c. 32-bit multiplication.

```
/* multiply two numbers R0=R1*R2        */

    .global  _start
_start:

    MOV R1, #20             @ R1=20
    MOV R2, #5              @ R2=5
    MUL R0, R1, R2          @ R0=R1*R2

    MOV R7, #1              @ exit through syscall
    SWI 0
```

You can assemble, link and run this using the following:

```
as -o prog6c.o prog6c.s
ld -o prog6c prog6c.o
./prog6c
```

Now print the result with:

```
echo $?
```

MLA is MuLtiply with Accumulate. It differs from MUL in that it allows you to add the results of a multiplication to a total. In other words, you can accumulate values. The format of the command is:

```
MLA (<suffix>) <dest>, <Op1>, <Op2>, <sum>
```

The rules stipulated at the start of this section still apply here. There is an extra operand, <sum>, which must be specified as a register. For example:

```
MLA R0, R1, R2, R3   @ R0=(R1 * R2) + R3
```

The register specified by <sum> may be the same as the <destination> register, in which case the result of the multiplication will be accumulated in the destination register, thus:

```
MLA R0, R1, R2, R0 @ R0=(R1 * R2) + R0
```

Example: let's adapt Program 6c to use it, creating Program 6d.

Program 6d. Using MLA.

```
/* multiply two numbers with accumulate   */

     .global   _start
_start:

     MOV R1, #20            @ R1=20
     MOV R2, #5             @ R2=5
     MOV R3, #10            @ R3=10
     MLA R0, R1, R2, R3     @ R0=(R1*R2)+R3

     MOV R7, #1             @ exit through syscall
     SWI 0
```

You can assemble, link and run this using the following:

```
as -o prog6d.o prog6d.s
ld -o prog6d prog6d.o
./prog6d
```

Now print the result with:

```
echo $?
```

The result returned will always be 10 more than the product of the two values in R1 and R2. This is because the value 10 was seeded into R3.

The ARM does not provide a division instruction, so dividing two numbers either requires a little bit of ingenuity or must be done using a long-hand subtraction method. This along with some other multiplication instruction examples are provided in Chapter 12.

Move Instructions

There are two data move related instructions. MOV and MVN are used to load data into a register from another register or to load register with a specific value. The instructions do not have an Operand1 and take the form:

```
MOV (<suffix>) <dest>, <Operand2>
MVN (<suffix>) <dest>, <Operand2>
```

Here are a couple of examples:

```
MOV R0, R1            @ Copy contents of R1 to R0
MOV R5, #0xFF         @ Place 255 in R5
```

If you look at the comment in the first example above, although the instruction is MOVe it is important to realise that the contents of the source register are unchanged. A copy is being made. Also, unless the S Flag is used the Status Register is not changed either. This instruction:

```
MOVS R0, #0
```

would load zero into R0 and set the Zero flag at the same time.

MVN is MoVe Negative. The value being moved is negated in the process. This means that 1s become 0s and 0s become 1s. This is to allow negative intermediate numbers to be moved into registers. You may need to pop back to Chapter 4 and revisit the section of twos complement numbers for a quick refresher on negative numbers in binary. Under the twos complement scheme the number 'n' is represented as:

```
(NOT n) + 1
```

To make MVN use a value of:

```
-n
```

we in fact specify:

```
n-1
```

So, to move -10 into a register we must place 9 into it, as:

```
(NOT 9)+1
```

At bit level this is (and we'll look at logical operations in the next chapter):

```
9:         0000 1001
NOT 9:     1111 0110
Add 1      0000 0001
Result     1111 0111
```

Here are some examples of the instruction:

```
MVN R0, #9            @ Move -10 into R0
MVN R0, #0            @ Move -1 into R0
MVN R1, R2            @ Move (Not R2) into R1
```

We will learn in Chapter 11 that there are restrictions on the value of contents being loaded into registers as immediate values. Put simply, there are some numbers you just can't use directly, and it is not because they are too big, for instance. This can also be an issue when dealing with addresses in memory. We'll examine why, and how to circumvent the problem in due course.

Compare Instructions

We encountered these instructions when we looked at the Status Register and flags in the previous chapter. They are two comparison instructions and they have the format:

```
CMP <Operand1>, <Operand2> ; Set flags of <Op1>-<Op2>
CMN <Operand1>, <Operand2> ; Set flags of <Op1>+<Op2>
```

These instructions do not move information or change the contents of any of the registers. What they do is update the Status Register flags. Since the purpose of CMP and CMN is to directly affect the Status Register flags there is no reason to use the S suffix. CMP works by subtracting Operand2 from Operand1 and discarding the result.

```
CMP R3, #0
```

The example above would only set the Zero flag if R3 itself contained 0, otherwise the Zero flag would be clear.

```
CMP R3, #128
```

Here, the Zero flag would be set if R3 contained 128. If R3 held anything less than 128 the Negative flag would be set. What would cause the Overflow flag to be set? If you are ever in any doubt what the result would be, then simply check it out longhand by doing the binary arithmetic!

CMN is the negative version of compare. This is good if you want to control a loop that has to decrement past zero. In such case you could use:

```
CMN R0, #1              @ Compare R0 with -1
```

The idea is the same behind the reason of the MVN instruction. It allows comparisons to be made with small negative immediate constants which could not be represented otherwise.

An important point to be wary of is that, in MVN, the logical NOT of Operand2 is taken. In CMN it is the negative of the operand that is used. Thus to compare R0 with minus 3 we would write:

```
CMN R0, #3
```

The ARM will automatically form the negative of Operand2 and then make the comparison.

As with CMP, the purpose of CMN is to affect the Status Register flags and the S suffix is not applicable.

7: Ins and Outs

When we use computers with installed operating systems we take an awful lot for granted. We type commands at the keyboard, the commands get actioned and we get feedback from the action of the command by way of what is displayed on the screen. There's a lot going on.

Consider a couple of what would seem relatively simple tasks, typing a command at the keyboard and then getting a response on the screen. These are things we do every time we interact with the command line. The question is then, how do we get input from the keyboard and write information to the screen in our machine code programs?

In the strictest sense you do it yourself. But this involves a good deal of knowledge about the various hardware components of the board you are using, because to write a message to the screen for instance, we have to know exactly where the hardware that drives the screen is located within the computer's memory and, in turn how to write the information to it. Equally, to read input from the keyboard we need to understand how the keyboard is mapped and how to read that matrix to identify which keys are being pressed.

Reading and writing to the hardware to do this is often termed *bare metal programming*, because you are 'talking' to the computer hardware directly. Whilst this in itself is potentially exciting, it is rather an advanced topic and not necessarily the domain of a beginner's book such as this. Equally though, unless you are specifically bare metal programming as an exercise there is absolutely no need for you to do it. Instead we can access the operating systems own routines to do these and several other bare metal style tasks!

SWI and SVR Commands

The SWI instruction allows you as the programmer to gain access to pre-defined routines or libraries of them. SWI stands for SoftWare Interrupt because when it is encountered it causes the flow of your program to be stopped and handed over to the appropriate routine. Once the SWI instruction has been completed, control is handed back to the calling program. The SWI command is also often referred to as SVR or Supervisor call as this is a mode of operation that is invoked in the ARM chip when it is called (quite advanced so no more on this until Chapter 27).

You will probably recall that we have used a SWI command in all our machine code programs so far. We used it to exit the code back to the command line prompt. This use took the form:

```
MOV R7, #1
SWI 0
```

All SWI calls are executed with SWI 0 (or SVR 0 can be used instead). The actual function to be performed is determined by the number held in register R7. This is called the Syscall number. In addition other registers may also have to be seeded with information, so a call to SWI 0 often requires some setting up before being executed. For example, to write a string of characters to the screen requires three other items of specific information to be placed in specific registers.

To use these SWI calls effectively then, we need to know what they do, what information has to be passed and in what registers. Information may be passed back by the SWI call and in such cases we need to know what information and in what registers.

A detailed description of all the SWI calls is not provided, but the more common and useful ones are described at various points in this book. No official list of Syscalls exist but there are various sources on independent websites, including the book support pages at www.brucesmith.info.

Let's look at what are arguably the two most important Syscalls at this stage in our learning —, printing to the screen and reading from the keyboard. These are important as we will use them a lot in the program examples in the rest of this book. In using them we will need to look at a few more features of the GCC assembler and also use a few assembly language techniques that we won't learn about in great detail until later (this is one of those occasions I mentioned at the start of this book!)

(If you are programming in A32 then SVR should be used. However, it is likely that any compiler you are using will compile SWI correctly.)

Writing to the Screen

To write a sequence or string of ASCII characters to the screen we need to use the 'write' function. This is Syscall 4. The parameters required by Syscall 4 are as follows:

```
R0= determines output stream, 1 for the monitor
R1= the address of the string of characters
R2= the number of characters to be written
R7= the number of the Syscall, so R7=4
```

The GCC assembler provides us with a facility to store an ASCII string of characters within the body of our machine code file (ASCII stands for American Standard Code for Information Interchange, and an ASCII code is a simple number used to represent the character. Appendix A contains the ASCII character table). Program 7a illustrates the setup for this. The key here is to note the GCC assembler directive .ascii on the last line. This directive informs the assembler that an ASCII string of characters follows (the string that is enclosed by quotes). You will also notice '\n' at the end of the string. The backslash character signifies that the next character is a 'control-character' and as such has an action. Here \n means generate a new line. A label is used to mark the start of the location of the string — in this case I have been original and called it string.

Program 7a. Using Syscall 4 to write a string to the screen.

```
/* How to use Syscall 4 to write a string */

        .global _start
_start:

        MOV R7, #4          @ Syscall number
        MOV R0, #1          @ Stdout is monitor
        MOV R2, #19         @ string is 19 chars long
        LDR R1,=string      @ string located at string:
        SWI 0

_exit:
                            @ exit syscall
        MOV R7, #1
        SWI 0
```

```
.data
string:
.ascii "Hello World String\n"
```

Create, assemble and link the program and try it out for yourself. The instruction:

```
LDR R1,=string
```

Can be read as:

```
LoaD Register R1 with the address of the label string:
```

When Syscall 4 is made it identifies the output stream, the 1 passed in R0 defines the standard output device, the monitor. It then extracts the length of the string from R2 and prints that number of characters out starting at the address held in R1. The number of characters held in R2 includes spaces and any punctuation. The final '\n' character is regarded as one character. Try altering the value loaded into R2 and see if you can predict the result. For example, try:

```
MOV R2, #11
```

You will also note that there is an extra directive in the program:

```
.data
```

This informs the assembler that what follows should be treated as a subsection containing data, as opposed to assembly language code.

The data subsection could have been placed at the start of the source file had we desired. We would then have needed to signify the start of the assembly language subsection by using a directive thus:

```
.text
```

How you structure your files is entirely a matter of which way you wish to work. I tend to prefer placing data and data areas at the end of programs to avoid any alignment problems. You may recall from Chapter 5 that ARM machine code must be assembled on four-byte word boundaries, in other words start at an address that is directly divisible by four. This may not be the case if a string of 10 characters was used, for example. This can be corrected by using an align directive, something discussed later.

ARM A32 Assembly Language

Reading From the Keyboard

To read a sequence (or string) of ASCII letters from the keyboard we need to use the 'read' function. This is Syscall 3. The parameters required by Syscall 3 are similar to that for Syscall 4 and are as follows:

```
R0= input stream, this is 0 for the keyboard
R1= the address of the buffer for the string of
    read characters to be placed
R2= the number of characters to be read
R7= the number of the Syscall, so R7=3
```

You can use Program 7a as a basis for the new program. You can make a copy of it at the command line by using the cp command as follows:

```
cp prog7a.s prog7b.s
```

Now edit the source file to contain the new _read routine. The entire program is given below.

Program 7b. Using Syscall 3 to write a string to the screen.

```
/* How to use Syscall 3 to read from keyboard */

    .global _start
_start:
_read:
                        @ read syscall
    MOV R7, #3          @ Syscall number
    MOV R0, #0          @ Stdin is keyboard
    MOV R2, #5          @ read first 5 characters
    LDR R1,=string      @ string placed at string:
    SWI 0

_write:
                        @ write syscall
    MOV R7, #4          @ Syscall number
    MOV R0, #1          @ Stdout is monitor
    MOV R2, #19         @ string is 19 chars long
    LDR R1,=string      @ string located at string:
    SWI 0
```

82

```
_exit:
    @ exit syscall
    MOV R7, #1
    SWI 0

.data
string:
.ascii "Hello World String\n"
```

Here we still need to define the ASCII string. I have purposely left the original text in place so that you can see what results from using the function. The label string: points to what is effectively a buffer or place for the input read from the keyboard to be placed. We could have just defined an empty string, for example:

```
.ascii "                              "
```

(There are other ways to reserve empty spaces in memory in programs and these will be discussed later.)

R2 is now used to hold the number of characters we want from the read process. It is important to remember that this is not the number of characters that can be typed. When _read: is executed it accepts all input at the keyboard until the Return key is pressed. Only at that stage does it extract the first x characters as defined by the value in R2. Thus typing:

```
123456789
```

At the keyboard would see 12345 (the first five characters) placed into the string buffer. The rest would then be dealt with as though a bash command had been entered and therefore generates an error message. (Bash being the name given to the command line shell you have been working within.) The _write: routine would print out the newly created string which in this instance would be:

```
12345 World String
```

12345 having overwritten 'Hello'.

Run the program again and just type in:

```
12
```

Now the string printed is:

```
12
lo World String
```

Note here that a newline has been generated. This is because the Return was inserted into the string buffer as well. We will come back to Syscalls in Chapter 18.

Makefiles

So far as we have developed new source files and we have assembled and linked the files by typing the commands at the command line. This is repetitive but made easier by the bash history feature. By using the up and down arrow keys you can scroll through previously entered commands, which in turn can be edited.

GNU also provide a very clever piece of software called *Make*. This is a tool that allows programmers to control the generation of executable files from a single controlling file. When you see a piece of software installing on your computer then chances are that the whole process is bring controlled by a Make file. Make is a very sophisticated tool and you can find out more about it from the GNU website.

Program 7c is a source file (although you save it without the '.s' suffix) that will automate the whole assemble and link process for you. It is extremely flexible and can deal with most possibilities.

Program 7c. Automate assembly and linking with makefiles.

```
PROGRAMS = prog7a prog7b

# If we've supplied a goal on the command line
# then set it as the list of programs we
# already know about.
ifneq ($(MAKECMDGOALS),)
    ifneq ($(MAKECMDGOALS),clean)
        PROGRAMS = $(MAKECMDGOALS)
    endif
endif

# The default rule if none specified on the
# command line
all: $(PROGRAMS)

# Make knows how to compile .s files, so all
```

```
# we need to do is link them.
$(PROGRAMS): % : %.o
        ld -o $@ $<

clean:
        rm -f *.o $(PROGRAMS)
```

Use Vim to create the above file and call it 'makefile' - there is no need to append an '.s' to the filename, just plain 'makefile'.

Also, note that the two lines:

```
ld -o $@ $<
```

and

```
rm -f *.o $(PROGRAMS)
```

must be indented by a single tab character for make to work.

If you type:

```
make
```

The variable PROGRAMS (first line in Makefile) is being used to hold the names of the source files to be assembled and linked. You can enter one or as many names as you like here, with each being separated by a space. And effectively that is all you need to do. The rest of the program will assemble each of the files, create the object files and then link them.

In listing above this would mean the source files called prog7a and prog7b. Note that the .s is implied and you do not need to include it.

```
PROGRAMS = prog7a prog7b
```

This implies the makefile exists in the same directory as your source code files! If the source files have previously been assembled and linked they will be overwritten provided the target files are older than their associated source files. If the files do not exist then make will complain with an error message.

If you want to assemble and link a specific file or files then you can enter the file name after the commands thus:

```
make prog6a
```

This would assemble and link the source file called 'prog6a' provided it existed.

It makes good sense to include a makefile in each and any directory where you create and save your source files that need to be assembled and linked.

eax and Others

Virtually all Linux Syscall documentation you come across will have been written with non-ARM machines in mind and specifically i386 processor systems. As such you will find yourself dealing with an alien set of register references. Figure 7a lists these registers and their ARM equivalents which should assist you in breaking down what needs to go where.

i386	ARM	Function
eax	R7	Syscall Number
ebx	R0	Argument 1
ecx	R1	Argument 2
edx	R2	Argument 3
esi	R3	Argument 4
edi	R4	Argument 5
eax (on Return)	R0	Return value or error number

Figure 7a. 386 v ARM registers for Syscalls.

8: Logical Operations

In computer terms, logic can be defined as the non-arithmetic operations performed that involve yes/no decisions. The ARM has three different logical operators, being AND, OR and EOR. In each case, the logical operation is performed between the corresponding bits of two separate numbers. As such there can only ever be two possibilities: yes or no, that is on or off. In binary these are represented as 1 and 0. These instructions are useful when it comes to identifying or forcing the state of individual bits in sets of data.

Each operation has the four distinct set of rules.

Logical AND

The four rules for AND are:

    0 AND 0 = 0   [Nought and nought is nought]

    1 AND 0 = 0   [One and nought is nought]

    0 AND 1 = 0   [Nought and one is nought]

    1 AND 1 = 1   [One and one are one]

The AND operation will only generate a 1 if both of the corresponding bits being tested are 1. If a 0 exists in either of the corresponding bits being ANDed, the resulting bit will always be 0.

Example:

```
        1010
        0011
   AND= 0010
```

In the result only bit 1 is set; the other bits are all clear because in each case one of the corresponding bits being tested contains a 0. It is important to remember in these logical operations that there is no carry bit. The tests are done on the individual bits, and we are not adding or subtracting numbers here.

The main use of the AND operation is to 'mask' or 'preserve' bits. To preserve the low nibble (bits 0 to 3) of a byte and completely clear the high nibble (bits 4 to 7) so that the byte is set to all zeros we use the AND operator, masking the original with the value 00001111. If the byte we wished to preserve was the low nibble of say, 10101100, we would logically AND it thus:

```
       10101100
       00001111
 AND=  00001100
```

Here, the top four bits are cleared and the lower four bits have had their condition preserved.

Logical OR

The four rules for OR are:

0 OR 0 = 0 [Nought or nought is nought]

1 OR 0 = 1 [One or nought is one]

0 OR 1 = 1 [Nought or one is one]

1 OR 1 = 1 [One or one are one]

Here the OR operation will result in a 1 if either or both the bits contain a 1. A 0 will only occur if neither of the bits contains a 1.

Example:

```
       1010
       0011
 OR=   1011
```

Here, only bit 2 of the result is clear, the other bits are all set as each pair of tested bits contains at least one 1.

One common use of the OR operation is to ensure that a certain bit (or bits) is set — this is sometimes called 'forcing bits'. For example, if you wish to force bit 0 and bit 7 you would need to OR the byte with 10000001.

```
       00110110
       10000001
 OR=   10110111
```

The initial bits are preserved, but bit 0 and bit 7 are 'forced' to 1. These two bits were originally clear.

Logical EOR

Like AND and OR, the Exclusive OR operation has the four rules:

    0 EOR 0 = 0   [Nought eor nought is nought]

    1 EOR 0 = 1   [One eor nought is one]

    0 EOR 1 = 1   [Nought eor one is one]

    1 EOR 1 = 0   [One eor one is nought]

This operation sets the bit if it is Exclusive to the OR operation. If both bits being tested are identical, 0 and 0 or 1 and 1 then the result is 0. A 1 will only result if both bits being tested are not alike.

```
         0101
         1110
    EOR= 1011
```

This instruction is often used to complement, or invert, a number. This is done by EORing the other byte with 11111111.

```
         00110110
         11111111
    EOR= 11001001
```

Compare the result with the first byte — they are completely opposite: 1s where 0s were and 0s where 1s were.

The MVN instruction introduced in the last chapter effectively performs an EOR on Operand2 to obtain its result.

Logical Instructions

The process remains the same no matter how wide the data is. The examples above are one byte wide. The operation is the same in four bytes (or as many bytes as you need). The operation takes place on the directly associated bits, and no Status Register flags are involved or taken into account, and there is no Carry involved at any point.

AND, ORR and EOR are the instructions used to perform the three main logical operations. The form is the same as previous commands:

```
AND (<suffix>) <dest>, <Operand1>, <Operand2>
ORR (<suffix>) <dest>, <Operand1>, <Operand2>
EOR (<suffix>) <dest>, <Operand1>, <Operand2>
```

ARM A32 Assembly Language

In these cases Operand1 is a register, while Operand2 can be a register or immediate value. The operations themselves do not set the Status Register flags but can be forced to do so with the suffix.

Here are a few examples of these instructions in use:

```
AND R0, R0, #1          @ preserve state of b0 in R0
ORR R1, R1, #2          @ ensure bit 1 in R1 is set
EOR R2, R2, #255        @ invert bits in low byte R2
```

Here's a short segment of code to look at:

```
MOV R0, #129
AND R0, R0, #1
ORR R0, R0, #2
EOR R0, R0, #255
```

The result is 0xFC and here's how we arrived at it (dealing with just the low byte of the word):

```
Load 129            10000001
AND with 1          00000001
Result              00000001
OR with 2           00000010
Result              00000011
EOR with 255        11111111
Result              11111100
```

Here are some practical examples of the ORR and EOR commands in use, with a typical application of each of them.

ORR to Convert Character Case

Program 8a illustrates how the ORR instruction converts a character from upper case to lower case. For example, it will take 'A' and convert it to 'a'. The ASCII value of the letter 'A' is 0x41 (65) and the ASCII character for 'a' is 0x61 (97). By comparing the hex numbers, we can see that the difference between 'A' and 'a' is 0x20.

As both these characters mark the start of their section of the alphabet, it follows that the difference between an uppercase and lowercase value would always be the same. Figure 8a shows how this pans out in 8 bits of binary.

I hope you can see that we can achieve this difference by using the ORR instruction with the binary value 0010 0000 or 0x20 (32).

ARM A32 Assembly Language

ASCII	Value	Binary
A	0x41	0100 0001
a	0x61	0110 0001
Difference	0x20	0010 0000

Figure 8a. Binary difference between ASCII 'A' and 'a'.

Program 8a. Converting character case.

```
/* Using ORR to toggle a character case */

        .global _start
_start:
_read:                          @ read syscall
        MOV R7, #3              @ Syscall number
        MOV R0, #0              @ Stdin is keyboard
        MOV R2, #1              @ read one character only
        LDR R1,=string          @ string at string:
        SWI 0

_togglecase:
        LDR R1, =string         @ address of char
        LDR R0, [R1]            @ load it into R0
        ORR R0, R0, #0x20       @ change case
        STR R0, [R1]            @ write char back

_write:                         @ write syscall
        MOV R7, #4              @ Syscall number
        MOV R0, #1              @ Stdout is monitor
        MOV R2, #1              @ string is 1 char long
        LDR R1,=string          @ string at start:
        SWI 0

_exit:
        @ exit syscall
        MOV R7, #1
        SWI 0
```

```
.data
string:    .ascii " "
```

Program 8a above does this in the section called _togglecase. The routine starts by reading a character at the keyboard (press a capital letter and press Return) which it then stores at 'string'. The togglecase routine then places the address of the stored character into R1 and uses a technique called indirect addressing to load the character into R0. (This form of addressing is discussed in Chapter 15.) The value in R0 is then masked with 0x20 or %100000 and the indirect addressing technique used to store the modified contents of R0 back at the address held in R1.

Note that no check is made here to ensure that the character entered is in the range A-Z. How would you adjust the program to convert a lower case character into an uppercase one?

Bit Clear with BIC

The BIC instruction sets or clears individual bits in registers or memory locations. Its format is:

```
BIC (<suffix>) <dest>, <Operand1>, <Operand2>
```

The Bit Clear instruction forces individual bits in a value to zero.

```
BIC R0, R0, #%1111   @ clear low 4 bits of R0.
```

If R0 held 0xFFFFFFFF then the example above would clear the lowest four bits to leave 0xFFFFFFF0.

```
R0:           11111111 11111111 11111111 11111111
BIC #0xF      00000000 00000000 00000000 00001111
Result is:    11111111 11111111 11111111 11110000
```

The BIC command performs an AND NOT operation on Operand1 with Operand2.

Flag Tests

There are two instructions whose sole purpose is to test the status of bits within a word. Like CMP there is no destination for the result, which is reflected directly in the Status Register (therefore the S suffix is not required). The two instructions are TeSt BiTs (TST) and Test EQuivalence (TEQ). The formats are:

```
TST   <Operand1>, <Operand2>
TEQ   <Operand1>, <Operand2>
```

TST is a test bits instruction, and Operand2 contains a mask to test on Operand1. It performs the equivalent of a logical AND with the outcome updating the Zero flag:

```
TST R0, #128  @ Test if b7 of R0 is set
```

TEQ is test equivalence and uses an EOR process. It is a handy way of seeing if particular bits in registers are the same.

```
TEQ R0, R1  @ Test if R0 & R1 are same
```

You can use suffixes with both the TST and TEQ instructions so that you can test for other conditions as well as that of the Zero flag (detailed in the next chapter).

Program 8b uses the TST instruction to convert a number entered at the keyboard into a binary number, which is displayed on the screen. The number to be printed is placed in R6. There are a few things of interest in this program which we have not encountered yet and they will be explained in detail in the following chapters. Note how the program is broken into clearly named sections.

Program 8b. Printing a number as a binary string.

```
/**** Convert number to binary for printing ****/

      .global _start
_start:
      MOV R6, #251            @ Number to print in R6
      MOV R10, #1             @ set up mask
      MOV R9, R10, LSL #31
      LDR R1, = string        @ Point R1 to string

_bits:
      TST R6, R9              @ TST no, mask
      BEQ _print0
      MOV R8, R6              @ MOV preserve, no
      MOV R0, #49             @ ASCII '1'
      STR R0, [R1]            @ store 1 in string
      BL _write               @ write to screen
      MOV R6, R8              @ MOV no, preserve
      BAL _noprint1
```

```
_print0:
    MOV R8, R6              @ MOV preserve, no
    MOV R0, #48             @ ASCII '0'
    STR R0, [R1]            @ store 0 in string
    BL _write
    MOV R6, R8              @ MOV no, preserve

_noprint1:
    MOVS R9, R9, LSR #1     @ shuffle mask bits
    BNE _bits

_exit:
    MOV R7, #1
    SWI 0

_write:
    MOV R0, #1
    MOV R2, #1
    MOV R7, #4
    SWI 0
    MOV PC, LR

.data
string:
    .ascii " "
```

The mnemonic LSL is used in a couple of places. This stands for logical shift left and is used to shuffle the bits in a word along — left in this case. In the program it is used as follows:

```
MOV R10, #1
MOV R9, R10, LSL #31
```

Here #1 is being placed into R10, and shifted 31 times to the left and the result placed in R9, so that only the most significant bit in the register is set. This is because we cannot load the value we require directly into the register due to constraints that are imposed on use of immediate values (more on this shortly).

So the line does this:

```
MOV R10, #1:    00000000 00000000 00000000 00000001
LSL #31         10000000 00000000 00000000 00000000
                <<   shift left by 31 places     <<
```

We now enter the 'bits' loop.

```
_bits:
        TST R6, R9              @ TST no, mask
        BEQ _print0
        MOV R8, R6              @ MOV preserve, no
        MOV R0, #49             @ ASCII '1'
        STR R0, [R1]            @ store 1 in string
        BL _write               @ write to screen
        MOV R6, R8              @ MOV no, preserve
        BAL _noprint1

_print0:
        MOV R8, R6              @ MOV preserve, no
        MOV R0, #48             @ ASCII '0'
        STR R0, [R1]            @ store 0 in string
        BL _write
        MOV R6, R8              @ MOV no, preserve
```

R6 holds the number ('no'). We know that the most significant bit of the mask is set (b31) and TST tests to see if it is in 'number' too. If it is, then the following BEQ will occur and a 1 will be printed. If not a 0 will be printed. Note that in each case we preserve the value in R6 as this is our number to be tested, and we need to use R0 to print the 1 or 0 in the _write routine. The ASCII value for '1' (49) or '0' (48) is placed in R0 and stored in string: in either case. (This should be familiar to you now as we have used this technique a few times in previous programs.)

In either case we now use the _write routine as a subroutine, This means that we only need to assemble it once in the program. The program uses:

```
        BL _write
```

to jump to the routine. BL stands for Branch with Link. When this occurs the address of the next instruction is saved and the program jumps to the named label. If you look at the end of the _write routine it ends with:

```
MOV PC, LR
```

This effectively puts the saved address (in the Link Register) back into the Program Counter (PC) thereby causing program flow to restart after the original BL instruction. These concepts are dealt with in some detail in Chapter 10, so all will become clearer then.

In the _noprint1 section we use a logical shift right to shift the mask bit along one place to the right, making sure that we update the Status Register flags using the S suffix. The program continues to loop, and print 1s and 0s as required, until all 32-bits have been tested.

```
_noprint1:
    MOVS R9, R9, LSR #1 @shuffle mask bits
    BNE _bits
```

This program is a great visual aid to see how bit patterns develop. When you run it, work your way up through the numbers from '1' to see the output. You should recognise the binary very clearly now.

You could have a go at improving this program by requesting a number to be entered at the keyboard and then displaying its value in binary. To do that though you would need to be able to convert an ASCII value into hex so you can store it in a register. A technique to do this is given later in the book.

Syscall Registers

One of the downsides of using Syscalls is that you need to be careful which registers you use in your own programs. As we have seen, several registers need to be seeded with information for use by the Syscall. So if you plan to use Syscalls, do plan your register usage from the start. It could save a lot of editing later.

9: Conditional Execution

The concept of the suffix was introduced in an earlier chapter to illustrate how S can be appended onto instructions to force the Status Register flags to be updated. For example:

```
ADDS R0, R1, R2  @ R0=R1+R2 & set flags
```

Without the S, using the instruction in its basic form, ADD has no effect on the Status flags. S is just one of many suffixes that exist and can be used in a similar way to expand the functionality of just about every operation in the ARM's instruction set.

Almost all ARM instructions can have a suffix applied to them that will only allow the command to be executed if the condition under test is true. If the condition is not met, then the instruction will be ignored. The suffix CS denotes Carry Set, so the instruction it is appended to will only be executed if the Carry flag is set at the time the ARM reaches the instruction. In programming terms, it gives you the ability to make every instruction a conditional operation.

The list of condition codes is extensive and is given in Figure 9a overleaf.

The GCC Assembler understands these conditional codes, and you can append them for use in your programs by adding the letters onto the end of the mnemonic. You can leave spaces between the mnemonic and the condition code as well if this aids readability. These two examples are both acceptable:

```
MOVCS R0, R1
MOV CS R0, R1
```

In these examples:

```
MOV CS R0, R1
```

the contents of R1 will only be moved into R0 if the Carry flag is set. Likewise:

```
MOV CC  R0,R1
```

will only move the contents of R1 into R0 if the Carry flag is clear.

Some suffixes alter more than one flag and in such instances these operations might require certain combinations of flags to be at a combination of set or clear. Thus, we can conveniently group the condition codes into two sets: those that are performed on the result of a single Status Register flag and those that are executed based on the result in two or more flags.

Suffix	Meaning
EQ	Equal
NE	Not Equal
VS	Overflow Set
VC	Overflow Clear
AL	Always
NV	Never
HI	Higher
LS	Lower than or Same
PL	Plus clear
MI	Minus set
CS/HS	Carry Set
CC/LO	Carry Clear
GE	Greater than or Equal
LT	Less Than
GT	Greater Than
LE	Less than or Equal

Figure 9a. ARM assembly language condition codes.

Condition codes act on the status of the flags; they do not set the Status Register flags in the first instance. You will need to use a compare instruction or an associated S suffix instruction to do that. A good understanding of binary and arithmetic operations will aid your understanding of how instructions are affected by these condition flags.

There are examples of the use of conditional execution throughout the programs in this book. Indeed, Chapter 10 also includes a perfect illustration of how the use of conditional codes can greatly reduce the size of your program.

Single Flag Condition Codes

Falling into this group are the suffixes:

```
EQ, NE, VS, VC, MI, PL, CC, AL, NV
```

These conditional flags are provided in complementary pairs. In the first set below, EQ and NE, they both act on the condition of the Zero flag — one when it is set, and the other when it is clear. If you are testing one condition and it is false then you do not have to test for the alternative condition as, by definition, it has to be true as it can only be one of two states.

EQ: Equal Z=1

Instructions that use the EQ suffix will only be executed if the Zero flag is set. This will be the case if the previous operation resulted in zero. Subtracting two numbers of the same value will result in zero and accordingly set the Zero flag. A compare operation would set the Zero flag if the two values being compared were the same. If the result of any operation is not zero then the Zero flag is clear (Z=0).

Example:

```
MOVS  R0, R1    @ Move R1 into R0 and set flags
MOVEQ R0, #1    @ If 0, load R0 with 1
```

Here, the Zero flag will be set if 0 is moved into R0 from R1. If this is the case then the next instruction will be executed, and 1 will be written into R0. The instruction will not be executed if the Zero flag is clear, thereby proving that the value in R0 was non-zero.

NE: Not Equal Z=0

Instructions that use the NE suffix will only be executed if the Zero flag is clear. This will be the case if the previous operation did not result in zero. Subtracting two unlike numbers will clear the Zero flag. A compare operation would set the Zero flag if the two values being compared were the same. If the result of any operation is not zero then the Zero flag is clear (Z=0).

Example:

```
CMP   R5, R6       @ Compare R6 with R5 & set flags
ADDNE R5, R5, R6   @ If not zero R5+R6 and put in R5
```

Here, the CMP instruction is used to compare contents of R5 and R6. If they are not the same (so that the Zero flag will be clear, Z=0) then R5 and R6 are summed and the result placed in R5.

VS: Overflow Set V=1
Instructions that use the VS suffix will only be executed if the Overflow flag is set. This flag is set as a result of an arithmetic operation producing a result which cannot be represented in the 32-bit destination register, creating a potential overflow situation. In cases like this, data placed in the destination register may not have value and thus require corrective action by the programmer. Examples of this can be found in Chapter 5.

VC: Overflow Clear V=0
Instructions that use the VC suffix will only be executed if the Overflow flag is clear. This flag is set as a result of an arithmetic operation producing a result which cannot be represented in the 32-bit destination register. That is, an overflow situation. If the flag is clear then no such overflow has occurred. This condition tests for the no overflow condition.

MI: Minus Set N=1
Instructions that use the MI suffix will only be executed if the Negative flag is set. This flag is set as a result of an arithmetic operation producing a result which is less than zero. This would occur if a large number is subtracted from a smaller one. Logical operations may also set the Negative flag if they cause bit 31 of the destination register to be set.

Example:
```
SUBS R1, R1, #1      @ Subtract 1 from R1 & set flags
ADDMI R0,R0, #15     @ If negative add 0x0F to R0
```

Here, the SUB instruction takes 1 from the contents of R1, and the S suffix is used to update the flags as the result is stored into R1. The ADD in the next line only takes place if the N flag is set and if so 15 is added to R0.

PL: Plus Clear N=0
Instructions that use the PL suffix will only be executed if the Negative flag is clear. This flag is cleared if the result of an arithmetic operation is positive, one that is greater than or equal to zero. Note that the EQ suffix will test for zero only, the PL instruction tests for a plus or non-negative result. It is important to note the subtle difference here.

Example:
```
SUBS  R1, R1, #1     @ Sub 1 from R1 & set flags
ADDMI R0, R0, #15    @ If neg add 0x0F to R0
ADDPL R0, R0, #255   @ If pos add 0xFF to R0
```

This example illustrates how compilations of conditional instructions act on alternative results. This builds on the MI example above: if the result was a positive number then 255 is added to the contents of R0 and stored there. As you can see, only one of these instructions can take place and both act on the result of the SUBS instruction. Because neither of the following ADD instructions has used the S suffix, the status flags will not have changed since the CMP instruction.

CS: Carry Set C=1 (HS: Higher or Same C=1)

Instructions that use the CS or HS suffix will only be executed if the Carry flag is set. This flag is set if an arithmetic operation creates a result bigger than 32-bits. The Carry flag can be thought of as the 33rd bit. The Carry flag can also be set by using an ARM shift operation which is examined in Chapter 11.

Example:

```
ADDS  R0,R0,#255 @ Add 0xFF to R0 and save in R0
ADDCS R1,R1,#15  @ Carry set add 0x0F to R1 save in R1
```

CC: Carry Clear C=0 (LO: Lower C=0)

Instructions that use the CC or LO suffix will only be executed if the Carry flag is clear. This flag is clear if an arithmetic operation creates a result that fits inside 32-bits. The Carry flag is also affected by using any ARM shift operation which are examined in Chapter 11

Example:

```
ADDS  R0,R0,#255  @ Add 0xFF to R0 and save in R0.
ADDCS R1,R1,#15   @ If C=1 add 0x0F to R1 save in R1
ADDCC R1,R1,#128  @ If C=0 add 0xF0 to R1 save in R1
```

As with the PL example, this has a definitive action that is controlled by the status of the Carry flag.

AL: Always

Instructions that use the AL suffix are always executed and do not rely on the setting of any of the Status Register flags. Given that instructions will always execute if there are no conditional suffixes, the AL suffix is the default setting for all appropriate instructions.

Example:

```
ADDAL, R0,R1,R2 @  Add R1 and R2 and save in R0
ADD R0,R1,R2    @  Add R1 and R2 and save in R0
```

These two instructions have exactly the same result.

A common use of the AL suffix is with the Branch instruction to provide a three letter mnemonic and greater clarity:

```
B start     @ Branch to start
BAL start   @ Branch to start
```

NV: Never

Instructions that use the NV suffix are never executed and do not rely on the setting of any of the status flags. This suffix is included for completeness. It can be used as a way of making space within a program as the instruction will be assembled. This space might be used to store data or modify the program itself at some point, and in more advanced cases, allow for pipelining effects (Chapter 12).

Example:

```
ADDNV R0, R1, R2     @ Never perform the addition.
```

Multiple Flag Condition Code

Falling into this group are six suffixes:

```
HI, LS, GE, LT, GT, LE.
```

These condition codes are executed based on the condition of two or more Status Register flags. They are most often used after a CMP or CMN instruction. This set of condition codes is further divided into two groups: those that operate on unsigned numbers (HI and LS) and those that operate on signed numbers (GE, LT, GT and LE).

HI: Higher (Unsigned) C=1 AND Z=0

Instructions that use the HI suffix will only be executed if the Carry flag is set and the Zero flag is clear. This happens in a comparison if Operand1 is greater than Operand2.

Example:

```
CMP R10, R5      @ Compare Registers R10 and R5
MOVHI R10,#0     @ If R10 > R5 then set R10 to zero.
```

It is important to remember that this condition assumes the two values being compared are unsigned and that negative values are not being used in a twos complement format.

LS: Lower Than or Same (Unsigned) C=0 OR Z=1

Instructions that use the LS suffix will only be executed if the Carry flag is clear and the Zero flag is set. This happens in a comparison if Operand1 is less than Operand2. Again it is important to remember that the condition assumes that the two numbers being compared are unsigned.

Example:
```
CMP    R10, R5        @ Compare Registers R10 and R5
ADDLS  R10,R10,#1     @ If R10<=R5 add 1 & save in R10
```

GE: Greater or Equal (Signed) N=1,V=1 OR N=0, V=0

This instruction will execute if both the Negative flag and Overflow flag are set or clear. In other words, the flags must be in the same condition. This happens when two values are being compared: Operand1 was greater than or equal to, Operand2.

Example:
```
CMP R5, R6          @ Compare contents of R5 and R6
ADDGE R5,R5,#255 @ If R5 >= R6 then add 0xFF to R5
```

It is important to remember that this condition assumes the two values being compared are signed quantities.

LT: Less Than (Signed) N=1,V=0 OR N=0, V=1

This instruction will execute if the Negative and Overflow flags are different. This happens if Operand1 is less than Operand2. Again the condition assumes that the two values being compared are signed quantities.

Example:
```
CMP R5, #255        @ Compare contents of R5 with 0xFF
SUBLT R5,R5,R6      @ If R5<0xFF subtract R6 from R5
                    @ save result in R5
```

GT: Greater Than (Signed) (N=1,V=1 OR N=0, V=0) AND Z=0

This instruction will execute if the result is a positive number and not zero. Here, Operand1 is greater than Operand2 and the assumption is that signed numbers are used. So both Negative flag, and Overflow flag must be set or the Negative, Zero and Overflow flags must all be clear.

Example:
```
CMP R5, R6          @ Compare R5 with R6
ADDGT  R0,R1,R2     @ If R5>R6 add R1+R2 & put in R0
```

LE: Less Than or Equal To (Signed)   N=1,V=0 OR N=0, V=1 OR Z=1

This instruction will execute if the result between two values, Operand1 is less than or equal to Operand2. The assumption is that signed numbers are used. To achieve this both Negative flag and Overflow flag must be different, or the Zero flag must be set.

Example:

```
CMP   R5, #10        @   Does R5 contain 0x0A?
SUBLE  R0,R1,R2      @   If R5<=0x0A subtract R2 from R1
                         and put result in R0
```

Mixing the S Suffix

The S suffix can be mixed with conditional suffixes. This ensures that the result of whatever action taking place will also update the Status Register flags. We saw in a couple of earlier examples how preserving the status of flags after an action means that it is possible to act on the outcome of a conditional execution for both results. This assumes that the Status Register flags are not updated. If you want the Status Register flags to be updated by the conditional operation then the S suffix should be added after the conditions suffix thus:

```
ADDCSS R0, R1, R2    @ Add R2 to R1 if Carry=1.
                     @ Update Status flags as well.
```

It is important to place the S suffix after the condition code otherwise the assembler will miss it if it is placed before. Trying to assemble:

```
ADDSCS R0, R1, R2
```

gives an error.

10: Branch and Compare

This chapter has a more detailed look at the use of the compare instructions and the most economical ways of using them.

Branch Instructions

The branch instruction allows the execution of a program to be transferred to somewhere else in the machine code, and continued from there. The two common variants have the format:

```
B (<suffix>) <label>
BL (<suffix>) <label>
```

In effect, combined with conditional flags, there is a branch for every occasion. Although it is perfectly possible to use the B instruction on its own, it is preferable to use the ALways suffix so as not to lose the 'B' in a bigger program:

```
BAL start
```

But this is also perfectly acceptable:

```
B start
```

The <label> is a marked position in the assembly language program. There is a physical limit to the distance a branch can occur. This is plus or minus 32 Mb, as this is the largest address that can be represented in the space allocated for the label position. An absolute address is not stored; what is stored is the offset from the current position. When the ARM encounters the Branch instruction it treats the value following as a positive (forward) or negative (backward) adjustment to the PC from the current position.

Chapter 13 looks at Register 15 in more detail and also discusses how branches are calculated.

The Link Register

The Branch with Link instruction, BL, allows you to pass control to another part of your program – a subroutine – and then return on completion. BL works like the normal branch instruction in that it takes its destination as an address, normally specified by a label in an assembly language program. However, before it branches it copies the contents of the Program Counter (R15) into the Link Register (R14).

```
BLEQ subroutine @ Branch & save PC if Z flag set
```

Once the subroutine has completed the contents of the Link Register, it can be transferred into the Program Counter to return control to the calling segment of code:

```
MOV R15, R14
```

This is arguably the least elegant instruction implementation on the ARM chip. It is effective and does the job; however, most other CPUs have specific subroutine call and return instructions. For example, on the 6502 chip the mnemonics JSR <label> and RTS were used for Jump SubRoutine and ReTurn Subroutine.

A MOV instruction is used to move the return address from R14 back into the Program Counter. This will have no effect on the Status Register flags, and therefore, flags are preserved from whatever was going on before the return.

It is important to remember that each time a BL instruction is executed the contents of R15 are copied into R14. This means that if the program is already in a subroutine and another is called, the original link address will be overwritten with the new link address.

If your program is going to nest BL calls inside one another, the Link Register must be preserved on each occasion. The Link Register can then be re-seeded with the return address each time the subroutine is completed. In such cases, housekeeping is important. Re-seeding the wrong address back into the Program Counter will most likely crash your program.

A common way to store these nested addresses is to utilise the stack as a store. This is described in Chapter 17.

Using Compare Instructions

Your machine code will regularly need to check the result of an operation and then, depending on that result, take a course of action. There are a range of instructions that allow you to do this and a couple also that jump, or 'branch' to another part of the program. These comparisons instructions directly affect the Status Register flags at which point you can act on what you find. The following segment will count from 1 to 50 and uses compare and branch instructions to control the loop to do so:

```
        MOV R0,#1            @Initialise count
loop:
        ADD R0,R0,#1         @ Increment count
        CMP R0,#50           @ Compare with limit
        BLE loop
```

This program continues to add 1 to the value in R0, which was initially set at 1. R0 is compared to 50, and a BLE occurs if Less than or Equal to is the result. So the loop continues until R0=50. Then the loop continues until R0=51, because R0 would have been incremented to 51 in the instruction before the CMP, which is the point when the BLE instruction fails to loop back to 'loop'.

This segment of code is perfectly acceptable, but we can reduce its length, by making the loop count down thus:

```
        MOV R0,#50           @ Initialise count
loop:
        SUBS R0,R0,#1        @ Decrement count
        BNE loop             @ Loop if not Zero
```

Here, we use the SUBS to decrement and set the flags and can therefore, get away with excluding the CMP instruction. If you are just counting a sequence of iterations and do not need the count value for anything then it is better and more efficient programming practice to count down. This means fewer instructions and therefore a faster execution.

Compare Forward Thinking

Because the only effect of the comparison instructions is to test the condition of Status Register flags, by thinking about what you require, you can actually get away without using them. Let's look at an example. The program below is a loop that will cycle until R0 and R1 are the same. If R0 is greater than R1 it will subtract R1 from R0 and place the result in R0. If on the other hand R0 is less than R1, it will subtract R0 from R1 and place the result in R1. When they are the same, the program will finish.

```
        MOV R0, #100         @ arbitrary values in R0 & R1
        MOV R1, #20
loop:
```

```
        CMP R0, R1          @ Are they the same: Z=1?
        BEQ stop            @ if so stop
        BLT less            @ if R0 < than R1 go to less
        SUB R0,R0,R1        @ otherwise sub R1 from R0
        BAL loop            @ branch always back to start
less:
        SUB  R1,R1,R0       @ subtract R0 from R1
        BAL loop            @ branch always to the start
stop:
```

While this code is perfectly acceptable and does the job, we can reduce it by taking full advantage of conditional execution of instructions:

```
        MOV R0, #100        @ arbitrary values in R0 & R1
        MOV R1, #20
loop:
        CMP R0, R1          @ Are they the same: Z=1?
        SUBGT R0,R0,R1      @ sub R1 from R0 if Great Than
        SUBLT R1,R1,R0      @ else sub R0 from R1 as Less
        BNE loop   @ branch is not equal
```

As we are testing for greater than and less than conditions we can make direct use of the GT and LT suffixes respectively and tag them onto the end of the SUB subtraction instruction.

Using Conditionals Effectively

In Chapter 8, we saw how to use the TST instruction to print out a binary number. There, Program 8b used the section of code below to select whether a '1' or '0' will be used for printing:

```
_bits:
        TST R6, R9          @ TST no, mask
        BEQ _print0
        MOV R8, R6          @ MOV preserve, no
        MOV R0, #49         @ ASCII '1'
        STR R0, [R1]        @ store 1 in string
        BL _write           @ write to screen
        MOV R6, R8          @ MOV no, preserve
        BAL _noprint1
```

```
_print0:
    MOV R8, R6              @ MOV preserve, no
    MOV R0, #48             @ ASCII '0'
    STR R0, [R1]            @ store 0 in string
    BL _write
    MOV R6, R8              @ MOV no, preserve
```

Program 10a. Conditional execution to improve program size.

```
/**** Convert to binary for printing ****/

    .global _start
_start:
    MOV R6, #251            @ Number to print in R6
    MOV R10, #1             @ set up mask
    MOV R9, R10, LSL #31
    LDR R1, = string        @ Point R1 to string
_bits:
    TST R6, R9              @ TST no, mask
    MOVEQ R0, #48           @ ASCII '0'
    MOVNE R0, #49           @ ASCII '1'
    STR R0, [R1]            @ store 1 in string
    MOV R8, R6              @ MOV preserve, no
    BL _write               @ write to screen
    MOV R6, R8              @ MOV no, preserve

    MOVS R9, R9, LSR #1     @ shuffle mask bits
    BNE _bits

_exit:
    MOV R7, #1
    SWI 0

_write:
    MOV R0, #1
    MOV R2, #1
    MOV R7, #4
    SWI 0
```

```
    BX LR

.data
string:    .ascii " "
```

On the face of things, this is a perfectly acceptable way to archive the result of printing either a 1 or 0 to the screen dependent on the result of a test. Indeed it is, but that is without a full understanding of the ARM instruction set. Now consider the listing for Program 10a and the new section of code from _bits down which, using conditional instructions, is half the size of the original segment.

Now, dependent on the result of the TST instruction one of the MOV commands — and only one — will get executed, dependent on the condition of the Zero flag. This is much more elegant and also easier to follow. The revised program is listed above.

Branch Exchange

The Branch Exchange (BX) and Branch with Link (BLX) offer a third way of branching within a program. However, it should be said they are most commonly used to effect an entry into Thumb code, a subject addressed in Chapter 25 and as such should be avoided until that point and when you are familiar with their added implications.

11: Shifts and Rotates

The ARM has an internal mechanism called the barrel shifter. This device moves the bits in a word left or right. Most microprocessors have standalone instructions that allow you to perform this directly. However, the ARM only allows these movements as part of other instructions. It is a significant process because moving bits left or right can be a simple way of multiplying or dividing numbers quickly.

There are three types of shifts that can be performed. They are logical, arithmetic and rotate. Rotate is the only one that does not have an arithmetic function — it is included purely to move bits. Figure 11a details the six types of bit moves available for use.

Mnemonic	Meaning
LSL	Logical Shift Left
LSR	Logical Shift Right
ASL	Arithmetic Shift Left
ASR	Arithmetic Shift Right
ROR	Rotate Right
RRX	Rotate Right with eXtend

Figure 11a. Shift instructions available for use.

Although the barrel shifter is in operation during shifts and rotates, practically, its operation is transparent to the user.

Logical Shifts

Logically shifting a number left or right by one position has the effect of doubling it or halving it. By increasing the number of logical shifts you can multiply and divide numbers accordingly.

Figure 11b shows how a single Logical Shift Left (LSL) moves the bits on a full word of data. In an LSL the most significant bit (b31) drops out and into the Carry flag and the hole made by b0 shifting along into b1 is filled with a 0.

111

LSL	C	Word									
Before	x	b31	b30	b29	b28	b27	...	b3	b2	b1	b0
After	b31	b30	b29	b28	b27	b26	<<	b2	b1	b0	0

Figure 11b. Logically shifting bits left.

Consider the single byte binary value 00010001. In decimal this is 17. If we perform a logical shift on this number by one place to the left (LSL #1) we get: 00100010 which is 34. We have effectively doubled, or multiplied the number, by two. This assumes that we drop off the top digit and insert a 0 at the least significant bit. This is illustrated in Figure 11c.

	b7	b6	b5	b4	b3	b2	b1	b0		
Before	0	0	0	1	0	0	0	1		#17
After	0	0	1	0	0	0	1	0	<0	#34

Figure 11c. Doubling a number with a single LSL

This is a single byte example. The ARM uses four bytes, so the whole word is shifted to the left in this fashion. The bit that was in b7 gets moved across into the next byte and into what is effectively b8, and so on. The bit that gets shifted out at the very top, bit 31, gets moved into the Carry flag. The Carry flag can be tested to see if there is an overflow in the number multiplication.

As mentioned, the ARM does not have any standalone shift instructions, but it does implement them as an add-on to Operand2 to use within instructions and they affect the whole 32-bits of the register specified. Using the example illustrated above, we might code it thus:

```
MOV  R1, #17
MOVS R0, R1, LSL#1
```

Note the structure of the syntax for this. Operand1 is the destination for the result (R0), and the LSL is performed on Operand2 (R1). Here, the logical shift is given as an immediate value, but it could also have been specified in a register, which makes it available for alteration. A value from 0 to 31 can be used in a shift command. Using:

```
LSL #5
```

would multiply a value by two, five times =32 (2 x 2 x 2 x 2 x 2). It would perform LSL five times. Here, the new spaces would be filled with 0s and the Carry flag would reflect the value of the last bit 'falling out' from b31. All the other bits moved out are 'lost'. This means that the multiplication only remains true provided we do not lose any significant bits through the

Carry flag. Therefore for large numbers care must be taken that significance is retained. In other words the result must fit inside 32-bits. This multiplication rule breaks down if we were using twos complement numbers.

Logical Shift Right

Figure 11d shows how a Logical Shift Right (LSR) affects the bits in a word of data. The most significant bit (b31) goes right with a 0 taking its place. The least significant bit, b0 drops into the Carry flag.

LSR	C	Word								
Before	x	b31	b30	b29	b28	b27	...	b3	b2	b1	b0
After	b0	0	b31	b30	b29	b28	>>	b4	b3	b2	b1

Figure 11d. Logically shifting bits right.

The effect of LSR is to divide the number by two. Figure 11e shows this using our previous example. We start with 34 and perform an LSR #1 to arrive back at our original value of 17. Here a 0 is drawn in at the top end (b31) and any value falling out on the right (b0) is taken into the Carry flag. As with LSL the Carry flag is used to capture what is falling out so it can be tested if required.

	b7	b6	b5	b4	b3	b2	b1	b0		
Before	0	0	1	0	0	0	1	0		#34
After	0	0	0	1	0	0	0	1	>0	#17

Figure 11e. Dividing a number by two with a single LSR.

Arithmetic Shift Right

In an arithmetical shift the sign bit is preserved. Here b31 is saved; everything else is shifted one place to the right with b0 dropping into the Carry flag. These examples are shifted by one place only, but the principle is the same for multiple shifts with b31, the sign bit being preserved, and the last bit moved out of b0 is dropped into the Carry flag. This is illustrated in Figure 11f:

ASR	C	Word									
Before	x	b31	b30	b29	b28	b27	...	b3	b2	b1	b0
After	b0	b31	b31	b30	b29	b28	>>	b4	b3	b2	b1

Figure 11f. Arithmetic shift right preserving sign bit.

The advantage of ASR is that the shift takes into account the sign of the data and so a twos complement number may be represented. It extends the original sign of the number from b31 to b30 and ensures the division is performed correctly for both positive and negative numbers.

```
MOV R1, #255
MOV R2, #1
MOVS R0, R1, ASR R2
```

When we execute the segment above it would leave a value of 0x7F (128) in R0 with R1 and R2 unchanged, but the Carry flag set.

The conditional tests can also be used as with a normal MOV instruction. This following line would only be executed if the Carry flag is set:

```
MOV CS S R0, R1, ASR R2
```

An arithmetic shift left (ASL) is identical in operation to LSL, and there is no difference between them in the result. As a matter of course, you should always use LSL instead of ASL as some assemblers may not compile it and issue an error message. Others may just give a warning.

Rotations

There are two instructions that allow you to rotate bits to the right and in conjunction with the Carry flag. Rotate Right (ROR) moves the bits out from the low end and feeds them straight back in the high end. The last bit rotated out is also copied into the Carry flag as well as being rotated around. Figure 11g illustrates how the bits move. The Rotate instructions have no arithmetic action of significance and are included to shift bit patterns.

ROR>	C	Word									
Before	x	b31	b30	b29	b28	b27	...	b3	b2	b1	b0
After	b0	b0	b31	b30	b29	b28	>>	b4	b3	b2	b1

Figure 11g. The Rotate Right instruction.

The following segment:

```
MOV R1, #0xF000000F
MOVS R0, R1, ROR #4
```

would give a result of 0xFF000000 with the Negative and Carry flags set. The ROR #4 shuffles the bits four places to the right.

The top bytes, 0xF000 move to the right by four giving 0x0F00; The low bytes 0x000F move to the right by four to give 0x0000; The 0xF, which has dropped out of the lower byte, is rotated to the top four bits of the high byte to give 0xFF00. Of course, the bits in the middle would all be shuffled along as well, but as they are 0s this is not noticeable. Finally, a copy is made of the last bit out, which was originally in the position bit 4, and placed in the Carry flag.

Extended Rotate

There is also an extended version or Rotate Right called RRX:

```
MOV R0, R1, RRX
```

This shift operation is unique in that you cannot specify the number of movements it makes as you are only allowed one. RRX always and only rotates data right by one position.

RRX>	C	Word								
Before	x	b31	b30	b29	b28	b27	...	b3	b2	b1	b0
After	b0	x	b31	b30	b29	b28	>>	b4	b3	b2	b1

Figure 11h. Rotate Right With Extend.

The Carry flag value is dropped into b31, and the value in b0 is moved into the Carry flag. Figure 11h shows how the bits are moved.

All bits are preserved albeit in a different order. RRX uses the Carry flag as a 32nd bit and so everything is preserved.

Uses of Shifts and Rotates

The shift and rotate commands can be used with any of the following data processing instructions:

```
ADC, ADD, AND,
BIC,
CMN, CMP,
```

```
EOR,
MOV, MVN,
ORR,
RSB,
SBC, SUB,
TEQ, TST
```

They can also be used to manipulate the index value of LDR and STR operations as described in Chapter 13. This also illustrates some handy uses for this group of modifiers.

Immediate Constant Range

We have seen the use of immediate constants in instructions:

```
SUB R0, R1, #3
```

Here the immediate constant (#3) is specified as Operand2. However, there is a limit to the size of the number that can be specified in this constant, and more particularly, some numbers just can't be used − 257, for example.

The reason for this is in the way ARM instructions are encoded. There are only 12-bits available for storing an immediate value as the operand. The encoding of ARM instructions is beyond the scope of this book. However, accepting that 12-bits are available, this is how the ARM uses these bits: The 12-bit field is split into two, one part of 8-bits and one of 4-bits. The 8-bit field is used to represent a numeric constant and the 4-bit field one of 16 different positions (each themselves then shifted by two) which the 8-bit value may be rotated to through an even number of positions.

Figure 11i summarises this scheme showing the position of the 8-bit value afforded within the 32-bits as defined by the position bits, 0-15. The '+' is used in the diagram to represent 0s, in the hope it makes it easier to read. The ROR column shows the value to be used in the shift.

A couple of examples should make this clearer. Suppose we wanted to use 173 as immediate constant. In binary this is:

```
00000000 00000000 00000000 10101101
```

This value can be presented in 8-bits, so no shift is required and the position bits will be set to 0.

Let's now examine the number 19,968. In binary across 32-bits this is:

```
00000000 00000000 01001110 00000000
```

ARM A32 Assembly Language

If we compare this to the patterns in Figure 11i, we can see this has the value placed at position 12. To create this number as an immediate operand we would use 78 (01001110) and rotate it right by 24.

This provides us with the second way that an immediate operand can be specified as a shifted operand, and this takes the format shown in the following line:

```
Instruction (<Suffix>)  <Op1>, <Op2>, <Op3> <Shift>
```

Here's an example:

```
MOV R1, #78
MOV R0, R1, ROR #24
```

```
Bit31                                  bit0    Psn   ROR
++++++++++++++++++++++++76543210        0     0
10++++++++++++++++++++++++765432        1     2
3210++++++++++++++++++++++++7654        2     4
543210++++++++++++++++++++++++76        3     6
76543210++++++++++++++++++++++++        4     8
++76543210++++++++++++++++++++++        5     10
++++76543210++++++++++++++++++++        6     12
++++++76543210++++++++++++++++++        7     14
++++++++76543210++++++++++++++++        8     16
++++++++++76543210++++++++++++++        9     18
++++++++++++76543210++++++++++++       10     20
++++++++++++++76543210++++++++++       11     22
++++++++++++++++76543210++++++++       12     24
++++++++++++++++++76543210++++++       13     26
++++++++++++++++++++76543210++++       14     28
++++++++++++++++++++++76543210++       15     30
```

Figure 11i. Immediate operands calculation.

Here, R1 is loaded with 78, then rotated right 24 places and the result placed in R0. The result generated would be 19,968. Of course, we can use all these values directly as immediate constants as the assembler will resolve them directly for us, so we can use:

```
MOV R0, #19968
```

and the assembler works it out. It is the values that cannot be calculated in this way through Figure 11i that are the issue.

Although 257 cannot be used as an immediate constant, it can be seeded by storing it in a register and then using the register to specify the value.

```
ADD R0, R1, #257
```

would cause an error, along the lines of:

```
Invalid constant
```

but the following would achieve the same result:

```
MOV R2, #256      @ Load R2 with 256
ADD R2, R2, #1    @ Add one to make 257
ADD R0, R1, R2    @ Add 257 to R1 and save in R0.
```

12: Smarter Numbers

In Chapter 6 we introduced the two basic multiplication instructions MUL and MLA. These were the original multiplication instructions wired into the ARM. Since version 3 of the ARM additional instructions have been added to deal with signed and unsigned numbers up to 64-bits long. We'll look at some of the more useful ones here. Several have very specific uses and are aimed at more complex tasks such as digital processing.

Long Multiplication

The SMULL and UMULL instructions offer signed and unsigned multiplication using two registers containing 32-bit operands to produce a 64-bit result, which is split across two destination registers. The format of the instruction is:

```
SMULL (<suffix>) <destlLo>, <destHi>, <Op1>, <Op2>
UMULL (<suffix>) <destlLo>, <destHi>, <Op1>, <Op2>
```

For signed multiplication the values passed through Operand1 and Operand2 are assumed to be in twos complement form. You cannot use the PC in these instructions and the SP should be avoided as it is not supported in some later ARM chips. It should go without saying that the two destination registers should be different.

The following example will produce the full 64-bits of a product of two unsigned 32-bit numbers, which assumes that the two unsigned numbers are in R1 and R2, and on exit R3 and R4 hold the result with the low word of the product in R3 and R4 the high word.

```
UMULL R3, R4, R1, R2
```

To give you an idea of how code-saving these newer instructions are, the segment presented in Figure 12a. will perform the same operation using just the original MUL instruction. As with the above example the routine assumes that the two unsigned numbers are in R1 and R2 and on exit R3 and R4 hold the result, with the low word of the product in R3 and R4 the high word. On exit, both R1 and R2 are non-defined.

The ADDS following the MULNE test is used in preference to MLA here as we need to preserve the Carry flag for the ADDCS that follows.

If you do not follow this example, try writing it out longhand, or work through it using GDB (discussed in Chapter 14) so that you can dump registers during a step-through process.

```
MOVS  R4,R1,LSR #16         @ R4 is ms 16 bits of R1
BIC   R1,R1,R4,LSL #16      @ R1 is ls 16 bits
MOV   R5,R2,LSR #16         @ R5 is ms 16 bits of R2
BIC   R2,R2,R5,LSL #16      @ R2 is ls 16 bits
MUL   R3,R1,R2              @ Low partial product
MUL   R2,R4,R2              @ 1st middle partial product
MUL   R1,R5,R1              @ 2nd middle partial product
MULNE R4,R5,R4              @ High partial product - NE
ADDS  R1,R1,R2              @ Add mid partial products
ADDCS R4,R4, #0x10000       @ Add carry to high partial
                            @ product
ADDS  R3,R3,R1,LSL #16      @ Add middle partial product
ADC   R4,R4,R1,LSR #16      @ sum into lo and hi words
```

Figure 12a. Long multiplication the hard way.

Long Accumulation

SMLAL and UMALA are the signed and unsigned equivalents of MLA. As with the previous instructions the signed or unsigned values acting at Operand1 and Operand2 are multiplied together, but in this instance the result is added to any value already in destLo and destHi.

```
SMLALS R1, R2, R5,R6
```

There are also a couple of interesting variants of the command which are only applicable with signed multiplication.

SMLAXY permits multiplication with accumulates using 16-bit operands with a 32-bit accumulator. This is interesting and the full syntax is:

```
SMLA<x><y> (<suffix>)><dest>, <Op1>, <Op2>, <Op3>
```

Here <x> and <y> can be either B or T which stand for Bottom and Top, referring to the bottom or top two bytes of Operand1 and Operand2 respectively. Operand3 contains the value to be added to the result of the multiplication of the bytes identified in Operand1 and Operand2.

For example:

```
SMLABTCC R0, R1, R2, R3
```

Here if the Carry is clear (CC) then the low half-word of R1 will be multiplied with the top half-word of R2. The result will be added to the value in R3 and the result stored in R0.

The SMLAWy instruction (Signed Multiply Wide) is very similar but in this circumstance either the top two or bottom two bytes of Operand2 are utilised to multiply with Operand1. The upper 32-bits of the result (which may be 48-bits long) are placed in the destination register. This is therefore a 16-bit by 32-bit multiplication with accumulation. The full syntax is:

```
SMLAW<y> <dest>, <Operand1>, <Operand2>, <Operand3>
```

For example:

```
SMLAWB R0, R5, R6, R7
```

Here the bottom half-word of R6 is multiplied with the full word in R5 and the value in R7 is added to the result, which is dropped into R0.

SMUAD and SMUSD work on 16-bit values and offer Signed Multiply with Addition and Signed Multiply with Subtraction, with the twist of allowing optional exchange of operand halves. The syntax for the commands is:

```
SMUAD<X> (<suffix>) <dest>, <Operand1>, <Operand2>
SMUSD<X> (<suffix>) <dest>, <Operand1>, <Operand2>
```

If 'X' is included in the instruction then the most and least significant half-words of Operand2 are exchanged. If 'X' is omitted then no exchange takes place. The instruction then multiplies the contents of the two lower half-words of Operand1 and Operand2 and saves the result, and then multiplies the contents of the two upper half-words of the operands and saves the result.

For SMUAD (Dual Signed 16-Bit Multiply with Addition) the two partial products are then added and the result placed in the destination register. For SMUSD (Dual Signed 16-Bit Multiply with Subtraction) the second partial product (the upper half-word) is subtracted from the first partial product.

Examples:

```
SMUADXEQ  R5, R6, R7
SMUSD     R5, R7, R9
```

Division and Remainder

The ARM does not provide a division instruction, so the following segment shows how you can perform one using two 32-bit values. It assumes that the dividend is in R1, and the divisor is in R2. On exit R3 holds the quotient, R1 the remainder and R2 the original divisor. No check is made to see if the divisor is zero, which will fail – but this is a simple check to add to your own function.

```
MOV R4,R2              @ Put the divisor in R4.
CMP R4,R1,LSR #1       @ Then double it until
                       @ 2 x R4 > divisor.
Div1:
MOVLS R4,R4,LSL #1
CMP R4,R1,LSR #1
BLS Div1
MOV R3,#0              @ Initialise the quotient

Div2:
CMP R1,R4              @ Can we subtract R4?
SUBCS R1,R1,R4         @ If we can, do so
ADC R3,R3,R3           @ Double quotient &
                       @ add new bit
MOV R4,R4,LSR #1       @ Halve R4
CMP R4,R2              @ Loop until we've gone
BHS Div2               @ past the original divisor
```

Figure 12b. Dividing two 32-bit values.

Smarter Simple Multiplication

We had a look at simple multiplication in an earlier chapter. Now armed with the knowledge of shifts and bit operators, we can look at easier ways to achieve multiplication results. In the examples that follow R0 is used as the main register, However, any register may be used.

If you want to multiply by a factor of 2 then you should use LSL directly:

```
MOV R0, R0, LSL #n
```

Where 'n' is the constant. Replacing n above by, say 4, would produce:

```
R0=R0 x 2 x 2 x 2 x 2
```

ARM A32 Assembly Language

This is, in effect, 2^n.

To multiply by $(2^n)+1$, examples being 3, 5, 9, 17 etc., use:
```
ADD R0, R0, R0, LSL #n
```
Again where n is the value.

Conversely to multiply by $(2^n)-1$, examples being 3, 7, 15 etc., use:
```
RSB R0, R0, R0, LSL #n
```
Where n is the value.

To multiply a number by 6 first multiply by three and then by two:
```
ADD R0, R0, R0, LSL #1
MOV R0, R0, LSL #1
```

Saturation and Q Flag

Saturation arithmetic is a version of mathematics in which all operations such as addition and multiplication are limited to a fixed range between a minimum and maximum value. If the result of an operation is greater than the maximum, it is set ("clamped") to the maximum; if it is below the minimum, it is clamped to the minimum. For example, if the valid range of values is from -50 to 50, then 30+10=40 and 40+20=50. The latter result is saturated at 50.

ARM provides instruction such as QADD and QSUB to test for this situation. This needs to be signalled in some way Bit 27 of the CPSR is a sticky overflow flag, also known as the Q flag. This flag is set to 1 if any of the following occurs:

- Saturation of the addition result in a QADD or QDADD instruction
- Saturation of the subtraction result in a QSUB or QDSUB instruction
- Saturation of the doubling intermediate result in a QDADD or QDSUB instruction
- Signed overflow during an SMLA<x><y> or SMLAW<y> instruction

The Q flag is *sticky* in that once it has been set to 1, it is not affected by whether subsequent calculations saturate and/or overflow.

For example:
```
MOV     R2,#0x70000000
QADD    R3,R2,R2
```

0x70000000 + 0x70000000 would become 0xE0000000, but since QADD is saturating, the result is saturated to 0x7FFFFFFF (the largest positive 32-bit integer) and the Q flag is set.

13: Program Counter

Register 15 is the Program Counter, and it's important. If you don't treat it with respect your program can crash. If this happens your board will most likely 'freeze' and will not recognise anything you do until you turn the power switch off and re-boot. Time consuming, annoying and frustrating. It will happen occasionally, but it's good for the soul to keep those occasions very infrequent!

R15 performs a simple function. It keeps track of where your program is up to in an executing machine code program. It holds the 32-bit addresses of a physical memory location. In fact, the PC holds the address of the next instruction to be fetched. So, if you happen to load it with a number which relates to your calorie count for the day, you will understand why the program might crash.

The PC can be used within instructions in a variety of ways. R15 can be used in data processing instructions, which means that it can be used as either Operand1 or Operand2.

Example:

```
ADD R0, R15, #8
```

This is an example of R15 acting as Operand1. This line would add 8 to the value (address) in R15 and save the result in R0.

```
SUB R0, R9, R15
```

Here, as Operand2, the value in R15 is subtracted from R9 and the result stored in R0.

R15 can also be used as the destination register in an instruction. In such instances, it should expect to be loaded with an appropriate value for the Program Counter as it will seek to fetch the next instruction from it.

```
MOV R15, R14
```

places the value held in R14 into R15. As R14 is the Link Register, this is an effective way of returning from a previously called routine. Generally it (or a variation of it) will be used to hand control back to the point from where the machine code was called.

Pipelining

It is important to understand how the ARM goes about fetching, decoding and executing instructions. The instruction pipeline is a design feature of the ARM that is fundamental to its execution speed. This is because when it comes to executing machine code the ARM is doing three things almost simultaneously: fetching, decoding and executing. As these operations cannot be performed on the same instruction at the same time, the ARM has three instructions on the go at once. It is executing one, decoding a second and fetching a third. When an instruction is executed everything gets shuffled along one place as a new instruction is fetched. The instruction that was previously fetched is then being decoded, and the one that was being decoded is now being executed. There is a continuous stream running through the pipeline as illustrated in Figure 13a.

	Fetched	Decoded	Executed
Cycle 1	Op1	empty	empty
Cycle 2	Op2	Op1	empty
Cycle 3	Op3	Op2	Op1
Cycle 4	Op4	Op3	Op2

Figure 13a. The Fetch, Decode and Execute cycle of the ARM.

It takes three cycles for the ARM to fill the pipeline when it starts operating. Once an instruction has been executed it is discarded as the next instruction overwrites it. It is because of this multi-tasking process that the ARM can achieve great processing speeds. During the process of decoding, the ARM is identifying what registers are going to be used in the instruction when it is executed.

In Figure 13a, on Cycle 4, the PC holds the address of Op4 — the next one to be fetched. Figure 13b shows where each cycle of the pipeline is relative to the PC.

This three-stage pipeline was the original design of the ARM chip. In fact today's ARM processors are even more sophisticated and the ARM chip has a pipeline that is no less than eight operations long. But for this book and the concepts we are evaluating the original model remains sound for evaluating the pipeline effect (although we'll come back to the subject in Chapter 28).

The effect of pipelining must always be taken into account. Otherwise in certain circumstances your program may not function as you might expect. Consider this instruction:

    MOV R15, R15

If you place this in your program then it will cause the next instruction to be skipped. This is because the address accessed from the PC is two words (eight bytes) more than the address of the MOV instruction. When written back into the PC by the operation, execution resumes a couple of words (instructions) further on, thereby skipping the instruction in between.

Remember that the address held in the PC is always eight bytes more than the address of the instruction being executed.

Contents	Action
PC	Next instruction to fetch
PC-4	Being decoded
PC-8	Currently executing
PC-12	Previously executed

Figure 13b. The PC relative to instruction processing.

Calculating Branches

We looked at branches in Chapter 10. Let's examine how they are handled by the Program Counter.

A branch typically takes this format:

    BAL label

Here 'label' is taken to be a label or a marked position in the assembly language program. Remember there is a physical limit to the distance a branch can occur; it is plus or minus 32 Mb as this is the largest address that can be represented in the space allocated for the label position. An absolute address is not stored. What is stored is the offset from the current position. When the ARM encounters the Branch instruction it treats the value following as a positive (forward) or negative (backward) adjustment to the PC from the current position.

Because of the way instructions are encoded, the branch value is a 24-bit signed offset in twos complement form. The word offset is shifted left by two places (bits) to form a byte offset. This offset is added to the PC. Look at the following example shown in Figure 13c:

```
Address   Label      Instruction
0x0100               BEQ     zero
                     ...
                     ...
0x0120               BL      notzero

0x1C30    zero:      <instructions>
                     ...
                     ...
0x2C30    notzero:   <instructions>
```

Figure 13c. Calculating branches.

The first column is the address of the instruction. Here we have two labels whose addresses are 0x1C30 and 0x2C30. The first instruction:

```
BEQ zero
```

is located at 0x0100, and the second instruction:

```
BL notzero
```

is located at 0x0120.

Because of pipelining when the BEQ zero instruction is executing, the instruction that is being fetched will be two instructions later, which is eight bytes later. So the byte offset for the BEQ instruction will be:

```
0x1C30 - 0x0100 - 8 = 0x1B28
```

So the word offset for the BEQ zero instruction is:

```
0x1B28 / 4 = 0x6CA
```

For the BL notzero instruction the calculation is:

```
0x2C30 - x0120 - 8 = 0x2B08
0x2B08 / 4 = 0xAC2
```

Backward branches work in a similar way but have to have the pipeline effect added to the calculation.

By using relative or offset values as branch destinations, it becomes possible to write machine code programs that are totally relocatable. In other words, they can be loaded and run into any part of memory. As soon as you hard code the actual definitive address into place it ties the machine code into one location.

14: Debugging with GDB

GCC comes with a complete debugging tool, GDB, which you will find very useful when the time comes to unravel your programs, and are trying to understand why something doesn't work the way you expected.

One of two things generally happens when your machine code program doesn't work correctly. The first is that the result returned is not the one expected. The second is that no result is returned, and the system freezes and requires a hard-reset. Of course, both situations can occur together as well!

For a wrong result, the likelihood is that a constant or address are out-of-kilter. The positive side is that your routine seems to be functioning, and there are no logical or branch errors. Here, it is a matter of trying to track down where the error is occurring. The type of result being returned might give you a clue, and you will need to examine this and make some deductions of your own. For example, if you are getting a result that is one more than you were expecting (and 'one' in this case might not be a number) then perhaps a loop is being executed one more time than it should. The loop counter might need adjusting, or your conditional branch instruction might need changing. Being able to see what a loop counter value is at this point would be useful. It may also be that values in registers have been mixed or not referenced correctly in your assembler — for instance, you might have used R1 when you should have used R3.

Frozen Cases

For a frozen machine things can be a bit more involved. Perhaps a routine is trapped in a continuous loop. The loop counter may not be decremented and so will continue to process while power is applied. It might also be that you have mismanaged a stack or corrupted the Program Counter.

Trapping all these types of errors will become an everyday programming task for you. It is part and parcel of programming. That is why it is useful to develop your programs in small sections or functions. Each has a purpose and each can be tested independently.

If you find that a program crashes or hangs, one key issue is to locate at what point this happens. The best way to do this is to get some visual feedback on how far the machine code gets before being upset. This allows you to at least narrow your search. For example, if you are getting screen output from your code then you will have some idea that most likely you ignore everything that went before the last item displayed.

Here is one way to produce screen output so you can get some visual feedback on the screen: If you are having issues with your code and cannot narrow down the segment creating the issue then you can populate your code with an instruction to print out a marker on the screen, to show you where you are, and therefore have a good idea exactly where the issue lies.

For example, let's say a machine code program has five main areas of operation. We could place an appropriate call to a _write style routine at the start of each one as illustrated in Figure 14a.

```
.area1
BL _write      @ Print A
...
.area2
BL _write      @ Print B
...
.area3
BL _write      @ Print C
...
.area4
BL _write      @ Print D
...
.area5
BL _write      @ Print E
...
```

Figure 14a. Locating issues by use of a _write style function.

Now when the program is run, as each area is reached, a letter will be printed to the screen. Let's say we had the following result:

ABC

before the program froze. This would show that the program had seized somewhere in area3, because 'D' was never printed.

Now you can concentrate your efforts in this area. You might add in additional calls to print out more letters or numbers inside area3. This will then narrow your search and allow you to concentrate your debugging efforts in the right area. Once you have narrowed the area down you can look more closely at the segment.

Assembling for GDB

GDB is the GNU project debugger. It is supplied with GCC and is run from the command line. It provides a wide range of tools that will allow you to interrogate your machine code programs in many different ways from within an enclosed environment. GDB can operate on many, many levels and it would be fair to say that it has a command for almost every occasion. It is customisable as well. As with most GNU software it has extensive documentation available online. In this chapter we'll look at some practical examples, and we'll use Program 10a as the centrepiece of the demonstration.

Before you can use GDB the core program has to be assembled using an additional directive so that it generates additional information that can be used by GDB:

```
as -g -o prog10a.o prog10a.s
ld -o prog10a prog10a.o
```

The -g option generates the additional data for the debugger. From your point of view nothing different has happened. You can start GDB as follows:

```
gdb <filename>
```

where <filename> is the name of the assembled file to be interrogated. So:

```
gdb prog10a
```

will launch the debugger and also load the information relating to prog10a. If you forget to specify a filename then you can use the FILE command at the gdb prompt:

```
file prog10a
```

Now typing:

```
list
```

will produce the output shown opposite in Figure 14b. (You may need to press the Return key to continue the listing.) The numbers at the start are simply line numbers. They relate to what you would see if you have line numbers enabled in Vim when editing your source code (using :set number in command mode). However, within GDB you can utilise these numbers with many of the commands that are at your disposal.

```
1  /**** Convert number to binary for printing ****/
2  /*                                                */
3  /* Registers: R6=number, R8= preserve, R9=mask    */
4  /* R7 needed for syscall, R1 points to string     */
5
6          .global _start
7  _start:
8
9          MOV   R6, #15           @ No to print in R6
10         MOV   R10, #1           @ set up mask
11         MOV   R9, R10, LSL #31
12         LDR   R1, = string      @ Point R1 to string
13
14 _bits:
15         TST   R6, R9            @ TST no, mask
16         MOVEQ                   R0, #48
17         MOVNE                   R0, #49
18         STR   R0, [R1]
19         MOV   R8, R6            @ MOV preserve, no
20         BL    _write            @ write to screen
21         MOV   R6, R8            @ MOV no, preserve
22
23         MOVS  R9, R9, LSR #1    @shuffle mask bits
24         BNE   _bits
25
26 _exit:
27         MOV   R7, #1
28         SWI   0
29
30 _write:
31         MOV   R0, #1
32         MOV   R2, #1
33         MOV   R7, #4
34         SWI   0
35         BX    LR
36
37 .data
38 string:
39         .ascii " "
```

Figure 14b. Listing a loaded file in GDB.

The Disassembler

A *disassembler* does the opposite to an assembler. It takes the values stored in memory and converts them back into an assembly language listing. For example, at the GDB prompt enter:

    disassemble _start

You should get output that looks something similar to that shown in Figure 14c below.

```
Dump of assembler code for function _start:
0x00008074   <+0>:    mov    r6, #15       ;0x0f
0x00008078   <+4>:    mov    r0, #1
0x0000807c   <+8>:    lsl    r9, r10, #31
0x00008080   <+12>:   ldr    r1, [pc, #60] ;0x80c4
                                            <_write+20>
End of assembler dump
```

Figure 14c. Disassembling a function in GDB.

One thing the -g option did when it assembled the source code was to create a list of the labels or functions defined in the original source code, which allows us to refer to these directly when using GDB.

The first column in the listing generated is the address in memory where the code is assembled. Note that this address may differ on your output. The second column inside the chevrons shows the number of bytes from the start of the function.

Notice the last line in this listing has disassembled to something a little different than was in our original source. It has converted the original:

    LDR R1, = string

into an absolute address. In this case:

    ldr   r1, [pc, #60]

This means load R1 with the address which is 60 ahead of the current PC address (R1=PC+60). So here pipelining is taken into account. The actual address is 0x80c4 and is given after the semi colon at the end of the line, as is the label it is referring to!

You can also disassemble an area of memory by specifying a start and end address. By using the '/r"switch at the start it is also possible to include the hexadecimal opcodes and operands.. For example:

```
Disassemble /r 0x8084, 0x80a0
```

will give (adjust the addresses for your situation if needed) the output shown in Figure 14d:

```
0x00008084   <_bits+0>:    09 00 16 e1   tst     r6, r9
0x00008088   <_bits+4>:    30 00 a0 03   moveq   r0, #48  ; 0x30
0x0000808c   <_bits+8>:    31 00 a0 13   movne   r0, #49  ; 0x31
0x00008090   <_bits+12>:   00 00 81 e5   str     r0, [r1]
0x00008094   <_bits+16>:   06 80 a0 e1   mov     r8, r6
0x00008098   <_bits+20>:   04 00 00 eb   bl      0x80b0 <_write>
0x0000809c   <_bits+24>:   08 60 a0 e1   mov     r6, r8
0x000080a0   <_bits+28>:   a9 90 b0 e1   lsrs    r9, r9, #1
```

Figure 14d. Using the /r switch when disassembling.

The third set of figures listed are the opcodes and operands for each of the instructions. If you look at the address line starting 0x8098 you can see that the offset for the BL instruction has been calculated (0x80b0). If the program is 'running' (discussed below) the current position of the PC is shown by a '=>' on the left of one of the addresses.

Figure 14e provides a summary of some of the more common disassembly options in GDB.

Command	Action
disas <function>	Disassemble the named function. Example: disas _start
disas <addr1>, <addr2>	Disassemble from address 1 to address 2. Example: disas 0x8084, 0x80a4
disas <no>	Disassemble around the line number specified. Example: disas 19
/r	Include hex codes in output. Example: disas /r _write
/m	Include listing information in output: Example: disas /m _write

Figure 14e. Common disassembly commands.

Breakpoints

The major debugging facility at your disposal is without a doubt the use of breakpoints, and the ability to step through commands one-by-one, called single stepping. and allow you to watch your program in action.

Breakpoints are temporary halt signs in a machine code program, which GDB allows you to place where and when you want, so that when you run your program from within GDB the program will be halted each time a breakpoint is reached, at the same point, preserving all registers. By inserting one or more breakpoints in a machine code program, we can stop and look at register and flag contents at any chosen point. This can come in very handy when a program is not working as it should. By examining the contents of registers and the setting of flags you should be able to narrow down and kill the culprit causing the problems.

Breakpoints can be set using labels or line numbers using the 'b' command at the GDB prompt thus:

```
b _bits
```

In the first case the breakpoint is set at the address where '_bits' is assembled. This will be confirmed visually thus:

```
Breakpoint 1 at 0x8084: file prog10a.s, line 14
```

Let's set a second breakpoint immediately after the two conditional MOV statements. From the file listing we can see this is at line 18:

```
b 18
```

Which returns:

```
Breakpoint 2 at 0x0890: file prog10a.s, line 18
```

Typing:

```
info b
```

will print a listing of any breakpoints set so far, as shown in Figure 14f:

```
1  breakpoint  keep  y   0x00008088   prog10a.s:14
2  breakpoint  keep  y   0x00008090   prog10a.s:18
```

Figure 14f. Breakpoint listings.

This shows the two breakpoints set. Deleting breakpoints is just as easy:

```
delete 2
```

ARM A32 Assembly Language

would delete breakpoint 2.

We can execute programs and get them to stop at defined breakpoints. If the above two breakpoints are in place, typing:

```
run
```

at the GDB prompt would produce:

```
Breakpoint 1, _bits () at prog10a.s:14
17              MOVEQ R0, #48
```

The program has run but has stopped before executing the command on line 17. We can now get a dump of all the register contents by typing:

```
info r
```

This would give a listing like that shown in Figure 14g:

```
r0      0x0             0
r1      0x100c8         65736
r2      0x0             0
r3      0x0             0
r4      0x0             0
r5      0x0             0
r6      0xf             15
r7      0x0             0
r8      0x0             0
r9      0x80000000      2147483648
r10     0x1             1
r11     0x0             0
r12     0x0             0
sp      0xbefff860      0xbefff860
lr      0x0             0
pc      0x8088          0x8088 <_bits+4>
cpsr    0x40000010      1073741840
```

Figure 14g. Register dump after breakpoint 1 has halted the program.

At this point in the program the code listed in lines 9-12 will have been executed and this is reflected in the contents of the registers. To continue to the next breakpoint type:

```
continue
```

and then list the register contents again. These are shown in Figure 14h.

ARM A32 Assembly Language

```
r0      0x30            48
r1      0x100c8         65736
r2      0x0             0
r3      0x0             0
r4      0x0             0
r5      0x0             0
r6      0xf             15
r7      0x0             0
r8      0x0             0
r9      0x80000000      2147483648
r10     0x1             1
r11     0x0             0
r12     0x0             0
sp      0xbefff860      0xbefff860
lr      0x0             0
pc      0x8090          0x8090 <_bits+12>
cpsr    0x40000010      1073741840
```

Figure 14h. Register dump after breakpoint 2 has halted the program.

Here we can see that the ASCII code for '0' has been placed into R0 so the MOVEQ command was the one that was executed. This is reflected in the CPSR where the Zero flag is set. Note how the PC reflects where we are in the execution cycle.

```
r0      0x1             1
r1      0x100c8         65736
r2      0x0             0
r3      0x0             0
r4      0x0             0
r5      0x0             0
r6      0xf             15
r7      0x0             0
r8      0xf             15
r9      0x40000000      1073741824
r10     0x1             1
r11     0x0             0
r12     0x0             0
sp      0xbefff860      0xbefff860
lr      0x809c          32924
pc      0x80a4          0x80a4 <_bits+32>
cpsr    0x10            16
```

Figure 14i. Register dump after breakpoint 3 has halted the program.

Try setting a third breakpoint at line 25 (this can be done while the program is 'running') and continue to the breakpoint. Listing the register contents will show output as depicted in Figure 14i.

R9 has been updated with the new mask value, and note now how the link register has an address in it. Compare the source listing so you can see where these new values have come from.

Command	Action
`break <function>`	Set a breakpoint at the named function. Example: b _start
`break <lineno>`	Set a breakpoint at the file line number given. Example: b 23
`break <offset>`	Set a breakpoint at specified lines forward/backwards from current position. Example: b +5
`break *<addr>`	Set a breakpoint at specified address. Example b *0x8074
`info break`	List and provide information about all set breakpoints
`delete (<no>)`	Delete the specified breakpoint(s). If no number delete all. Example: delete 2

Figure 14j. Common breakpoint commands.

You can execute your program in GDB a line at a time by simply pressing the 's' key. This is called single-stepping. You should try this and watch the program cycle through the _write function as well. You can also print the register contents at any point. GDB is totally interactive and Figure 14j lists some of the more popular commands to experiment with.

Memory Dump

You can look at sections of memory, including your code and data areas. The latter is useful to see how data is changed in response to your program's operation. If you know that you have cleared memory, or filled a section with 0s before running your program, you can be sure that what is there after you have.

The 'x' (for examine) command produces output in a variety of formats. To get a hex dump of memory of the program itself type the following at the GDB prompt:

```
x/22xw 0x8074
```

This will produce a listing similar to that shown in Figure 14k.

```
0x8074 <_start>:     0xe3a0600f   0xe3a0a001   0xe1a09f8a   0xe59f103c
0x8084 <_bits>:      0xe1160009   0x03a00030   0x13a00031   0xe5810000
0x8094 <_bits+16>:   0xe1a08006   0xeb000004   0xe1a06008   0xe1b090a9
0x80a4 <_bits+32>:   0x1afffff6   0xe3a07001   0xef000000   0xe3a00001
0x80b4 <_write+4>:   0xe3a02001   0xe3a07004   0xef000000   0xe12fff1e
0x80c4 <_write+20>:  0x000100c8   0x00174120   0x65610000   0x00696261
0x80d4: 0x00000d01   0x08020600
```

Figure 14k. A hex dump of memory in GDB.

The command format is as follows:

```
x/nfu <addr>
```

Here the '/' is used to signify a change in the defaults; f being format which is hexadecimal by default; and u the unit size. <addr> is the start address from which this is to happen. In the example above 'w' specifies word or four-byte wide units and to show 22 of them, starting at 0x0874. Other unit sizes that are available are: b=bytes, h=halfwords (two bytes), g=giant words (eighth bytes).

When you specify a unit for x then that becomes the default value until it is changed again. When GDB is started the default value is 1.

The 'i' command in combination with 'x' can be used as an alternate way to produce a disassembly listing. Here:

```
x /13i 0x8074
```

will disassemble the _bits function.

The combinations are almost endless and it is a good investment of time to print a copy of the GDB Manual out and keep it bound and close to hand. GDB is really one of those tools that you will always be looking to get more from, and a printed copy is a good place to make notes and keep track of your favourite formats.

Finally, if you are wondering, typing 'quit' will exit GDB and return you to the command line.

15: Data Transfer

In most of the examples we have used so far, all data instructions used have come from either the contents of a register or an immediate constant — a specified value, like these examples:

```
ADD R0, R1, R2
SUB R0, R1, #7
```

There is only so much information that can be held in a set of registers, and registers have to be kept clear to perform operations on data. In general, data is created and then held at known memory locations. In such cases, we need to manage these memory blocks. To load and store data in memory we must know two things. First, the actual address of the data, and second, its ultimate destination – where it's coming from or going to. Registers are used in both circumstances, and the method of doing so depends on the addressing mode used. There are three addressing modes offered by the ARM:

- Indirect Addressing
- Pre-Indexed Addressing
- Post-Indexed Addressing

These methods load or store the contents of a specified register, but in each case the data source or destination is different.

ADR Directive

In Chapter 6 we examined the use of immediate constants and saw that although the MOV and MVN instructions can be used to load constants into a register, not all constant values are accessible in this way. The knock-on of this is that they cannot be used to generate every available memory address for the same reason. Therefore, the GCC Assembler provides a method that will load any 32-bit address. In its simplest form it looks like this:

```
ADR <Register>, <Label>
```

An example would be:

```
ADR R0, datastart
```

Despite its appearance, the ADR is a directive and not an ARM instruction. It is part of the assembler. What it does is take the hard work out of calculating the right number for you. When the assembler encounters this directive it does the following:

- Notes the address of where the instruction is being assembled.
- Notes the address of the specified label.
- Calculates the offset between the two memory positions.

It will then use this information as part of an appropriate instruction, normally ADD or SUB, to reconstruct the location of the address or label containing the information.

It's worth looking at what we write in an example program and what actually gets assembled to illustrate the point. Look at the listing given in Program 15a:

Program 15a. Use of the ADR directive.

```
/**** using the ADR directive ****/

    .global _start
_start:
    ADR R0, value
    MOV R1, #15

_exit:
    MOV R7, #1
    SWI 0

value:
    .word 255
```

Program 15a does nothing really, other than point ADR at the data label and show R0 as the destination register. When this is assembled it will produce something similar to what is shown in Figure 15b. If you use GDB and enter:

```
x/4i _start
```

the ADR directive has not assembled an address. It has assembled a relative address that will be used as an offset for the Program Counter,. Here the

ADD instruction is used to add 8 to the PC, the address of value which comes right after the last instruction.

```
0x8054    <_start>:      add    r0, pc, #8
0x8058    <_start+4>:    mov    r1, #15
0x805c    <_exit>:       mov    r7, #1
0x0860    <_exit+4>:     svc    0x00000000
```

Figure 15a. Disassembly of Program 15a

Note also that the instruction:

    SWI 0

Has been disassembled to:

    SVC 0

Showing the two commands are interchangeable. The preferred method is probably SVR these days, but I am still old hat and tend to use SWI.

In GDB type:

    x/5w _start

The output will be similar to that shown in Figure 15b.

```
0x8054 <_start>:  0xe28f0008 0xe3a0100f 0xe3a07001
       0xef000000
0x0864 <value>:   0x000000ff
```

Figure 15b. Hex dump of Program 15a.

Here the 255 stored at the label marked by value can clearly be seen. This illustrates another new feature of the assembler. You may recall in an earlier chapter that we used the directive called .string to load an ASCII character string into memory. Here the '.word' directive allows us to store a word — or four bytes — into memory. The format of this is shown clearly in Program 15a and it can be referred to by using a named label. (We'll look at .word and other directives in Chapter 18.)

This also illustrates another very important aspect of the ADR pseudo-instruction. The values it references must always be within the .text or executable section of the code. You will recall that use of the .string directive, which was being accessed by the LDR instruction, was placed in the .data section of the code. If you try and use ADR to access information in a data

ARM A32 Assembly Language

area you will get an error message. Okay, let's get back to the subject of addressing modes.

Indirect Addressing

The ARM is constructed with a 'load and store' architecture, but you cannot access memory locations directly. You can only access them indirectly via a register. The beauty of indirect addressing is that it enables the whole of the ARM's memory map to be reached through a single register.

There are two instructions that read and write memory data:

```
LDR         LoaD Register from memory
STR         STore Register to memory
```

Indirect addressing provides an easy method to read or write to a memory location. The address of the location is held in a register. So the address location is accessed indirectly. The advantage of this method is that you can change the source or destination location simply by changing the contents of the register. This makes it a handy way to dip into tables of data. Rather than writing a separate routine for each, a general purpose one can be developed, with the address operand being 'seeded' on each occasion that the routine is called.

In its simplest form indirect addressing takes the format:

```
LDR (<suffix>) <Operand1> [<Operand2>]
STR (<suffix>) <Operand1> [<Operand2>]
```

For example:

```
LDR R0,[R1]    @ Load R0 with contents at location in R1
STR R0,[R2]    @ Store R0 at memory location in R2
```

Executing the above two instructions would effectively transfer a word of data from one point in memory to another. Figure 15c illustrates this and is based on the instruction:

```
LDR R0, [R1]
```

At the onset R1 holds the memory address, here 0x9308, and that memory address contains the value 0xF80A. This value is loaded into R0. So on completion of the instruction R0 will contain 0xF80A. The value in R1 is unaltered.

All the addressing modes allow use of suffixes to effect conditional execution. So, for example:

```
LDREQ R0, [R1]
```

143

Here, the load operation into R0 from the address in R1 will only take place if the Zero flag is set.

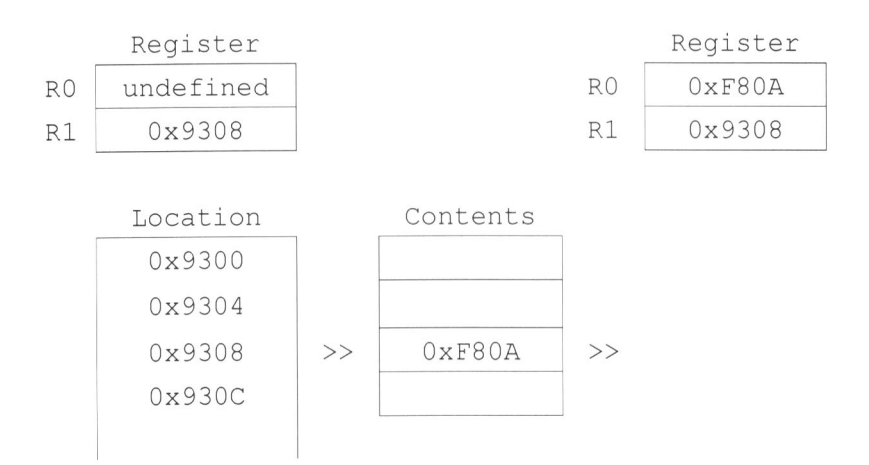

```
       Register                              Register
  R0 | undefined |                      R0 |  0xF80A  |
  R1 |  0x9308   |                      R1 |  0x9308  |

       Location        Contents
       0x9300     |            |
       0x9304     |            |
       0x9308  >> |   0xF80A   | >>
       0x930C     |            |
```

Figure 15c. Indirect addressing of memory using LDR R0, [R1].

ADR and LDR

In previous examples we have seen that LDR can be used in a pseudo-instruction manner to load the address of a label directly into a register. For example:

```
LDR R0, =string
```

would load R0 directly with the address of the label called string. The advantage of LDR used in this way is that it can access memory across the board, and is the preferred method if you are using data sections specifically to hold information. Labels accessed by ADR must be within .text sections of code and within the executable code area. This can be useful if you are creating data pools on the fly as you code.

Immediate Constants

Although we have used ADR to provide the correct address, it is still possible to use immediate constants with the MOV and MVN commands. The only problem that will arise is when you encounter a constant that you can't load. In these instances you will need to work out ways to synthesise the address. This might be as the nearest immediate value to which you would then add or subtract an appropriate amount to arrive at the required address.

Pre-Indexed Addressing

Pre-indexed addressing provides the ability to add an offset to the base address to give the final address. The offset can be an immediate constant or a value in a register, or indeed, the shifted contents of a register. The format of the instruction is:

```
LDR  (<suffix>) <destination>, [(<base>,(<offset>)]
STR  (<suffix>) <destination>, [(<base>,(<offset>)]
```

The modifying constant or register is simply placed as part of Operand2, separated by a comma, within the square brackets. For example:

```
LDR R0, [R1, #8]
```

Here, 0x08 is added to the address in R1 and the four-byte value at that address (R1+8) is placed in R0. Note that the value of R1 is not changed or adjusted by the constant. This is depicted in Figure 15d. R1 contains the memory address 0x9300. This is added to the specified constant value 8, to give a final source address of 0x9308. The contents of this location, 0xFB0A are loaded into R0.

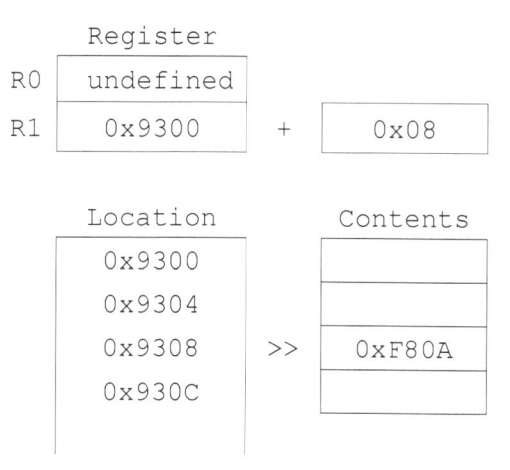

	Register
R0	undefined
R1	0x9300

+

0x08

Location		Contents
0x9300		
0x9304		
0x9308	>>	0xF80A
0x930C		

Figure 15d. Pre-Indexed Addressing.

You can use two registers inside the square brackets too:

```
STR R0, [R1, R2]
```

This instruction, when executed, would store the value in R0 at the address given by adding the contents of registers R1 and R2 together. R1 and R2 are not adjusted in any way.

ARM A32 Assembly Language

You can also subtract the offset as well, simply by placing a minus sign in front of the offset:

```
LDR R0, [R1, #-8]
STR R0, [R1, -R2]
```

Finally, the offset operand may be rotated using one of the shift operations thus:

```
LDR R0, [R1, R2, LSR#4]
```

The value in R2 is shifted right by two bits and added to R1. This gives the address of the data to be loaded into R0. This final construction is useful when it comes to moving through data held in memory, given that it is located in four-byte blocks (ie, 32-bits and the size of a register) and that an LSL #2 operation (which is 2 x 2 = 4) moves you elegantly to the next word boundary.

The following segment replaces the third item in a four-byte wide list with the second item in the list, with the address of the start of the list held in R1, in this example held as 0x9300:

```
MOV R2, #4              @ four byte offset
LDR R4, [R1, R2]        @ load R4 from (0x9300+4)
STR R4, [R1, R2, LSL #1] @ store R4 at(0x9300+8)
```

Here, 4 is given as the offset as the first item is stored at offset #0 (ie, the base address). Then the LSL #1 shifts the bits along by four places. The #4 in R2 becomes #8 which is added to the address in R1. The value in R2 does not change itself. If you wanted to locate the next item in this list you would need to increment either R1 or R2 by four. But there is a far more elegant way as we shall see.

Accessing Memory Bytes

Program 15b illustrates the use of pre-indexed indirect addressing, using an offset to extract characters from a string located at a base address. It also uses the instruction, LDRB to load a register with a single byte, and STRB to store a single byte.

ASCII characters are represented in single bytes, so LDRB will allow us to load single bytes of memory, rather than a word, at the location specified. To start with, R1 is loaded with the address of the string, and 26 as an offset into R2. The STRB instruction is complementary to LDRB in that it writes a single byte of information into memory. Program 15b overleaf uses both of these commands to overwrite one string with another:

Program 15b. Use of pre-indexed indirect addressing.

```
/**** Use pre-indexed addr to move chars ****/
/*                                           */

        .global _start
_start:

        LDR R1, =string        @ Get 1st string location
        LDR R3, =numbers       @ Get 2nd string location
        MOV R2, #26            @ chars in alphabet

_loop:
        LDRB R0, [R1, R2]      @ get byte at R1+R2
        STRB R0, [R3, R2]      @ save byte to R3+R2
        SUBS R2, R2, #1        @ decrement and flag set
        BPL _loop              @ and loop while positive

_write:
        MOV R0, #1
        LDR R1, =numbers
        MOV R2, #26
        MOV R7, #4
        SWI 0

_exit:
        MOV R7, #1
        SWI 0

.data
string:
        .ascii "ABCDEFGHIJKLMNOPQRSTUVWXYZ"
numbers:
        .ascii "01234567891011121314151617"
```

At entry, _start sets up R1 and R3 with the address of the two strings. R2 is used to hold the counter which is initialised at 26 — the number of letters in the alphabet.

The LDRB instruction loads the byte at R1+R2 into R0 and this is then stored at R3+R2. So first time around the last character in string: is stored over the last character in numbers: R2 is decremented by one and while the number is not zero or below the loop cycles again. When R2 reaches zero, the read/write is completed and the _write routine prints the new string out.

Although we haven't used immediate constants in these examples, they are certainly available to you and may also be specified as negative values. Here are a couple of examples:

```
STR R0, [R1, #0xF0]
LDR R0, [R1,#-4]
```

In the latter example, R0 would be loaded with data taken from an address which is one word lower than the address contained in R1.

Address Write Back

In calculating the location in memory of the word or byte, the ARM adds the contents of the items held inside the square brackets, the first being a register with an address, and the second being a register or immediate constant. Once the result of the addition of these values has been used it is discarded.

It is sometimes useful to retain the calculated address, and this can be done in pre-indexed addressing, using a method called 'write back'. This is done by including a '!' at the end of the instruction, after the closing square bracket:

```
LDR R0, [R1, R2]!
LDRB R0, [R2, #10]!
```

In the first example, if we refer to our earlier programs, let's assume that R1 holds the address 0x9300 and R2 contains the index initially set at 26. Now, on the first iteration R1 and R2 point to the address given by 0x9300+26 which is 0x931A. This address is used to source the information and then 0x931A is written back into R1.

To step through an array of data held in memory we might use the instruction:

```
LDR R0, [R1, #4]!
```

The value 4 will be added to R1 and thus create a single word step. The value in R1 is updated to reflect R1+4. By including this in a loop we can quickly step through memory with little hindrance.

Post-Indexed Addressing

Post-indexed addressing uses the write back feature by default. However, the offset field isn't optional and must be supplied. The offset is also handled differently. Post-indexed addressing takes this format:

```
LDR (<suffix>) <Destination>, [<Operand1>],<Operand2>
```

The first thing to note is that the compulsory Operand2 is based outside the square brackets to signify the difference in addressing mode. Here are a few examples of how the instruction is formatted:

```
LDR R0, [R1], R2
STR R3, [R4], #4
LDRB R6,[R1], R5, LSL#1
```

When post-indexed addressing is used, the contents of the base register alone are taken as the source or destination address (word or byte depending on the format of instruction). Only after the memory has been extracted or deposited are the contents of the offset field (Operand2) added to the base register and the value written there. Thus the offset is added post and not pre memory access. Figure 15e below illustrates this diagrammatically for the command:

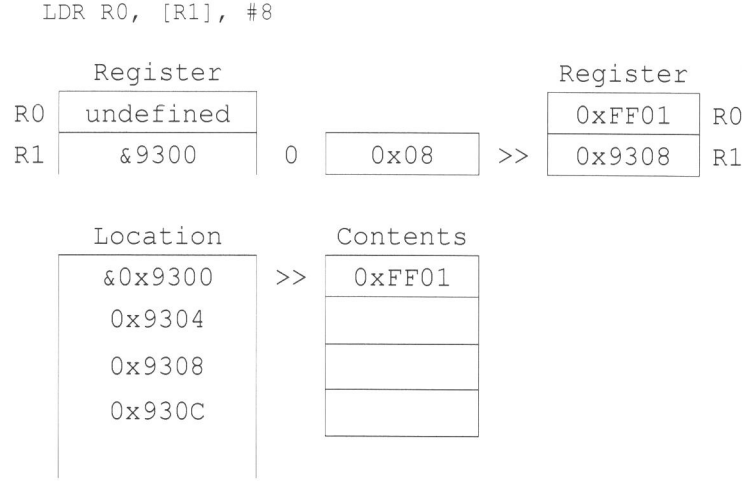

```
LDR R0, [R1], #8
```

	Register					Register	
R0	undefined					0xFF01	R0
R1	&9300	0	0x08	>>		0x9308	R1

	Location		Contents
	&0x9300	>>	0xFF01
	0x9304		
	0x9308		
	0x930C		

Figure15e. Post indexed addressing process.

The left hand side of the diagram shows the situation before the command executes. The contents of R0 are undefined at this stage. R1 contains the address 0x9300. The location 0x9300 contains 0xFF01, and this is taken and placed in R0. The intermediate value 8 is then added to the contents of R1

(0x9300+08) and the result written back into R1, leaving R1 now containing 0x9308 as now reflected on the right hand side of the diagram.

Program 15c. Using post-indexed addressing.

```
/**** Use post-indexed addr to concat strings ****/
/*                                                */
     .global _start
_start:
     LDR R2, =string1      @ load locations
     LDR R3, =string2      @ of both strings
_loop:
     LDRB R0, [R3], #1     @ Get string2 byte & +1
     CMP R0, #0            @ is it end of string?
     BNE _loop             @ no, then get next byte
     SUB R3, R3, #1        @ Yes, decrement back 1

_copyloop:
     LDRB R0, [R2], #1     @ get byte from string 1
     STRB R0, [R3], #1     @ add to end of string 2
     CMP R0, #0            @ is it 0?
     BNE _copyloop         @ if not get next char

_write:
     MOV R0, #1            @ is 0 so print new
     LDR R1, =string2
     MOV R2, #24
     MOV R7, #4
     SWI 0

_exit:
     MOV R7, #1
     SWI 0

.data
string1:
     .asciz "ABCDEFGHIJKL"
string2:
     .asciz "012345678910"
```

```
padding:
    .ascii "                    "
```

If the LDR line was executed again then the contents of 0x9308 would be extracted and deposited in R0, and after 8 is added to it R1 would contain 0x9310.

Program 15c will create a machine code routine that uses post-indexed addressing to join two strings to create one single string.

Note that in the data definitions for the string we use a slight twist on the .ascii directive. Here we use .asciz — which will place a zero byte (0x0) at the end of the string, and we use this to see if we have reached the end of the strings during the load and compare portions of the program.

Byte Conditions

Conditional suffixes may be used with the load and store instructions in a similar fashion to others. However, when you are using the byte modifier with conditionals, you should express the conditional instruction first, thus:

```
LDREQB R0, [R1]
```

Note the condition test EQ comes before B, the byte modifier. If they are not in this order, an error message will result when you try to assemble the program.

PC Relative Addressing

Besides pre and post index addressing, the GCC Assembler implements an additional pseudo-addressing mode itself – PC relative addressing. We have already used this in previous examples, but it is worth highlighting its usefulness under a separate sub-heading here.

The general format of instructions that use PC relative addressing is as follows:

```
LDR <dest>, <address>
```

As before, the destination is always a register, into which — or from which — the data is transferred. The address is either an absolute number or an assembler label. In the latter case, the label marks the address from where the data will be placed or gathered. Let's look at a couple of examples:

```
LDR R0, 0x9300
```

```
    STR R0, data
```

In the first case, the word located at 0x9300 would be loaded into R0. In the second, the location which the label 'data' was assembled at would be used as the destination of the word to be held in R0.

When the Assembler encounters an instruction in such a format it looks at the address or location of the address and calculates the distance from where it is to the specified location. This distance is called the offset, and when added to the program counter would provide the absolute address of the data location. Knowing this, the assembler can compile an instruction that uses pre-indexed addressing. The base register in this instruction will be the program counter, R15. If we ignore effects of pipelining, the PC will contain the instructions address when executed. The offset field contains the absolute offset number as previously calculated by the assembler, with a correction for pipelining. (This is a similar method to the one described for branches in Chapter 12).

It is important to remember that there is a set range restriction in the offset that can be used in pre-indexed addressing. This is -4096 to 4096, and the offset in PC relative addressing must be within this range.

16: Block Transfer

Efficiency is one of the key design concepts behind the ARM chip. With the large number of registers and the consistent need to manipulate and move data, it would be very inefficient to have to sequence a whole series of instructions to transfer the contents of a set of registers from one place to another. The LDM and STM instructions simplify multiple load and store between registers and memory.

The format of the instruction is:

```
LDM <Options>(<Suffix>) <Operand1>(!), {<Registers>}
STM <Options>(<Suffix>) <Operand1>(!), {<Registers>}
```

Registers is a list of the registers, inside curly brackets and separated by commas, to be included in the transfer. The registers can be listed in any order, and a range of registers can be specified with the use of a hyphen, ie, R5-R9.

Reg			Memory	Contents
R0	0x9300	>>	0x9300	0xFF00FF00
R1	0xFF00FF00		0x9304	0x2A0D4AA
R2	0xFF		0x9308	0x953A
R3	0xA8FB		0x930C	0xF36BCA
R4	0xAF2		0x9310	0x101
R5	0x2A0D4AA			
R6	0x953A			
R7	0xF36BCA			
R8	0x101			

Figure 16a. Storing register contents in memory.

Operand1 is a register which contains the address marking the start of memory to be used for the operation. This address is not changed unless the write back operator ! is used in the instruction.

Here's an example:

```
STM R0, {R1, R5-R8}
```

Here, the contents of the registers R1, R5, R6, R7 and R8 (five words or 20 bytes in total) are read and stored sequentially, starting at the address held in R0. If R0 held 0x9300 then R1 would be stored here; R5 at 0x9304, R6 and 0x9308 and so forth as illustrated in Figure 16a.

Counting Options

The example in Figure 16a assumes that we want data to be stored in successively increasing memory address locations, but this need not be the case. The ARM provides options that allow memory to be accessed in an ascending or descending order, and also in which way the increment step is handled. In fact, there are four options as listed in Figure 16b.

Suffix	Meaning
IA	Increment After
IB	Increment Before
DA	Decrement After
DB	Decrement Before

Figure 16b. Suffixes for memory direction setting.

The I or D in the suffix defines whether the location point is being moved forwards (increasing) or backwards (decrementing) through memory. In other words, the base address is being increased four bytes at a time or decremented four bytes at a time.

After each instruction, the ARM will have performed one of the following:

Increment: Address = Address + 4 * n

Decrement: Address = Address - 4 * n

where 'n' is the number of registers in the register list.

The A or B options determine where the base address has the defined adjustment before or after the memory has been accessed. There is a subtle difference, and if you are not careful it can lead to your information being a word askew to what you might have expected. This is illustrated in Figure 16c and Figure 16d.

ARM A32 Assembly Language

In Figure 16c the left hand model shows the storage pointer in Incrementing After mode. After the first register has been stored (R0), the storage pointer has four added to it and is incremented to Base+4 where the contents of R1 are placed. On the right hand side of the model Incrementing Before is in operation. When the command is executed 4 is added to Base and the contents of R0 is stored at that address.

In Figure 16d the actions are the same except that in each case 4 is subtracted from Base either After or Before as illustrated.

```
STMIA Base,{R0-R6}           STMIB Base,{R0-R6}
```

			R6	Base+28
R6	Base+24		R5	Base+24
R5	Base+20		R4	Base+20
R4	Base+16		R3	Base+16
R3	Base+12		R2	Base+12
R2	Base+8		R1	Base+8
R1	Base+4		R0	Base+4
R0	<<Base			<<Base

Figure 16c. The effect of IA and IB suffixes on STM.

Write Back

Unless the instruction asks for write back to occur, then the address held in the specifying register remains unaltered. Its contents remain the same as they were when the command was first fetched. If we want write back to take place, the '!' operator must be included. For example:

```
LDMIA R0!,{R2-R4}
STMDA R0!,{R5-R8, R10}
```

The value written into the address register (R0) is the address calculated after the last register in the list has been processed.

STMDA Base,{R0-R6}		STMDB Base,{R0-R6}	
			<<Base
R0	<<Base	R0	Base-4
R1	Base-4	R1	Base-8
R2	Base-8	R2	Base-12
R3	Base-12	R3	Base+16
R4	Base-16	R4	Base-20
R5	Base-20	R5	Base-24
R6	Base-24	R6	Base-28

Figure 16d. The effect of DA and DB suffixes on STM.

The STM and LDM instructions have a variety of applications. One of the most obvious is that used in combination they can be used to preserve and restore the contents of all the registers. If R0 holds the address of a free memory block then save all the registers with:

```
STMIA R0, {R1-R14}
```

And restore them later with:

```
LDM R0, {R1-R14}
```

assuming that R0 again has the address of the memory block.

A word of caution about including R15 in a list like this. If you block restore with LDM and include R15 you will most likely set your program into a continuous loop. A real case of Ground Hog Day.

This write back feature in this block data transfer instruction is provided to simplify the creation of stacks, which is the subject of the next chapter.

Block Copy Routine

Program 16a shows just how simple it is to copy a block of data from one place in memory to another. In fact, just four lines of assembler is all it takes, and this routine is robust enough to copy a block of memory that can be any length provided it is divisible by 8.

It uses registers R3 and R4 to first load and then store the data, so any information in them will be destroyed unless preserved first. R0, R1 and R2 hold addresses that point to the start and end of the data and the start address of its ultimate destination, respectively.

To see this work you can use GDB. Make sure you assemble with the -g option. Enter GDB and load the file:

```
gdb prog14a
```

Set a breakpoint at the _exit routine (this is right after the block copy loop):

```
break _exit
```

Now run the program:

```
run
```

The program will run to the breakpoint, at which point type:

```
x/2x &dest
```

The '&' is used here to mean the 'location of' dest. If you do not use the ampersand then the data labels will not be recognised. When the two words of memory are displayed you will see that all the bits are now set (all Fs) proving the block copy worked, as they were 0s originally.

The routine can be extended to handle bigger blocks of memory. For example by changing the two load and store instructions to read

```
LDMIA R0!, {R3-R12}
STMIA R2!, {R3-R12}
```

you can work in blocks of 40 bytes (10 registers by 4 bytes each). Your data areas will need to be adjusted accordingly, or rather than using labels you may need to invoke absolute memory addresses.

Program 16a. Moving blocks of memory.

```
/**** Block copy routine ****/
/*                          */
    .global _start
```

ARM A32 Assembly Language

```
_start:
    LDR R0, =start      @ load locations
    LDR R1, =end        @ of both strings
    LDR R2, =dest       @ addr of destination

_blockcopy:
    LDMIA R0!, {R3-R4}
    STMIA R2!, {R3-R4}
    CMP R0, R1
    BNE _blockcopy

_exit:
    MOV R7, #1
    SWI 0

.section .data
start:
    .word 0xFFFFFFFF
    .word 0xFFFFFFFF
end:
    .word 0
    .word 0
dest:
    .word 0
    .word 0
```

17: Stacks

Stacks have been a fundamental feature of computer systems since just after the day dot. In many respects they are exactly what you might think them to be, stacks of data, but they are stacks of data that you as the programmer own and control. Their management is a fundamental component of designing programs. Do it well and the program flows well. Do it badly and you'll be reaching for the power switch.

The general analogy is a stack of plates. In theory, you can continue putting a plate on top of a plate. Unless you are attempting a trick, if you want to take a plate off the stack it will be the last one you placed on it. In this respect the last one on is the first one off. We refer to this as a LIFO structure, last in, first out. Try to take a plate out from the middle (or the bottom!) and, unless you do so very carefully, the lot comes crashing down. It's a good analogy.

Push and Pull

In the early days of home computers on systems such as the BBC Micro, stacks were built in a simple fashion. You pushed data onto the stack and pulled data off the stack. For the most part you didn't even know where the stack was — that was managed by the CPU. However, as a programmer you did need to keep track of what order things went on to the stack. Generally the concept is still true today in that a sequence of data pulled from the stack is always pulled from it in the reverse order it was pushed.

The instructions STM and LDM and their derivatives are what we use for pushing (STM) and pulling (LDM) data onto and off ARM stacks. These stacks are areas of memory that we as the programmer define. There is no limit to the number of stacks that can be used. The only restriction is the amount of memory available to implement them.

R13, also known as the Stack Pointer or SP, is designated to be used to hold an address relating to the location of the stack, but you can use any of the available registers for the purpose. If you are running several stacks you will

ARM A32 Assembly Language

need to allocate more registers or manage where you store the addresses in memory. Figure 17a illustrates a very simple stack.

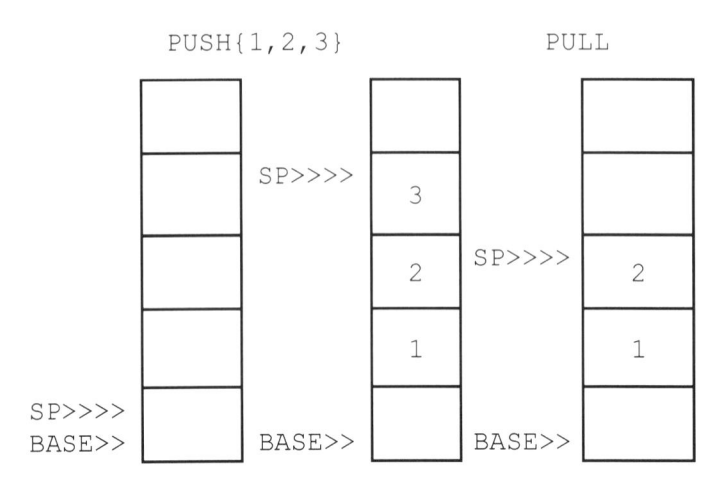

```
      PUSH{1,2,3}              PULL
    ┌───┐                    ┌───┐
    │   │                    │   │
    ├───┤                    ├───┤
    │   │SP>>>>              │   │
    │   │     ┌───┐          │   │
    ├───┤     │ 3 │          ├───┤
    │   │     ├───┤          │   │
    │   │     │ 2 │SP>>>>    │ 2 │
    ├───┤     ├───┤          ├───┤
    │   │     │ 1 │          │ 1 │
SP>>>>        │   │          │   │
BASE>>└───┘   BASE>>└───┘    BASE>>└───┘
```

Figure 17a. A simple stack where each stack item is four bytes wide.

To implement a simple stack we can use the following instructions. The important thing to note is that the options for the STM instructions are always reversed for the LDM instruction.

```
STMIA SP!,{R0-R12, LR} @ push registers onto stack
LDMDB SP!,{R0-R12, PC} @ pull registers from stack
```

The IA and DB suffix options (introduced in the last chapter) are used in tandem to move up through memory to push them on, and then down through memory to pull them off. The LR and PC registers are used to save the Program Counter's address, therefore this two line combination is an effective way to save register contents before calling a subroutine and restoring everything on return.

The use of the write back function is absolutely vital. Without write back the Stack Pointer will not be updated, and the stack will effectively be corrupted as we will not know our relative positive within it.

You may implement a stack with two pointers. The first is the base point, and this locates to the memory location where the stack begins. The second is the stack pointer which is used to point to the top of the stack. The base pointer remains a static address; the stack pointer might be a moving address or an offset from the base pointer. Hopefully, you can now understand how different addressing modes could be used to organise different types of stacks. Whichever way you fall, you will always need to keep a record of where the stack starts and the point where it must end. Without defining these two end limits, you could get into all sorts of trouble. Also, does the Stack Pointer provide the address of the next free space in the stack or the last space used? To make this situation easier to manage and to manage the balancing of pushes and pulls more easily some additional options are provided.

Stack Growth

In ARM architecture stacks are grouped by the manner in which they grow through memory. Stacks can ascend through memory as items are pushed onto them, and they can descend through memory as data is pushed onto them. It's like being in space — there is no up and down, and the term is relative. Stand on the 10th floor of an empty 20 storey building. The 10th floor is the only entry and each floor, above and below, has four apartments. Eight families arrive; you can accommodate them on two floors up or two floors down. How do you want to do it?

In computer memory terms a stack that grows up — or ascends through memory — is one where the address grows larger. So as an item is pushed into it, the Stack Pointer increases its address by four bytes. A stack that grows in memory by going down the memory address decreases; this is called a descending stack.

In all, there are four types of stacks as listed in Figure 17b:

Postfix	Meaning
FA	Full Ascending Stack
FD	Full Descending Stack
EA	Empty Ascending Stack
ED	Empty Descending Stack

Figure 17b. The four types of ARM stack.

When the stack pointer points to the last occupied address on the stack it is known as a full stack. When the stack pointer indicates the next available free space on the stack, it is called an empty stack. Note that in this empty stack scenario the stack can have data on it; it is used to signify the condition of the next free word on the stack.

The option of full, empty, ascending or descending will often force itself on you and may just be decided by the way you are looping through your data. It may be easier to implement a descending stack as your code lends itself to a decrementing count and it's easier to test for the Zero flag.

There are instructions in the instruction set that cater for these types of stacks and these are shown in Figure 17c.

Instruction Pair	Meaning
STMFD / LDMFD	Full Descending Stack
STMFA / LDMFA	Full Ascending Stack
STMED / LDMED	Empty Descending Stack
STMEA / LDMEA	Empty Ascending Stack

Figure 17c. Instruction set to access stacks.

Here are some examples:
```
STMED R13!, {R1-R5, R6}
LDMFD R13!, {R1-R4, R6}
```

There is nothing to stop you using different types of stacks within the same program. Just don't mix them up! Equally, you will understand now why write back is compulsory in the construction of these instructions.

Examples of these stacks are illustrated in Figure 17d and Figure 17e. By default, the ARM implements a full descending stack if a format is not specified.

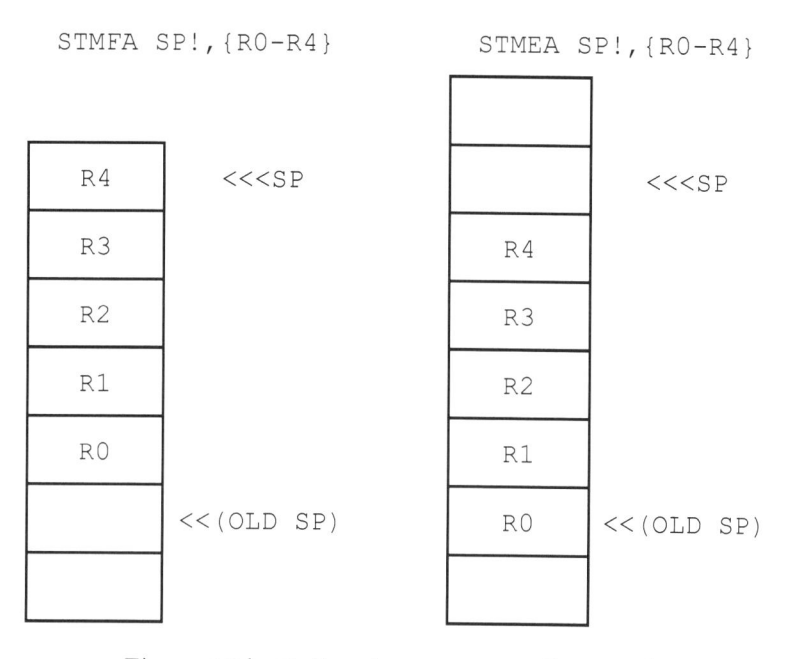

```
STMFA SP!,{R0-R4}              STMEA SP!,{R0-R4}

                                   
   ┌─────────┐                     ┌─────────┐
   │   R4    │ <<<SP               │         │ <<<SP
   ├─────────┤                     ├─────────┤
   │   R3    │                     │   R4    │
   ├─────────┤                     ├─────────┤
   │   R2    │                     │   R3    │
   ├─────────┤                     ├─────────┤
   │   R1    │                     │   R2    │
   ├─────────┤                     ├─────────┤
   │   R0    │                     │   R1    │
   ├─────────┤                     ├─────────┤
   │         │ <<(OLD SP)          │   R0    │ <<(OLD SP)
   ├─────────┤                     ├─────────┤
   │         │                     │         │
   └─────────┘                     └─────────┘
```

Figure 17d. Full and empty ascending stacks.

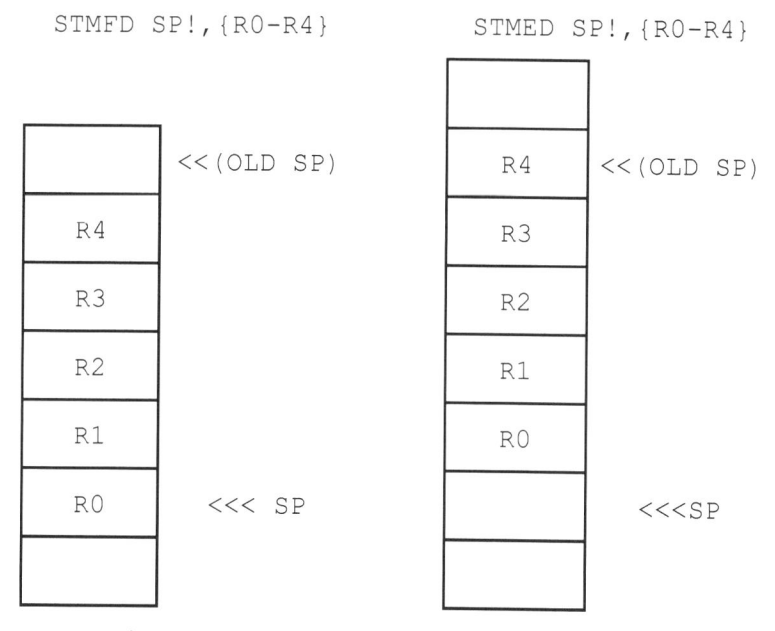

```
STMFD SP!,{R0-R4}              STMED SP!,{R0-R4}

   ┌─────────┐                     ┌─────────┐
   │         │                     │         │
   ├─────────┤                     ├─────────┤
   │         │ <<(OLD SP)          │   R4    │ <<(OLD SP)
   ├─────────┤                     ├─────────┤
   │   R4    │                     │   R3    │
   ├─────────┤                     ├─────────┤
   │   R3    │                     │   R2    │
   ├─────────┤                     ├─────────┤
   │   R2    │                     │   R1    │
   ├─────────┤                     ├─────────┤
   │   R1    │                     │   R0    │
   ├─────────┤                     ├─────────┤
   │   R0    │ <<< SP              │         │ <<<SP
   ├─────────┤                     ├─────────┤
   │         │                     │         │
   └─────────┘                     └─────────┘
```

Figure 17e. Full and empty descending stacks.

The best way to understand stacks and their manipulation is to experiment with them. Try seeding an area of memory with known values, and then see if you can move this section of memory to another location via a stack, with the information and its order remaining intact.

Stack Application

Stacks have a multitude of applications, and we have already mentioned a few of them:

- Saving register contents
- Saving and processing data

A third use is to save link addresses when subroutines are called. By pushing the link addresses from the Link Register onto the stack, it is possible to create nested (one inside another) routines without fear of losing control in the program. As you link to a routine you push the link register onto the stack. You can then return from each subroutine by pulling the link addresses off the stack and popping them back into the Program Counter.

The stack also makes it relatively simple to swap register contents around without ever having to go through another register. You simply push the required registers in the stack and then pull them in the order you need them. Imagine this situation where register contents need to be swapped:

Source	Destination
R0	R3
R1	R4
R2	R6
R3	R5
R4	R0
R5	R1
R6	R2

At first sight, this looks complex. However, the following four lines will manage it:

```
STMFD SP!, {R0-R6}
LDMFD SP!, {R3, R4, R6}
LDMFD SP!, {R5}
LDMFD SP!, {R0, R1, R2}
```

The first line pushes R0 to R6 onto the stack. The top three items on the stack are (in descending order) R0, R1 and R2. From the chart above these have to go into R3, R4, and R6 respectively, and this is what line two does.

The Stack Pointer is now positioned at R3, which is transferred into R5. This leaves just R4, R5 and R6 on the stack which, in the final line, is pulled into R0, R1 and R2 respectively. What looks to be a complex task at the onset is in fact a simple one.

18: Directives and Macros

GCC provides many additional tools to help in the writing of machine code programs. This includes instructions that allow you to store data within your programs and the ability to pass information to them when they are called from the prompt. All assembler directives begin with a period or full-stop and there are a lot of them with GCC. We have already seen several of these in action in earlier programs. In this chapter we'll look at some of them in more detail.

Data Storage Directives

To store character string information within our programs, there are two options:

```
.ascii "This is the string to print."
.asciz "This string has a zero added to the end"
```

A string is written between double-quotes. The 'z' in the second option stands for zero and a zero byte (0x00) is appended at the end of the string. This is a useful way to end mark a string in memory as it allows for a simple Zero flag test when you are looking for the end of it. Both directives allow for control or escape code characters to be embedded within them by use of a backslash character, '\'. Figure 18a gives some of the more popular and useful ones:

```
Option     Effect
\b         back space
\f         form feed
\n         newline
\r         return
\t         tab
\\         allows printing of '\' in the string
\"         allows " to be printed in the string
```

Figure 18a. Popular backslash controls for use in strings.

The following:

```
.ascii "1\t2\t3\r\n4\t5\t6\r\n7\t8\t9\r\n"
```

would print out a simple but neatly formatted table using any of the write routines shown in this book. (Remember to change the string length count accordingly.)

As your programs become more sophisticated and have real application you will need to store information in them. This might be in the form of constants, addresses or messages to be printed. For the latter, we have used the string operator. By placing the data within the body of the machine code, we can be safe in the knowledge that it is 'protected'.

In the block move example from Chapter 15 we saw a clear indication how this could be done by using the .word directive to write four-byte words of information to memory. As well as .word there are other directives that can create space in a similar way. Program 18a shows two of these, .byte and .equ.

Program 18a. Use of .byte and .equ directives.

```
/* Use of byte and equ to sum a set of numbers */
    .global _start
_start:

    LDR R1, =values
    LDR R2, =endvalues
    MOV R0, #0

_loop:
    LDRB R3, [R1], #increment
    ADD R0, R0, R3
    CMP R1, R2
    BNE _loop

_exit:
    MOV R7, #1
    SWI 0

.data
.equ increment, 1
```

```
values:
    .byte 1,2,3,4,5,6,7,8,9
endvalues:
```

The .byte directive allows for a sequence of values separated by commas to be stored sequentially in memory. As the directive suggests these values must be in the range 0-255.

The .equ directive allows an immediate value to be assigned to a name. The name can then be used in your source files. This is handy in that if you need to change the value at any point you just have to change the .equ definition and not any and every reference to it in the source.

If you look at the .data section of Program 18a you can see that the constant 'increment' has been assigned the value 1. You can see how this is used as the post-indexing counter at the start of the _loop routine.

The label values: is used to mark the start of the .byte definition. A second label called endvalues: is used to mark the end of the .byte sequence. This is a handy technique to use when dealing with tables or arrays of data as a simple CMP test sees if the end of the sequence has been reached. The program illustrates this.

If you assemble, link and run Program 18a and then enter:

```
echo $?
```

you will get the value 45 returned, which is the sum of the bytes.

Figure 18b below summarises a few important data directives.

Directive	Function
.equ	Assign immediate value to named label. Example: .equ one, 1
.byte	Store byte sized values, separated by commas into memory. Example: .byte 1,2,3,55,255
.word	Store four-byte values, separated by commas into memory. Example: .word 0xFFFFFFFF, 0xFF

Figure 18b. The common data storage directives.

ARM A32 Assembly Language

ALIGNing Data

If you intend to store data within your executable segments, in other words within the .text sections of your program, then this can create problems. All assembled opcodes must start on a word boundary. If you insert text or data that does not completely fill the space to a four-byte boundary then the assembler will freak and issue you with an:

```
Unaligned opcodes detected in executable segment
```

error.

Consider Program 18a. If you add these extra lines at the end of the _start: section:

```
    BAL _loop
_string:
    .ascii "12345"
```

and try to assemble the code you will get the above error. This can be corrected by adding the following after the .ascii definition:

```
    .align 2
```

This pads out the space with 0s to the next word boundary. You can check this out by using GDB.

Note that there is generally no reason to use the .align directive outside of the executable sections of your code. Any definitions made in data sections are normally stored at the end of the file by the assembler to avoid such problems.

Macros

A macro is a fragment of code – which can be of any length – and is defined by a name. The macro definition can be called from within the program by using the macros name. During assembly, the assembler block that constitutes the macro definition is inserted whenever the macro name is encountered in the listing.

Many programmers set about writing their library of macros that they can use in a variety of circumstances. They simply load the macros they need and then call the macro from their program when need. This differs from the pseudo-code given in Figure 2a at the start of the book which uses sub-routine calls to jump to different parts of the program. Macros create linear code – one long program! Both permit a group of instructions defined as a single entity.

Macros are not a substitute for subroutines since the macro is replaced with the code and therefore makes the program execution linear in nature. Long macros that are used many times in a program will result in an enormous expansion of the code size. In this case, a subroutine would be a better choice, since the code in the body of the subroutine is not inserted into source code when called.

Macros are useful when you have some difficult or complex calculations to do and where it may be easy to make a typo mistake. You can use the constant data inside the macro and pass the variable information to the macro each time you can do it. Macros are also useful to avoid the overhead of a subroutine call and return when the subroutine itself is but a few instructions.

Program 18b defines a simple macro, call 'multtwo' that takes two parameters, val1 and val2, which get stored in R1 and R2 respectively, and are multiplied together with their product stored in R0..

Program 18b. Implementing a simple macro.

```
/* Implement a simple macro    */
    .global _start
_start:

.macro multtwo val1, val2
    MOV R1, #\val1
    MOV R2, #\val2
    MUL R0, R1, R2
.endm

    multtwo 2, 2
    multtwo 3, 4

    MOV R7, #1              @ exit through syscall
    SWI 0
```

The '.macro' directive is used to define the macro which we give a name, 'multtwo' and I have chosen to call the two parameters 'val1' and 'val2'. As you can see the macro definition is terminated by the directive '.endm'.

Note that inside the macro definition the two named parameters are preceded with a backslash '\' character. This is to signify to the compiler that they are parameters and not absolute values. The most common mistake when writing macros is to omit the backslash before parameters.

Calling, or 'invoking' the macro is simple, just insert the name in the assembler and include the parameters. If you run Program 18b and then type:

```
echo $?
```

You'll get the result.

Program 18c. Multi-calling a macro.

```
/* Implement a simple macro #2    */

    .global  _start
_start:

    MOV R0, #0

.macro multtwo val1, val2
    MOV R1, #\val1
    MOV R2, #\val2
    MLA R0, R1, R2, R0
.endm

    multtwo 2, 2
    multtwo 3, 4
    multtwo 5, 6

    MOV R7, #1           @ exit through syscall
    SWI 0
```

Program 18c shows a midfield version of this which uses the MLA instruction to add the products of each multiplication together. This time we use the 'multtwo' macro three times to pass three successive sets of values to the macro to calculate:

(2*2)+(3*4)+(5*6)

Program 24d in Chapter 24 contains a macro that shows off how effective they can be and has a good mix of techniques.

19: Using libc

The assembler and linker we have been using to write and create machine programs so far is just a small part of the GCC Compiler. As I said at the onset the GNU GCC compiler is a C Compiler. It will take programs written in the C programming language and convert them into machine code. Broadly speaking, it takes the C source file and translates it into an assembly language source file, which in turn gets translated into an executable machine code program which is linked together. As you can see we have been dealing with the last couple of processes here. But that is only just the tip of the iceberg.

This is not a book about C programming, but that is not to say we cannot use many of the features that C and the GCC Compiler provides. This includes libc, which is the standard function library of C. As we saw in an earlier chapter we can use the Syscall interface to perform common operations such as input/output, memory management, string manipulation, and so forth.

Using C Functions in Assembler

Likewise the C language has no built-in facilities for performing these functions but provides the interface to allow access to them, without necessarily needing to know a lot about the underlying Syscall itself. In addition, many of the things you may be looking to program for yourself may already be found in libc or available in other C libraries, and they can be included and linked into your own assembly source. So there are in reality libraries to be found that are pre-packed and ready to be included by the compile process. Figure 19a illustrates diagrammatically how libc sits within the overall interface.

Syscalls	User Space	
Kernel	libc	Procedures

Figure 19a. libc and user space.

The kernel in our case is the OS. The area above it (which normally starts at about 0x8000 in the memory map under Linux) is the user space. This is where our files sit. Recall the addresses that were being displayed when we used GDB to disassemble our programs. The libc code sits directly on top of the kernel and any of our application code sits on top of this. Although it makes no real difference operationally, diagrammatically we can see how easy it is for the libc functions to tap into the kernel. For the most parts when an application is written, because it is often written in C, it uses the libc interface to tap into the Syscalls. Rarely in this situation would a programmer go directly to the Syscall.

The main reason for using the Syscalls directly and not using libc would be one of space and speed. Some might also consider it a purer method of programming and not the rather disjointed code that integrating libc creates. The libc library is of a certain size and much of its basic configuration might be redundant. This is not normally an issue, but for a tight, small routine where speed and memory overhead might be critical then it may be a critical consideration.

From a user point of view a copy of 'The GNU C Library Reference Manual' is essential. Not to learn C (but that isn't a bad thing to do — you will become increasingly aware of how fundamental it is to system and application programming) but for the detail of the various functions you can access. This contains information required and returned. In this chapter we'll be looking at some worked examples on these and using the above document as our source. The GNU C Library Reference Manual can be found on the GNU website for download or a link to it is available on the book support website via www.brucesmith.info. Another very good source of instant help is the online manual. At the command line prompt type:

```
man printf
```

and you will get a lot of text output relating to the use and directives available within this particular C function. Here 'man' stands for 'manual' and it will provide information relating to the function name after it.

Source File Structure

The format of the source file used with the full GCC compiler is a little different from what we have been using to date. It is no more difficult to create and is in fact a lot simpler to compile as we do not need to do the assembly and link stages separately — they can be done with a single command. Have a look at Program 19a. This is a revised version of the write string code that formed Program 7a.

Program 19a. GCC source file structure.

```
/**     Printing a string using libc    **/
/**     entry requirements change       **/
/**     and string must end with 0      **/
/**     when using printf function      **/

        .global main
        .func main
main:

        STMFD SP!, {LR}         @ save LR
        LDR R0, =string         @ R0 points to string
        BL printf               @ Call libc
        LDMFD SP!, {PC}         @ restore PC

_exit:
        MOV PC, LR              @ simple exit
.data
string:
        .asciz "Hello World String\n"
```

The first thing to notice is that the global _start definition has been replaced with global main thus:

```
        .global main
        .func main
 main:
```

The structure used is important as this is used by the compiler to tell libc where the main program is located. Because all C and lib C routines are written as named functions then we have to declare this main part of our code as a function and then use a label to mark exactly where the function starts. These three lines do that. (As you can see they effectively undertake the same task that _start does when using the assembler-linker only, notwithstanding the addition of the function definition.)

The two instructions at the start and end of the main function save and then restore the link register on the stack. These commands and their use were discussed in Chapter 17. Strictly speaking they are not necessary here but it is often an accepted convention just to preserve the link register when a function is entered. So we'll stick with it for now.

The libc function **printf** is used to print the asciz string defined at the end of the listing. printf is not a C command but is a function defined in the library that we can use. It is a very versatile function and all that is required before we call it is for R0 to be given the address of the string. In all cases printf requires that the string be terminated with a zero and this is why the asciz directive is — and should always — be used.

Finally, we have abandoned our normal exit function for the much simpler MOV instruction. The SWI version would have worked equally as well, but the full GCC compiler will accept this exit method which is more common in the wider programming world. You can continue to use the SWI method if you like the option of using the echo command to display return contents.

If you have tried to assemble and link this command in the way we have described so far it will have failed because there is no _start entry point. Compiling with GCC can be done in a single step thus:

```
gcc <options> <destination_name> <input_name.s>
```

So for Program 19a you might use:

```
gcc -o prog19a prog19a.s
```

and run the program with:

```
./prog19a
```

Investigating the Executable

At this stage it is worth looking at the code that is compiled using GDB. Recompile including the –g option to create the debugging data:

```
gcc -g -o prog19a prog19a.s
```

and then enter the disassembler:

```
gdb prog19a
```

If you now disassemble some code using:

```
disassemble main
```

or

```
x/44i main
```

you should see by the labels used that the library component of the file is tagged on after _exit: However, if you look through the listing you should also see branches to addresses before your main entry point. Inspect these areas. You will see that the labels associated in the listing indicate that this is libc initialisation code. Your program has almost been wrapped within libc! As you look at the listing you will probably notice some instructions that we haven't discussed so far (but will with the next program example).

Investigating listings in this way is a great way to learn about machine code programming. Remember, you can step through this code and print register values out at any time using GDB, so you can get a good insight into what is happening and how.

The **printf** function is amazingly versatile and I could fill a book with examples. Program 19b shows how values can be passed into printf and used in printing results.

Program 19b. Passing parameters to printf.

```
/****   Printing a string using libc and  ****/
/****   passing parameters to function    ****/
/****   for use in printf                 ****/

        .global main
        .func main
main:
        PUSH {LR}               @ use pseudo directive
        LDR R0, =string         @ R0 points to string
        MOV R1, #10             @ first value in R1
        MOV R2, #15             @ second value in R2
        MOV R3, #25             @ result in R3
        BL printf               @ Call libc
        POP {PC}                @ restore PC with pseudo

_exit:
        MOV PC, LR              @ simple exit

.data
string:
        .asciz "If you add %d and %d you get %d.\n"
```

The first thing to notice here is that the entry and exit instructions for main: have changed. We are using PUSH and POP. These are actually compiler directives and not ARM instructions but they have the same effect as the ones used in Program 19a. They are a lot easier to use as you don't have to think too much about what type of stack you are going to use and what order the stack adjusters are used in. (However, it is worth remembering that should you decide to use another assembler, directives may change and not be compatible with your existing code. That said, you will almost certainly have to make adjustments to your code format with a new assembly program.)

The string definition here includes three parameters within it. These are signified by the preceding '%'. If you compile and run this program you will see that its output is:

```
If you add 10 and 15 you get 25.
```

Looking at the listing for Program 19b we can see that these three values were passed in R1, R2 and R3. When using libc functions such as printf there is a standard way to pass and return information into them and we'll look at this in the next chapter which deals with writing functions.

The table in Figure 19b below lists some of the output options available to use within printf. This list is by no means extensive but it does provide some options for you to experiment with, by editing the above program.

Code	Function
%d	Print an integer as a signed decimal number.
%o	Print an integer as an unsigned octal number.
%u	Print an integer as an unsigned decimal number.
%x	Print an integer as an unsigned hexadecimal numbers using lower-case letters
%X	Print an integer as an unsigned hexadecimal number using upper-case letters.
%c	Print a single character.
%%	Print a literal '%' character.

Figure 19b Output parameters recognised by printf.

Number Input with Scanf

You could be forgiven for thinking that **scanf** performs the reverse task of printf, but it does not. scanf takes a string of characters entered at the keyboard and converts it into its numerical value and stores it in memory. For example, if when using scanf you typed:

```
255
```

when requested scanf would store the binary equivalent in memory. In hex this would be:

```
0xFF
```

The reason for discussing this routine at this point, rather than the string-input routine equivalent of printf is that it illustrates another way a libc function expects and uses data. Not all functions expect data in the same way. This is a concept that you will need to bear in mind as you come to learn how to access libc functions and write your own (discussed, as I said earlier, in the next chapter).

However, as with printf, scanf recognises many, many different formats and you could spend a great deal of time learning and experimenting with them both. For this example we'll stick with the use of integer values. This is the %d format introduced in the previous program example.

The format for use of scanf is as follows (this is stylised — it is not how it would be coded in C):

```
scanf <input_format>, <variable>
```

or:

```
scanf "%d", integernumber
```

The steps for using scanf are these:

- Declare a memory variable holding the address of the formatting string. This will be a string "%d" for this example.
- Declare a memory variable holding the address of where the value is to be placed.
- Make space on the stack for the converted ASCII string to be stored.

Notice how in this case we are pointing to the information indirectly; we are passing the addresses of the relevant information. This is important to know because it means that to use the indirect addresses we have to declare the variables, and here we are talking about the .word directive, within the text area, in other words within the executable code area. The string definitions themselves should remain outside the text section and be defined in the data segment of the code. The other thing you need to know is that scanf stores its result on the stack, so to prevent it being corrupted we need to adjust the stack point by a word to make a safe place for it. Program 19c should help disperse the mist.

Program 19c. Reading and converting a number with scanf.

```
1   /******  Reading a number using scanf    *****/
2   /******  via registers and the stack     *****/
3
4   .global main
5   .func main
6   main:
7       PUSH {LR}
8       SUB SP, SP, #4      @ Make room on stack
9       LDR R0, addr_format @ get addr of format
10      MOV R1, SP          @ place SP in R1 and
11      BL scanf            @ store entry on stack
12      LDR R2, [SP]
13      LDR R3, addr_number
14      STR R2, [R3]
15      ADD SP, SP, #4
16      POP {PC}            @ restore PC
17
18  _exit:
19      MOV PC, LR          @ simple exit
20
21  /* as scanf needs addresses of strings we */
22  /* assemble them in the text area         */
23
24  addr_format:            .word scanformat
25  addr_number:            .word number
26
27      .data
28  number:     .word 0
29  scanformat: .asciz "%d"
```

The line numbers are there to help in the description of the program and should be omitted when you are entering the listing. You can turn them on in Vim by using the 'set number' command in command mode.

Let's look at the listing. Lines 6 and 18 should be familiar and should be considered part of standard procedure. Line 8 is where we adjust the stack pointer by four bytes to make some space for scanf. Before we call scanf we need to place the SP address into R1 (line 10) and the address of the format string in R0 (line 9). The format string should indicate the details of the value that will be entered at the keyboard and read by scanf. This ensures that the value is converted correctly.

After calling scanf (line 11) the converted binary value is now held on the stack, so this is retrieved (line 12) and the address of where it is to be saved is placed in line 13. Then using indirect addressing the value is stored (line 14). To tidy up, we should reset the stack point by subtracting the 4 additional bytes we originally added to it (line 15).

Lines 25 to 29 show how we create addresses to point to the actual data to be utilised. The actual data is in the .data subsection (lines 27-29) and the addresses of these two places are held in word length addresses within the text area defined by lines 24 and 25. Thus on assembly the four-bytes of space created by line 24 will hold the address of the string "%d". This is the formatting string we encountered earlier. Line 25 creates a place for the address of where the result returned by scanf will be placed.

When you run this program there will be no prompt. Just enter a number such as 255 and press the return key. The prompt will be returned. If you have compiled the program with debugging information enabled (the –g option) then you can use GDB to single step through the code and interrogate the registers at each stage. This is a very worthwhile exercise and what seems a convoluted way to do something is in fact very simple once you have your head around it!

Program 19d overleaf extends the above routine to provide some interaction using printf to request the value and then print the result.

Note that in this program the information is expected to be entered in decimal format, but the result is actually displayed in hex — see the very last line of the program.

Getting This Information

If you have no experience with C then you may be wondering how best to get all this information and then understand how to use it. Good question.

The bald answer is that there is no central resource and that it comes down to investigation and interrogation. Websites and user forums are a good source of detail for one. The other way is actually look at what the function itself does and by generating the source code for it and then using GDB you may understand what it is doing. As your knowledge of ARM machine code increases then this will become a more common option and we'll have a look at just how to go about it in a later chapter.

Program 19d. Combining scanf and printf.

```
/******   Reading a number using scanf    *****/
/******   and printing it with prinf      *****/

        .global main
        .func main
main:
    PUSH {LR}               @ use pseudo directive
    SUB SP, SP, #4          @ make a word on stack

    LDR R0, addr_messin     @ get addr of messagein
    BL printf               @ and print it

    LDR R0, addr_format     @ get addr of format
    MOV R1, SP              @ place SP in R1
    BL scanf                @ and store entry on stack

    LDR R1, [SP]            @ get addr of scanf input
    LDR R0, addr_messout    @ get addr of messageout
    BL printf               @ print it all

    ADD SP, SP, #4          @ adjust stack
    POP {PC}                @ restore PC

_exit:
    MOV PC, LR              @ simple exit

addr_messin:    .word messagein
addr_format:    .word scanformat
addr_messout:   .word messageout
```

```
.data
messagein:      .asciz "Enter your number: "
scanformat:     .asciz "%d"
messageout:     .asciz "Your number was 0x%X\n"
```

20: Writing Functions

Functions are the basic building blocks from which you can construct your assembler programs. A function has a name and a purpose and it is written in such a way that it provides a result each time it is called. The function will accept information and produce a result based on the information it is given. It may also pass information back to the calling program. All functions have a pre-defined structure, and if we want to write a function ourselves then we should also follow that structure.

Ideally, before sitting down to write a program you should give its structure some thought and as we saw in Chapter 2, try and plan your program as a set of routines called from within a main controlling program. Each of these routines may themselves call smaller routines. When breaking down these routines any section of code that is used more than a few times could be worth writing as a function, especially if you may look at using it in other programs. Effectively we are creating reusable code.

However, there is an overhead in doing this, because a function must conform to certain standards which relate to entry and exit conditions. Clearly therefore the length of the function must be more than a few lines to make it worthwhile coding.

Often when programming we don't always plan as well as we should. One thing I like doing is returning to code after completion and trying to re-structure it. This can be very rewarding and a way to do this is to look at what can be broken down into functions.

Function Standards

A couple of the libc functions we looked at in the last chapter, namely printf and scanf, both expected to receive and return information. We also saw that we can pass information into these functions using the registers R0, R1, R2, and R3. This is determined by a standard called the Application Binary Interface (ABI) which was carefully devised and defines how functions should run. The point being that if everyone follows the standard and writes their functions in the same way, then everyone will be able to use each other's functions. (C programmers use the AAPCS standard which goes into things in a little more detail). As far as we are concerned they achieve the same result at code level but it is worth getting online and investigating both in a little more detail at some point.

Register	Role	Contents Preserved
R0	Argument and Result	No
R1	Argument	No
R2	Argument	No
R3	Argument	No
R4	General	Yes
R5	General	Yes
R6	General	Yes
R7	General	Yes
R8	General	Yes
R9	General	Yes
R10	General	Yes
R11	General	Yes
R12	General	Yes
LR	Return Address	No
SP	Stack Pointer	Yes

Figure 20a. Register designations in a function call.

Figure 20a details the purpose of each register when a function is called. In summary a function should adhere to the following:

- It may freely modify registers R0, R1, R2 and R3 and expect to find the information in them that it requires to carry out its task.

- It can modify registers R4-12, providing it restores their values before returning to the calling routine.

- It can modify the Stack Pointer providing it restores the value held on entry.

- It must preserve the address in the Link Register so that it may return correctly to the calling program.

- It should make no assumption as to the contents of the CPSR. As far as the function is concerned the status of the N, Z, C and V flags are unknown.

So let's break this down in a bit more detail.

Register Use

It is this standard that says R0, R1, R2 and R3 (in that order) will be used as inputs to a function. But this is only if the function requires four inputs. If it only needs one then this goes in the first register — R0, if it needs a second that must be placed in R1 and similarly for R2 and R3. If it only needs one input then it does not matter what is in the other registers as they will not be used. If the function returns a value it will always go in R0 (that's why we can use the Bash echo $? command to return a value).

The second point made is that the other registers R4-R12 inclusive must be preserved so that when the calling program gets control back from the function the contents of R4 through to R12 inclusive must be the same as when the function was called. Now that is not to say we can't use them. If your function needs them, then one of the first things it should do (but not necessarily the very first as we shall see) is to push their contents onto the stack and then restore them from the stack before finishing. These two complementary instructions would do the job:

```
STMFD SP!, {R4-R12}    @ save registers R4 thro R12
LDMFD SP!, {R4-R12}    @ restore R4 through R12
```

More Than Three

You may be asking at this point what happens if we need to pass more than four items to the function we are calling. The answer lies in the next 'rule' in that we can modify the Stack Pointer (SP) again provided we ensure that it is set correctly on completion of the routine. However, this is not always strictly true, because if we need to pass more information into the function the control of the SP has to be managed by the calling routine, especially if the amount of data is unknown. If a function must have an additional four items of data each and every time, then the function can manage the SP, but you need to be wary of this.

You will recall in Program 19b we called printf to display three items of information by passing the data through R1-R3. Program 20a extends this to pass six values to the calling routine. The listing has lines numbered for ease of discussion.

Program 20a. Passing function values via the stack.

```
1       /** Printing a string using printf **/
2       /** and passing parameters to it   **/
3       /** via registers and the stack    **/
4
5           .global main
6           .func main
7       main:
8           PUSH {LR}           @ use pseudo directive
9           LDR R0, =string     @ R0 points to string
10          MOV R1, #1          @ first value in R1
11          MOV R2, #2          @ second value in R2
12          MOV R3, #3          @ result in R3
13          LDR R7,=value1      @ get address of param
14          LDR R8, [R7]        @ load value1 into R8
15          PUSH {R8}           @ put on stack
16          LDR R7,=value2      @ repeat for value2
17          LDR R8, [R7]
18          PUSH {R8}
19          LDR R7,=value3      @ repeat for value3
20          LDR R8, [R7]
21          PUSH {R8}
22          BL printf           @ Call libc
23          ADD SP, SP, #12     @ balance stack
24          POP {PC}            @ restore PC
25
26      _exit:
27          MOV PC, LR          @ simple exit
28
29          .data
30      string:    .asciz "Values are: %d, %d, %d and %d\n"
31      value1:    .word 4
32      value2:    .word 5
33      value3:    .word 6
```

The program is pretty much identical until we get to line 13 where we start taking the word values stored in lines 31-33 inclusive and pushing them onto the stack. By the time we reach line 21 we have the address of the string in R0 whilst R1, R2 and R3 hold the values 1, 2 and 3 respectively. Then the stack holds (at the top) 6, and below that 5 and below that 4. Despite being single digits these are all words with values and occupy four bytes each. If you run the program the result you will see on screen is:

```
Values are: 1, 2, 3 and 6
```

This is because we only instructed printf to print an extra value, and it looked for it on top of the stack. Adding in a couple more d% into the printf string will provide the means to print the two additional values. You would also need to swap the push order onto the stack if you wanted to ensure that the numbers were displayed in the correct order.

Line 23 is the interesting one. We adjusted the SP by 12 bytes because of the three PUSH instructions. This line moves the SP back those 12 places and ensures that the system is hunky dory. This could have been achieved with three POP instructions equally as well; however, this is a neat way to restore the status quo if you are dumping a lot of data on the stack.

If this function had required the use of the other registers then we would have needed to save their contents as per the rule earlier. The simplest way to do this would have been to push the values straight onto the stack, but this would have forced the required data down the stack and out of sync with the function expectations (unless we are able to push them first). In situations such as these the best answer is to save them to an area of memory that you have set aside for workspace. Alternatively, you can look to push the data on the stack first and prior to pushing the function parameters there.

If you are writing a function that needs additional information passed to it on the stack and the registers saved, then you can use the stack for all of it as you are managing the stack. If your function expected three items on the stack and you needed to save R4 then you can access the stack directly at the three locations using a simple immediate offset, something like this:

```
    LDR R4, SP+4    @ Get first data word on stack
```

The second item would be at SP+8 and the third at SP+12.

Remember that these instructions do not adjust the SP so you must reset it on completion as already described.

Preserving Links and Flags

One thing you must always remember when writing functions is that on completion the function is going to need to return program control back to whence it came. This means that it is imperative to preserve the integrity of the Link Register. If you intend to call another function or routine at some point then you may well use a BL or BLX instruction to do so. If you do this then the contents of the LR will be overwritten and lost. Therefore they must be stashed away safely in your memory workspace somewhere or pushed onto the stack for later restoration.

There is no requirement for preserving the Status Flags. As far as the function is concerned these are generally unknown. That said, your function may have a requirement for the flags as a signal back to the calling line and this is a valid way to signal information back, especially as R0 is the one standard way of returning a value. For example, the N flag might be set on return to signal that an error occurred.

21: Disassembling C

As I have already stated this isn't a book about learning to program in C, but the fact is as you delve deeper into ARM assembler you will probably be drawn towards C. At the very least you will probably want to learn more about the libc functions so that you can take advantage of them in your own programs. You might want to look at the machine code that constitutes the libc functions to see how they work, and learn from them. This is called reverse engineering and it plays a major part in all software development, as programmers look at how other programmers have achieved certain results and seek to improve on those themselves.

While the libc functions are well documented from a C programmer's perspective, there is not a lot of detail about using them at the lower machine code level. I guess this is understandable. But given that C is relatively straightforward and there are literally thousands of program examples available to you (in manuals, on-line and in forums) it is very easy to write a very small C program containing a particular function that you can compile into an assembly language source file and then examine it, investigate it and refine it for your own purposes. With GCC and GDB you have the tools to do so at your disposal. This chapter provides an introductory primer towards that goal. You may well encounter some frustrating times, but as you become more familiar with the way GCC converts C into machine code then you will become more familiar with the code it is generating.

GCC - The Swiss Army Knife

GCC is a bit like a Swiss Army Knife, it has to be able to deal with all situations and it goes about it in a methodical manner. The use of the assembler and linker as standalone tools in the earlier part of this book shows that GCC isn't a single beast; it is more a controller for several GNU programs, running them one-by-one in order to produce a result. But the good thing is that we can stop the process at any point in that chain and this is to our benefit.

GCC can compile a C program to an executable file with just a single command line thus:

```
gcc -o tornado  tornado.c
```

This will take a C program called tornado.c and convert it to an executable file called tornado. It does this using a number of separate steps:

Preprocessor (CPP)   This takes the C source and gathers information about the #defines and #includes so that it has a list of all the variables and additional bits of information and files it will need.

GCC   Creates the assembly language source listing. It does this by using some basic rules and building the sections of code needed as a series of building blocks which calls functions in libc. It effectively organises your data and information using the functions rules we discussed in the previous chapter and then inserts the function call. It then assembles the code required to handle any information returned before starting the process again. Once this is complete the source file, with a '.s' extension, is complete.

AS   The assembler takes the source file and converts it into an object file (.o) as described much earlier in this book.

LD   The linker takes the object code file and adds to it all the additional files and libraries required. Again, this process was described in an earlier chapter.

In Chapter 14 we saw that by using GDB the final executable code produced by GCC is not a straightforward start-to-finish linear flow but an integrated suite of code that can provide a solution to every legal C program given to it. Think about that, it's mind-blowing!

What GCC does not give you is tight, highly refined machine code. If space and speed are critical then you need to code at the lowest level. Most Operating systems are written mostly in C and compiled. But critical areas of it are coded directly in assembler. Compiled code can be optimised at the source stage and GCC provides some automated options for doing this. However, this is outside the scope of this book. But in a way, when looking at the assembler source file created to execute a particular function, what we will be doing is to optimise the source, cutting away everything that is not needed, until we have the bare bones assembler to do what we need.

A Simple C Framework

The framework for a C program is simple enough. Program 21a illustrates the use of the C function putchar to print a single ASCII character to the screen. It has six lines.

Program 21a. A simple C program to print an asterisk.

```
#include <stdio.h>

int main()
{
    putchar('*');
    return 0;
}
```

The first line tells the compiler that the file stdio.h should be included in the compilation. This is the file that includes the standard input-output interfaces and includes functions such as printf and the one we are interested in now — putchar. This is the part of the file that would be handled by the pre-processor described earlier, and this is the case for any line that begins with a hash.

The actual program starts with the function named main(). All functions begin with an opening brace ({) and end with a closing brace (}). Everything between the opening and closing braces is considered a part of the function. main(), like all C functions, must state what kind of value it returns. The return value type for 'main()' is int, which means that this function returns an integer to the operating system when it completes. Here, it returns the integer value 0. A value may be returned to the operating system to indicate success or failure, or using a failure code to describe the cause of failure.

Hopefully you will have already cottoned on to how the main() in the C program above ties in with the main function in our assembler source files to date (and to a lesser extent the start function in the assembler listings that we looked at the start of this book).

In amongst all this we have the crux of the program — putchar — being instructed to print an asterisk to the screen.

Program 21a can be entered with Vim and the file should be created with the .c extension:

```
vim prog21a.c
```

To compile this C program into an executable and run it we use:
```
gcc -o prog21a prog21a.c
./prog21a
```
You will see an asterisk printed on the screen before the prompt.

Getting the Assembler

Given what we have learnt in the past few chapters you might be able to take a pretty good guess at what you would expect to see in the assembly language source code generated for this C program. The function prints a single character. We would expect therefore that, as specified by the AAPCS standard, the ASCII code for the character to be printed would be loaded into R0. No other information is passed. The routine will complete with a return value of 0, so we should also expect to find this passed back in R0 as per standard. Let's C!

To create an assembler listing from a .c file we use the –S directive (note must be capital S), thus:
```
gcc -S -o prog21a.s prog21a.c
```
GCC will create a file called prog21a.s and this will hold the assembler listing. Open this in Vim and you should see something very similar (it may not be identical) to what is shown in Figure 21a.

You should be able to identify quickly the body of the program in here. In fact of the 30 lines of assembler only a handful of them are of significance relative to what we are after. All the additional information can ultimately be discarded but was an important transformation step for GCC when it did the initial conversion. This conversion is very methodical and is a case of one size fits all using a brute force method of working. GCC has to create some workspace for each function it is dealing with in the conversion process, and has to protect this workspace for its needs. In broad terms it does this by partitioning an area on the stack for the function's use. This is called to the stack frame and this has its own pseudo-register called the Frame Pointer, FP. This marks the start of the stack frame and each function creates its own stack frame to manage local variables. The stack frame is therefore an important aspect of a C program but they are less important in creating assembler. However, understanding what it does is important in allowing us to deconstruct C derived assembler, more on which in due course.

ARM A32 Assembly Language

Back to the listing. It is good at this point to create a backup of this initial assembly file. You will want to start deleting lines and adjusting code to create a smaller compact source file that you can assemble and test. Thus:

```
cp prog21a.s prog21a.so
```

would create a copy with the .so indicating to you that it is source original.

```
            .arch armv6
            .eabi_attribute 27, 3
            .eabi_attribute 28, 1
            .fpu vfp
            .eabi_attribute 20, 1
            .eabi_attribute 21, 1
            .eabi_attribute 23, 3
            .eabi_attribute 24, 1
            .eabi_attribute 25, 1
            .eabi_attribute 26, 2
            .eabi_attribute 30, 6
            .eabi_attribute 18, 4
            .file "Prog18a.c"
            .text
            .align 2
            .global    main
            .type main, %function
    main:
            @ args = 0, pretend = 0, frame = 0
            @ frame_needed = 1, uses_anonymous_args = 0
            stmfd sp!, {fp, lr}
            add fp, sp, #4
            mov r0, #42
            bl  putchar
            mov r3, #0
            mov r0, r3
            ldmfd sp!, {fp, pc}
            .size main, .-main
            .ident "GCC: (Debian 4.6.3-14+rpi1) 4.6.3"
            .section  .note.GNU-stack,"",%progbits
```

Figure 21a. The assembler generated by GCC from the C program.

Building Blocks

Our purpose here is to cut this source down so that we can assemble and link it directly and produce the same result as the original C program. GCC has constructed the assembler source using some basic building blocks. The first 15 lines provide various items of information. There is a directive identifying the instruction set for which this code is to be compiled (armv6) and the specific floating point unit to be used (vfp). The eabi_attributes define various options that are present or absent on the CPU. They are not important and so can be deleted. There follows the file name and definition of the .text section. Again, for our small assembler construct these can both be deleted. The '.size main' directive is used by the linker to indicate the size of the function. Again, we do not need this and it can be discarded.

```
1         .global main
2         .typemain, %function
3    main:
4         @ args = 0, pretend = 0, frame = 0
5         @ frame_needed = 1, uses_anonymous_args = 0
6         stmfdsp!, {fp, lr}
7         add   fp, sp, #4
8         mov   r0, #42
9         bl    putchar
10        mov   r3, #0
11        mov   r0, r3
12        ldmfdsp!, {fp, pc}
```

Figure 21b. The C assembler source with directives removed.

Having done all that we are left with the listing shown in Figure 21b, with line numbers for ease of reference. The first three lines define the main() function and we will need to edit these slightly for use in our assembly listing. This is followed by a couple of comments (lines 4 and 5) provided by the compiler in relation to management of the stack frame for this routine. Again, we will not need these and they can be deleted.

Lines 6 and 12 act in tandem to preserve the addresses held in the Frame Pointer and link register The FP is of no importance to us here but we do need to preserve the LR before calling the putchar routine so a suitable PUSH and POP instruction can be substituted here. Line 7 can also be removed as we do not need to process anything relating to the FP, but we can see from this instruction that the FP is being give the value of SP+4.

The crux of our code comes down to lines 8 and 9. The ASCII code for the asterisk (42) is moved into R0 and putchar is called. Lines 10 and 11 are then used to place a 0 in R0, You will recall that the original C function is to return 0. For our purposes, we do not strictly need these two lines and they can be removed. What we are left with is the listing presented as Program 21b.

Program 21b. The final putchar listing.

```
      .global main
      .func    main
main:
      PUSH {LR}
      MOV R0, #42
      BL   putchar
      POP  {LR}
      MOV  PC, LR
```

You could remove the last two lines and return simply by using:

```
POP {PC}
```

This listing will assemble and run correctly. Although the original C program was relatively trivial the methodology used to create and reduce the assembler source that it creates is sound and can be applied in virtually all cases.

A printf Example

We have already examined the use of printf in assembly language programs but we'll look at it again, this time from the C perspective as it provides a good insight into how C programs are constructed that will be useful when looking at the assembler. Program 21c is the C file for the famous "hello world" program. On the face of it, this is really not much different from our previous putchar example. But in fact it is.

Program 21c. C listing for the 'hello world' program.

```
#include <stdio.h>
int main()
{
  printf("hello world");
```

```
    return 0;
}
```

You can convert this to assembler using:

```
gcc -S -o prog21c.s prog21c.c
```

```
            .section.rodata
            .align   2
.LC0:
            .ascii   "hello world\000"
            .text
            .align   2
            .global main
            .typemain, %function
main:
            @ args = 0, pretend = 0, frame = 0
            @ frame_needed = 1, uses_anonymous_args = 0
            stmfdsp!, {fp, lr}
            add   fp, sp, #4
            ldr   r3, .L2
            mov   r0, r3
            bl    printf
            mov   r3, #0
            mov   r0, r3
            ldmfdsp!, {fp, pc}
.L3:
            .align   2
.L2:
            .word.LC0
```

Figure 21c. The compiled assembler for the C printf program.

Figure 21c lists the derived assembler minus the initial header and footer directives.

Given our knowledge of printf and applying what we learned above, the main: section of the program should be straightforward — nothing new to learn here. It is the other areas that are of interest —notably the areas marked by the labels LC0, L3 and L2. The L3 label is not required nor is the align 2 directive — the label will clearly be on a word boundary as it comes directly behind code. L2 marks a reserved word to hold the address of the 'hello world' text marked by LC0. This was a technique that we used when playing with the scanf function in Program 19c but is different to the method we used in our original printf program, Program 19a. It is worth comparing the two side by side.

As a final exercise you might want to try compiling a scanf example, as this combines a few of these techniques and also accesses the stack for information. Program 21d is what you will need. If you compile and run this the keyboard will wait for you to enter a number. There will be no additional responses as it is the bare function we are concerned with.

Program 21d. A C listing for using the scanf function.

```
#include <stdio.h>

int main()
{
int myvariable;
    scanf("%d", &myvariable);
    return 0;
}
```

A reminder here that scanf uses the stack to store and pass its converted numeric value, so you will need to manage the stack pointer in the assembler.

Frame Pointer Variables

Just a word to the good about the Frame Pointer relative to dissecting your listings in this way. If the original C programs contains variables then the Frame Pointer will be used to point to these values, so it becomes important in your deconstruction. Consider these two lines of assembler:

```
LDR R2, {FP, #-8}
MOV R0, R2
```

The first line shows that a variable is located at the position given by FP-8 and this result is accessed and moved into R0. If the original C listing has several variables you will need to identify where each one is located on the stack, by seeking out similar code lines. Of course your assembler will not have a Frame Pointer, or it would be assigned a value it is often set equal to the SP by the code, so you will need to translate these into labelled locations.

(In ARM, R11 is normally used as the Frame Pointer register, although this may vary between Operating Systems.)

Disassembling Syscalls

In Chapter 7 we had a look at Syscalls and how to interface with the actual operating system calls directly with them. Of course, we have since learned of libc and how we can make use of its own functions such as printf. Using libc comes with a memory overhead which you might not be prepared to live with when space is tight, and at these times Syscalls can come into their own. This is fine in principle but the trouble is that hard detail about Linux Syscalls is rather scarce on the ground. For popular Syscalls such as printing a string to the screen you will find many examples if you search the net. The same cannot be said if you wanted to create a directory, or produce a directory listing. But the information is there if you use a bit of common sense and are prepared to do a little reverse engineering. Doing this with a few examples will test your knowledge of the ARM and the way it works, and you will learn heaps from doing it.

The book support website contains links to unofficial site where you can find out more information on Syscalls – unfortunately it is rather sketchy on the ground. One other option is to have a go at working it out for yourself!

Let's consider how we can use a Syscall to make a new directory; this is Syscall 39. Common sense would tell me that I need at least one item of information, this being the name and location of where the new directory should be created. I am also going to probably need information regarding the read/write privileges for the directory. This is harder to work out.

Program 21e. A C program to create a new directory using mkdir.

```
#include <sys/stat.h>
#include <stdio.h>

void main()
{
int status = mkdir("tempdir", 0511);
    if (status != 0) {
        printf ("mkdir failed!\n");
    }
}
```

With a knowledge of Linux I could search around for this information (and it exists because I've done it), or I could also find a C program that uses the mkdir function and compile the assembler source to look at it. The C program I came across is listed as Program 21e.

Looking at this I can see that this example uses an integer value 0511. This must be the value for privilege settings. However, the program shows me some significant new information. It shows me that the operation can fail and in doing so return an error. This makes sense. For example, if the directory already exists we will not be able to create it. And the following lines suggest that the function returns 0 if the directory is created and something else if not. If a function returns a value it will always be in R0 (due to the functions standards), so my assembler would need to check for this.

You can compile the above program and run it once to ensure that it creates the directory, and then a second time to see the error message.

At this stage we have enough information to create the assembler to use the mkdir Syscall. But one last check is always in order, compiling the file and creating the source file:

```
gcc -S -o prog21e.s prog21e.c
```

Figure 21c is the resultant assembler which I have sanitised by removing the various attribute settings at the start and end. I've also added line numbers to aid description here.

Line 1 contains a new directive .rodata. I have kept this in the final program. Normally data segments are read-write, by using .rodata we are specifying a read-only (r-o) data section.

Lines 3-8 set up the strings for the directory name and message if the operation fails. Line 19 contains the call to the mkdir function so the detail I need is before this. Line 17 loads R0 with the address of the string and line 18 loads R1 with the 'mode' value. However, if I look at line 33 for the value to be sent for 'mode' I see it is 329 and not 0511. The 329 is a decimal value and the 0511 is an octal value (a number to base 8). Generally any value that specifically starts with a 0 as in the original C program you should identify as an octal value.

Finally if we look at line 22 we can see that the code is testing if a zero was returned (lines 20-21) then move it into R3 from R0 in a tortuous manner. If it was then the program is exited; if not then the warning message is displayed through lines 23 and 24.

```
1               .section    .rodata
2               .align      2
3   .LC0:
4               .ascii      "tempdir\000"
5               .align      2
6   .LC1:
7               .ascii      "mkdir failed!\000"
8               .text
9               .align      2
10              .global     main
11              .type       main, %function
12  main:
13
14              stmfd       sp!, {fp, lr}
15              add         fp, sp, #4
16              sub         sp, sp, #8
17              ldr         r0, .L3
18              ldr         r1, .L3+4
19              bl          mkdir
20              str         r0, [fp, #-8]
21              ldr         r3, [fp, #-8]
22              cmp         r3, #0
23              beq         .L1
24              ldr         r0, .L3+8
25              bl          puts
26  .L1:
27              sub         sp, fp, #4
28              ldmfd       sp!, {fp, pc}
29  .L4:
30              .align      2
31  .L3:
32              .word       .LC0
33              .word       329
34              .word       .LC1
```

Figure 21d. Source listing generated by C program.

Program 21f provides the final source listing that will create a directory using the mkdir Syscall. Note I have made a slight change to the directory name to illustrate how you can use the full path of a destination to create a

ARM A32 Assembly Language

directory in somewhere other than the current directory, which is where the earlier examples will be created.

Remember, you should use the assembler and linker to create this file as we do not require libc attached.

You may like to look at writing the assembler to rename your directory and remove your directory using Syscalls 38 and 40 in a similar fashion. Why not add in functions to allow the user to input the details directly from the keyboard for the directories to be used?

Program 21f. The final mkdir program using Syscall.

```
/* Create a directory using Syscall */
        .section .rodata
string:
      .ascii "tempdir\000"
       .global _start
      .text
       .align 2
mode:      .word 0511

_start:
      @ mkdir syscall
      MOV   R7, #39
      LDR   R0,=string
      LDR   R1,mode
      SVC   #0

      @ exit syscall
      MOV   R7, #1
      MOV   R0, #0
      SVC   #0
```

In Summary

The examples above are ones we have encountered and already explained and this is done deliberately to make it easier to explain what GCC is doing in its compile process. You may not be forewarned with such knowledge when looking at new functions. But GCC goes about its business in a pre-defined way and the processes will not vary. Information is passed in registers and on the stack (and via the frame pointer) so it is often just a matter of identifying what is where and then working back from there.

You may also find it easier to open a second Vim window and set about creating a new assembly listing alongside the one created with GCC, rather than editing the original one. This is especially sound advice if the listing contains a lot of data access as the tables tend to flop all over the place.

22: Floating Point

In our everyday use of computers, we take floating point numbers for granted. After all what use would a bank have a computer that couldn't work out decimal points? When we use spreadsheets, calculators and even some word-processing packages, we accept the ability to perform simple calculations down to several decimal points without a second thought. But what about in assembly language? All the number action we have looked at to date, and there's not been that much in reality, has been dealing with integer numbers, values without any fractional part.

The management and manipulation of floating point numbers take lots of processing grunt. This grunt is supplied by something called a co-processor and not, in the first instance, the ARM chip. As we will see in Chapter 28, the many ARM chip releases form part of a series of chips known as a SoC or System-On-a-Chip device. It is more than just the ARM chip itself, and one of these additional items is some other hardware circuitry that handles floating point maths. This co-processor as it is known is the VFP or Vector Floating Point coprocessor, and this supplies new architecture, including registers and instructions. With this, we can include floating point operations in assembly language programs. Better still GCC and GDB support these too and do so as the IEEE 754 definition they conform to standardises the format of floating point numbers to provide a standard format across computer platforms.

With the release of ARMv8, the term co-processor becomes redundant as the new architecture is inherently built in with the ARM design – it is part of the ARM.

We'll look at how the floating point architecture implementation over the next couple of chapters and the instructions which we can use to include real numbers in our programs. This knowledge will provide you with more than enough information to use them in a practical way, and display your results for the world to see.

VFP, SIMD and NEON Architecture

Modern software, mainly media codecs and graphics accelerators, operate on large amounts of data that is less than word-sized. 16-bit data is common in audio applications, and 8-bit data is standard in graphics and video, and there is lots of it. When performing these operations on a 32-bit microprocessor, parts of the microprocessor are unused but continue to consume power. To make better use of this excess, wasted processor capacity, Single Instruction Multiple Data (SIMD) technology introduced the use of a single instruction to perform the same operation in parallel on multiple data elements of the same type and size. This way, the hardware that frequently adds two 32-bit values instead performs four parallel additions of 8-bit values in the same amount of time.

ARMv7 architecture introduced the Advanced SIMD extension as an optional extension to the ARMv7-A and ARMv7-R profiles. It extends the SIMD concept by defining groups of instructions operating on vectors stored in 64-bit D, double-word, registers and 128-bit Q, quad-word, vector registers. All Advanced SIMD instruction mnemonics begin with V, for example, VMAX.

All Neon, as Advanced SIMD is now known, and VFP instructions are available in both ARM and Thumb states. From ARMv8 Neon is king and adds instructions targeted primarily at audio, video, 3-D graphics, image, and speech processing.

Neon instructions perform many functions including:

- memory accesses
- data copying between Neon and general purpose registers
- data type conversion
- data processing.

The biggest benefit of Neon is if you want to execute the operation with vectors, video encoding/decoding. It can also perform single precision floating point(float) operations in parallel. VFP is a classic floating point hardware accelerator. It is not a parallel architecture like Neon. It performs one operation on one set of inputs and returns one output. Its purpose is to speed up floating point calculations.

Some devices such as the ARM Cortex-A8 have a cut-down VFPLite module (to further add to the melting pot) instead of a full VFP module. The trade-off here is speed as VFPLite requires roughly ten times more clock cycles per float operation.

For now, we'll concentrate on the VFP and look at how floating point values are manipulated. We'll look at the Neon architecture in a bit more detail in due course.

VFP Types

Let's take a step back and look at VFP in depth which provides low-cost, high-performance floating-point computation. VFP extends the processor functionality to provide support for the ARMv7 VFPv4 instruction set, which was previously done by being part of an add-on co-processor but is now part of the core.

The VFP provides support for single precision and double precision numbers. As the name implies, the latter can represent numbers in more detail than the former. To this end, a single precision number occupies a word of memory (32-bits or binary32), while a double occupies two-words of memory (64-bits or binary64). You will recall that the ARM can use 32-bit numbers for its standard values and this begs the question: are the single precision floating point numbers that are available as big as the integer ones? The answer is yes they are, and they can be much larger as it boils down to the way in which they are represented. The following are examples of floating point or real numbers:

```
0.2345
546.6735268
1.001011010
4E7
```

In the latter case, the number is 4*10 to the power of 7 or 4×10^7. The 7 is the exponent and means 'raised to the power of'. In single and double precision numbers the values can be encoded into the bits so that they have a sign bit, an exponent portion and a fractional or mantissa portion. In this way, very large or very small numbers can be depicted.

The various VFP architectures and what they provide are detailed below:

VFPv1   Obsolete

VFPv2   An optional extension to the ARM instruction set in the ARMv5TE, ARMv5TEJ and ARMv6 architectures. VFPv2 has 16 64-bit FPU registers.

VFPv3   Implemented on most Cortex-A8 and A9 ARMv7 processors. It is backwards compatible with VFPv2, except that it cannot trap floating-point exceptions. VFPv3 has 32 64-bit FPU registers as standard, adds VCVT instructions to convert

	between scalar, float and double, adds an immediate mode to VMOV such that constants can be loaded into FPU registers.
VFPv3-D16	As above, but with only 16 64-bit FPU registers. Implemented on Cortex-R4 and R5 processors and the Tegra 2 (Cortex-A9).
VFPv3-F16	Uncommon; it supports IEEE754-2008 half-precision (16-bit) floating point as a storage format.
VFPv4	Implemented on the Cortex-A12 and A15 ARMv7 processors, Cortex-A7 optionally has VFPv4-D32 in the case of an FPU with Neon. VFPv4 has 32 64-bit FPU registers as standard, adds both half-precision support as a storage format and fused multiply-accumulate instructions to the features of VFPv3.
VFPv4-D16	As above, but it has only 16 64-bit FPU registers. Implemented on Cortex-A5 and A7 processors (in the case of an FPU without Neon).
VFPv5-D16-M	Implemented on Cortex-M7 when single, and double-precision floating point core option exists.

Figure 22a below shows how a single precision and double precision number are laid out. In the circumstance of double precision numbers the two words must occupy consecutive memory locations and be word-aligned.

```
Single Precision format

31 30              23 22                              0
┌───┬────────────────┬──────────────────────────────┐
│ S │   Exponent     │           Fraction           │
└───┴────────────────┴──────────────────────────────┘

Double Precision format

63 62              52 51                             32
┌───┬────────────────┬──────────────────────────────┐
│ S │   Exponent     │           Fraction           │
└───┴────────────────┴──────────────────────────────┘

31                                                    0
┌──────────────────────────────────────────────────┐
│                    Fraction                      │
└──────────────────────────────────────────────────┘
```

Figure 22a. Construction of single and double precision numbers.

Sign (S): This can be 0 or 1 to represent positive or negative values respectively. It is held in the most significant bit of the number.

Exponent: The exponent is the value we need to shift the mantissa along to the left to restore it to its original value. It is held between the sign bit and fraction.

Fractional: Also called the mantissa, this is the number following the point and it can obviously be a binary value to represent the real number. The mantissa will have been normalised, that is shifted along to the right until we are left with a single digit on the left of the dot. In double-precision numbers it occupies the whole of the least significant word and part of the most significant word.

In a single-precision floating point the mantissa is 23-bits (+1 for the integer one for normalised numbers) and the exponent is 8-bits, meaning the exponent can range from -126 to 127. In a double-precision the mantissa is 53-bits (+1 as for single) and the exponent is 11-bits, so the exponent ranges from -1022 to 1023).

For completeness there is also a third type of number representation. This is called NaN which stands for Not a Number! This is used in special circumstances where a value cannot be represented in single or double precision manner. It is a fascinating topic — not least as there are also two different types of NaN, and is worth investigating further if you are interested in this type of thing. We will not be using them here and I am glad to take the cop-out on this one!

The Register File

The load and store architecture of the ARM chip persists in VFP and to deal with floating point values it provides a set of registers specifically for the purpose. There are 32 in all with the prefix S and numbered S0-S31. These registers are used to hold single precision values as they are all one word wide. For the manipulation of double precision numbers these registers can be paired up to form up to 16 two-word width registers. The prefix D is used to denote this and they are numbered D0 to D15. Figure 22b illustrates this in principle.

You should be clear that these registers are one and the same and although the values in registers may be either single or double they can only contain one value at a time. Thus S0 and S1 can be used individually for two single precision values or combined as D0 for a double precision value. If D0 is loaded with a value then the contents of S0 and S1 are wiped. It is perfectly possible to have single precision value in S0 and S1 and a double precision value in D1 as D1 is composed of S2 and S3.

Please note that there are no warning devices or alarm systems to tell you what is in what register. That is up to you to look after – this is machine code after all. You are the manager. These registers are grouped into Scalar (S0-S7/D0-D3) and Vectorial banks (S8-S31/D4-D15) for usage purposes – and the group determines how they are accessed, which we'll look at with some examples later on.

S0	S1	<< >>	D0
S2	S3		D1
S4	S5		D2
S6	S7		D3
S8	S9		D4
S10	S11		D5
S12	S13		D6
S14	S15		D7
S16	S17		D8
S18	S19		D9
S20	S21		D10
S22	S23		D11
S24	S25		D12
S26	S27		D13
S28	S29		D14
S30	S31		D15

Figure 22b. The VFP Register File. The Sx registers may be used individually or paired to create a double precision register, Dx.

As you might expect there are instructions to deal specifically with moving both single and double precision values to and from memory and registers and a variety of instructions for arithmetic functions. Let's look at a simple example first that will also show how to use printf to display a floating point number.

ARM A32 Assembly Language

Managing and Printing

Program 22a illustrates a few basic operations involving floating point numbers and also how to use printf to display a floating point value on the screen.

This is important as it will allow you to display the results of any operations you do. The first thing to note is that you cannot load a floating point value directly into a register; you have to do it indirectly via a register. This concept should be familiar and also the way the code is structured, as shown below.

Program 22a. Printing a floating point value with printf.

```
/* Printing a floating point number */
    .global main
    .func main
main:

    LDR R1, addr_value1     @ Get addr of value1
    VLDR S14, [R1]          @ Move value1 into S14
    VCVT.F64.F32 D5, S14    @ Convert to B64

    LDR R0, =string         @ point R0 to string
    VMOV R2, R3, D5         @ Load value
    BL printf               @ call function

    MOV R7, #1              @ Exit Syscall
    SWI 0

addr_value1:
    .word value1

    .data
value1:   .float 1.54321
string:   .asciz "Floating point value is: %f\n"
```

The first line of code loads the address of value1 into R1. In the next line this is used as the indirect address of the value to be loaded into S14. The VLDR stands for Vector LoaD Register. The third line then converts the value into a double precision one. This is because printf can print double

210

precision values but not single precision ones, which is the format of the value in S14. The instruction is complex but is surprisingly easy to read and construct when you know how:

```
VCVT        Vector Convert instruction
.F64        Convert to Binary64 - viz double precision
.F32        From Binary32 - viz single precision
D5          Destination double precision register
S14         The source single precision registers
```

The order is the important thing to remember here: the target comes before the source. We'll come back to this with some more examples shortly.

The next three lines are all about getting printf ready to use. As before R0 has to point to the string to print. Normally R1, R2, and R3 are used to pass additional values to printf. However, we can only get one double precision value in those three registers, so the definition is that R2 and R3 are used (R1 is ignored). VMOV moves D5 into R2 and R3. The %f directive is used in the print string and printf is smart enough to know that this directive indicates a double precision value and so just looks in R2 and R3 for it. (If you call other libc functions then you may be able to pass two double-precision values through to it as R0-R3 are allocated for the purpose in normal ARM use.)

You can also see in the data section that the .float directive is used to store the floating point value.

Printing more than one double precision value with printf follows the same route as previously. The additional items are pushed onto the stack. However, PUSH and POP or their equivalents become a little redundant here as we are dealing with two-word values for each double precision number. Program 22b builds on the previous listing to do this.

The load and conversion process remains the same, but obviously using different registers, and the VPUSH instruction is used to place the value on the stack. Additional values can be added in the same way.

Note that most floating-point numbers that a computer can represent are just approximations. One challenge in programming with floating-point values is ensuring that the approximations lead to reasonable results. If the programmer is not careful, small discrepancies in the approximations can snowball to the point where the results become meaningless.

Assembling & Compiling FP Code

There are some additional rules you need to be aware of when compiling floating point material. One of the advantages using the full gcc compile method is that GCC will invariably handle all the behind the scenes leg work for you. So when it parses the assembler it understands you are using floating point opcodes and therefore attaches and assembles the additional information required. However, we must tell it what type of FPU we are using. For instance, in the previous example using:

```
gcc -o prog22a prog22a.s
```

Will present likely tell you that it does not recognise the VFP instructions. So, we must specify it thus:

```
gcc -mfpu=vfp -o prog22a prog22a.s
```

The option 'mfpu' should be used to specify to the compiler which floating-point hardware (or hardware emulation) is available on the target, in this case, 'vfp'.

If you are assembling and linking code with the 'as' and 'ld' commands then you must include the option in the 'as' line, ie:

```
as -mfpu=vfp -o prog22a.o prog22a.s
ld -o prog22a prog22a.o
```

Load, Store and Move

As with the standard ARM instruction set the VFP instruction set provides a versatile set of instructions to shift information around. VLDR and VSTR load and store single register quantities using indirect addressing. Here are a few examples:

```
VLDR S1, [R5]      @Load S1 with F32 value at addr in R5
VLDR D2, [R5, #4]  @Load S2 with F64 value addr+4 in R5
VSTR S3, [R6]      @Store F32 value in S3 at addr in R6
```

Here, pre-indexed addressing is used in the second example to add 4 to the address held in R5 before the operation completes.

ARM A32 Assembly Language

Program 22b. Manipulating and printing two or more fp values.

```
/* Printing two floating point numbers */

      .global   main
      .func main
main:
      SUB SP, SP, #16        @ Make space on stack

      LDR R1, addr_value1    @ Get addr of value1
      VLDR S14, [R1]
      VCVT.F64.F32 D0, S14

      LDR R1, addr_value2    @ Get addr of value2
      VLDR S15, [R1]
      VCVT.F64.F32 D1, S15

      LDR R0, =string        @ point R0 to string
      VMOV R2, R3, D0        @ first value
      VSTR D1, [SP]          @ second on stack
      BL printf
      ADD SP, SP, #16        @ restore stack

      MOV R7, #1             @ Exit Syscall
      SWI 0
addr_value1:    .word value1
addr_value2:    .word value2

      .data
value1:    .float 1.54321
value2:    .float 5.1
string:    .asciz "The FP values are %f and %f\n"
```

We can also use pre-indexed addressing with write back as well, to update the address in the indexing register. This is useful when dealing with operations working on sets of registers, as shown here:

```
VLDMIAS R5!,{S1-S4}  @ Copy S1, S2, S3, S4 & update R5
```

In this example the values in the four registers S1, S2, S3 and S4 are copied sequentially to the word location starting at the address held in R5. When the operation is completed the length of space used for the storage is added to R5. This means that R5 will now point to the next address — the one after S4. If the instruction had read:

```
VLDMIAS R5!, {D1-D4} @ Copy D1, D2, D3, D4 & update R5
```

then the same operation would have taken place, but the instruction would have allowed two-words (8 bytes) per register and added 32 to the value in R5. If you do not wish to update R5 then exclude the '!' from the instruction.

The addressing modes in operation here are similar in fashion to those described in Chapter 15, but notice how the registers and information are arranged differently. Note also that there is no post-indexed addressing operation.

VPUSH and VPOP can be used with curly brackets to transfer several items to and from the stack:

```
VPUSH {S1-S4}   @ put S1, S2, S3, S4 onto stack
VPOP  {S5-S8}   @ pull them into S5, S6, S7 and S8
```

The VMOV instruction allows values to be freely transferred between different register sets. When there is a transfer between a VFP register and an ARM register then the transfer is done bit-by-bit and no conversion takes place.

```
VMOV S1, S2           @ Copy S2 into S1
VMOV S1, S2, R3, R5   @ Copy R3 to S1 and R5 to S2
VMOV R2, R4, D1       @ Copy loD1 to R2 & hiD1 to R4
```

In the last example a double precision value (8 bytes) is being transferred into two registers. In such instances it is important to be aware of the order of the hi and lo bytes of the floating point value as failure to do so can radically alter the value saved. Once again no conversion is performed and it is a bit-for-bit transfer. The value is preserved if the transfer is reversed as nothing has changed.

You can use the VMOV instruction to copy information from ARM to VFP registers and thus you can use the command to allow you to store ARM register contents in the Register File if you are looking for extra space:

```
VMOV S1, R1           @ Store R1 in S1
```

Precision Conversion

Both programs at the start of this chapter included conversion from single to double precision values. This was done as the printf function directive %f requires a double precision value as its source to work correctly. The VFP architecture allows for conversion to work in several directions. It can also perform double-precision to single precision transformation, but it can also simplify signed and unsigned integer values conversions. You should bear in mind that conversion can lead to a loss of precision and some rounding of values, particularly where a floating point number is transformed into an integer.

There are four operators that can be used with VCVT to define the conversion source and targets, two of which must always be used, one as the source and one as the target. These are detailed in Figure 22c.

The basic syntax of VFP instructions are thus:

```
VCVT <Target><Source>   <Reg-Target>, <Reg-Source>
```

The suffixes .F32 and .F64 can be appended to arithmetic or conversion instructions to determine whether the quantities being manipulated are single or double precision. We have already seen an example of this in the conversion process in both programs above.

Suffix	Meaning
.F32	Single Precision, 32-bit one word width values.
.F64	Double Precision, 64-bit two word width values
.S32	Signed integer, 32-bit one word values width values
.U32	Unsigned integer, 32-bit one word values width values

Figure 22c. Suffixes which can be used in number conversion.

The example used in Program 22a was:

```
VCVT.F64.F32 D5, S14
```

This took the single precision (F32) value in S14 and converted it into a double-provision (F64) value to be stored in D5. A few more examples with short explanations are listed below:

```
VCVT.F32.F64 S10, D2    @ Convert double in D2 to
                        @ single in S10
```

```
VCVT.F32.U32 S10, R2    @ Convert Unsigned integer in
                        @ R2 to single in S10
VCVT.D64.S32 D4, R2     @ Convert signed integer in R2
                        @ into double in D4
```

Vector Arithmetic

The VFP instruction set provides a comprehensive range of instructions to perform all the arithmetic operations you might expect. The format follows the standard form illustrated so far with F32 and F64 being used to specify single and double precision values. Operations are performed on one precision format value in each instruction line as single and double precision values cannot be mixed. An example for each instruction available is given below, remembering that there are .F32 and .F64 flavours of each:

```
VADD.F32 S0, S1, S2     @ Addition S0=S1+S2
VSUB.F64 D0, D2, D4     @ Subtraction D0=D2-D4
VDIV.F64 D4, D5, D1     @ Divide D4=D5/D1
VMUL.F32 S2, S4, S1     @ Multiply S2=S4*S1
VNMUL.F64 D4, D3, D2    @ Multiply and negate
                        @ D4=-(D3*D2)
VMAL.F64 D4, D3, D2     @ Multiply and accumulate
                        @ D4=D4+(D3*D2)
VSUB.F64 D0, D1, D2     @ Multiply and Subtract
                        @ D0=D0-(D1xD2)
VABS.F32 S0, S1         @ Absolute S0=ABS(S1)
VNEG.F32 S2, S3         @ Negate S2=-S3
VSQRT.F64 D0,D1         @ Square Root D0=SQR(D1)
```

GDB VFP Update

GDB provides debugging tools for operation with the VFP and Neon (which we will cover in more depth in Chapter 24). All of the options outlined in Chapter 14 are valid, and GDB will disassemble machine code files correctly. You can also access the VFP and Neon registers by adding the extension 'all' to the info command line thus:

```
info r all
```

This will list the D and S registers, plus the Q registers used by Neon. You will notice that this also lists D registers up to D31, whereas we only identified registers to D15 earlier. The D register set is extended to correlate with the Neon Q registers as we shall see.

The 'all' function provides a lot of data. You can limit the amount of data displayed by specifying individual registers:

```
info r $s0 $s1 $d0
```

Would display the contents of S0, S1 and D0.

Using GDB is a good way to learn what instructions do, and how the various combinations of actions affect the flags and results.

23 : VFP Control Register

The VFP co-processor provides three system registers. The most important of these from our perspective is the Floating Point Status and Control Register or FPSCR. You can think of this as the CPSR for the normal ARM instruction set, in that it provides flag status information. Indeed the N, Z, C and V flags are all present and have the same application. Figure 23a shows how the register is set out for the programmer whilst Figure 23b details the function of the register bits that we'll be discussing here.

FPSCR Format	Rd		Vector	Exception	CEB
31 28 24	23 22	21 20	18 17 16	12 7	4 0
N Z C V	Rmode	Stride	Len		

Figure 23a. Floating Point Status and Control Register layout.

The operation and function of several of these flag sets will be covered in these pages. However, the operation of exceptions, although introduced in a forthcoming chapter for the ARM chip itself is not detailed to any degree.

Bit	Flag Set	Detail
31-28	Condition Flags	Negative, Zero, Carry, Overflow
23-22	Rounding Mode	Controls how values are rounded.
21-20	Stride	Controls the step size taken in vector banks
18-16	Len	Controls the Vector length
12-8	Exception Status	Enables trapping of exception types.
4-0	Cumulative Exception	Trap cumulative exceptions

Figure 23b. Register function summary.

Conditional Execution

We first looked at these condition codes in Chapter 10. The precise meanings of the condition code flags differ depending on whether the flags were set by a floating-point operation or by an ARM data processing instruction. This is because floating-point values are never unsigned, so the unsigned conditions have no meaning. (There is also another reason involving NaN values but as we have not delved into these in this overview they are not significant at this point.)

Without exception the only VFP instruction that can update the status flags is VCMP and this sets the relative bits in the FPSCR. However, condition flags and instructions are controlled by the APSR (Application Program Status Register — CPSR) and so the FPSCR flags have to be copied across into the APSR. There is a specific instruction to do this:

```
VMRS APSR_nzcv, FPSCR
```

The VCMP instruction comes in .F32 and .F64 flavours and can be used thus:

```
VCMP.F32 S0, S1    @ S0-S1 and set condition flags
VCMP.F64 D2, D3    @ D2-D3 and set condition flags
```

The entire contents of the FPSCR can also be transferred to an ARM register thus:

```
VMRS R4, FPSCR     @ Copy FSPCR into R4
```

And likewise the FPSCR can be loaded with the contents of an ARM register allowing the bits to be pre-determined and set:

```
VMSR FSPCR, R4     @ Copy R4 into FPSCR
```

Using the bitwise operators (AND, ORR, EOR) this instruction allows you to mask individual bits and also provides a mechanism to test specific condition flags with the FPSCR. This is used specifically in dealing with the bits associated with 'len' and 'stride' which we'll discuss shortly. Figure 23c overleaf details the meanings of the condition code mnemonics for both ARM and VFP side by side for comparison.

Remember that one of the huge befits of using conditional execution is to reduce the number of branch instructions required and thereby reduce the overall size of your code. Branch instructions also carry a bigger overhead in execution timings — typically three cycles to refill the processor pipeline. For example:

```
VADDEQ.F32 S0, S1, S2  @ Execute only if C=1
VSUBNE.F64 D0, D2, D4  @ Execute only if negative
```

Code	Meaning after ARM instruction	Meaning after VFP VCMP instruction
EQ	Equal	Equal
NE	Not equal	No equal, or unordered
CS	Cary set	Greater than or equal, or unordered
HS	Unsigned higher or same	Greater than or equal, or unordered
CC	Carry Clear	Less than
LO	Unsigned lower	Less than
MI	Negative	Less than
PL	Positive or zero	Greater than or equal, or unordered
VS	Overflow	Unordered
VC	No Overflow	Not unordered
HI	Unsigned Higher	Greater than, or unordered
LS	Unsigned Lower or same	Less than or equal
GE	Signed Greater than or equal	Greater than or equal
LT	Signed Less Than	Less Than, or unordered
GT	Signed Greater Than	Greater Than
LE	Signed Less Than or equal	Less Than or equal, or unordered
AL	Always	Always

Figure 23c. Condition code comparison ARM v VFP

Program 23a shows how easy it is to use these commands. This simply loads values into S14 and S15 and then compares them using the VCMP instruction. This sets the flags in the FPSCR. The VMRS instruction is then used to copy the NZCV flags across into the ARM Status Register. Then depending on the status of the C register R0 is loaded with 0 or 255.

You can play with the values of the constants being loaded into the two single-precision registers and use GDB to check the register values to watch the process for yourself. You might like to try extending the program to create a loop that counts down in 0.1 increments, printing them on the screen as you do so and exiting when zero is reached.

Program 23a. Demonstrating conditional execution based on the outcome of a VFP operation.

```
/*** Conditional execution in VFP code ***/

        .global   main
        .func main
main:

        LDR R1, addr_value1     @ Get addr value1
        VLDR S14, [R1]
        VCVT.F64.F32 D1, S14

        LDR R1, addr_value2     @ Get addr value 2
        VLDR S15, [R1]
        VCVT.F64.F32 D2, S15

        VCMP.F32 S14, S15       @ Compare S14 and S15
        VMRS APSR_nzcv, FPSCR   @ Copy flag set across

        MOVEQ R0, #0            @ If C=1, R0=0
        MOVNE R0, #255          @ If C=0, R0=255

        MOV PC, LR

addr_value1:    .word value1
addr_value2:    .word value2

        .data
value1:    .float 1.54321
value2:    .float 5.1
```

Scalar and Vector Operations

In the previous chapter when looking at the Register file I mentioned that the registers can be divided into scalar and vectorial banks for access purposes. Figure 23d illustrates how this architecture is arranged.

In the earlier examples we have implied that all operations are working on individual registers. However, the VFP can group registers into vectors or groups of registers. For vector operations, the VFP register file can be viewed as a collection of smaller banks. Each of these smaller banks is treated either as a bank of eight single-precision registers or as a bank of four double-precision registers. The number of registers used by a vector is controlled by the LEN bits in the FPSCR. Practically the register banks can be configured as one of the following:

- Four banks of single-precision registers, S0 to S7, S8 to S15, S16 to S23, and S24 to S31

- Four banks of double-precision registers, D0 to D3, D4 to D7, D8 to D11, and D12 to D15

- Any combination of single-precision and double-precision banks.

Bank 0	Bank 1	Bank 2	Bank 3
S0 S7	S8 S15	S16 S23	S24 S31
D0 D1 D2 D3	D4 D5 D6 D7	D8 D11	D12 D15

Figure 23d. The four VFP banks and associated registers.

Normally the value of LEN is set to 1 so that an instruction will only operate on the registers defined in the instruction. However, by increasing the value of LEN we can make the instruction operate on the rest of the registers in the associated bank of registers. So, a vector can start from any register and wrap around to the beginning of the bank. In other words if a vector ends beyond the end of its bank, it wraps around to the start of the same bank. Figure 23e shows how this works in tabular form.

It is important to note that a vector cannot contain registers from more than one bank, so if the length wraps back to the start the operation stops at that point, once the bank is full.

Referring to Figure 23e, the first entry has a LEN of 2. This means that the number of registers to be operated on is two. The start register is D11. Looking at Figure 23d we can see that D11 is at the last register in Bank 2. Wrap around means that the next register in the bank is in fact D8 (D12 is in Bank 3).

The first register used by an operand vector is the register that is specified as the operand in the individual VFP instructions. The first register used by the destination vector is the register that is specified as the destination in the individual VFP instructions.

LEN	Start Register	Registers Used
2	D11	D11, D8
3	D7	D7, D4, D5
4	S5	S5, S6, S7, S0
5	S22	S22, S23, S16, S17, S18

Figure 23e. LEN and its effect on bank wrapping.

In the table above the registers accessed have been consecutive ones, in other words they followed the numeric order allowing for wrap around. However, they can also occupy alternative registers and this is defined by the setting of the STRIDE bits in the FPSCR. In the examples given in Figure 23e the STRIDE setting would have been 1 as the registers used are consecutive. But a STRIDE setting of 2 would have forced alternative registers to be used. Figure 23f illustrates this in tabular form also.

LEN	STRIDE	Start Reg	Registers Used
2	2	D1	D1, D3
3	2	S1	S1, S3, S5
4	2	S6	S6, S0, S2, S4
5	1	S22	S22, S23, S16, S17, S18

Figure 23f. How LEN and STRIDE affects vector wrap-around.

As we have said, a vector cannot use the same register twice, so the combinations of LEN and STRIDE settings are limited.

Consider the following instruction:

```
VADD.F32 S8, S16, S24    @ S8=S16+S24
```

ARM A32 Assembly Language

By default LEN=1 and STRIDE=1 and so the contents of S16 and S24 are added together with the result placed in S8. However, if we set LEN=2 and STRIDE=2 and execute the same instruction, it will be the same as executing the following two instructions with 1+1 settings:

```
VADD.F32 S8, S16, S24    @ S8=S16+S24
VADD.F32 S10, S18, S26   @ S10=S18+S26
```

In turn setting LEN=4 and STRIDE=2 and performing the same instruction would actually execute as though the following four instructions had taken place:

```
VADD.F32 S8, S16, S24    @ S8=S16+S24
VADD.F32 S10, S18, S26   @ S10=S18+S26
VADD.F32 S12, S20, S28   @ S12=S20+S28
VADD.F32 S14, S22, S30   @ S14=S22+S30
```

As you can see this is a potent programming method and is especially useful when it comes to matrix operations on blocks of numbers.

Which Type of Operator?

Essentially VFP arithmetic can be performed on scalars, vectors or both together. When LEN=1 (default) then all VFP operations are scalar in nature. When LEN is set to anything else then they can be any scalar, vector or mixed. How this works is in your control only by your selection of the register banks used or source and destination registers.

For most purposes Bank 0 (S0-S7/D0-D3) is a scalar bank and the remaining three banks are vector banks. A mixed operation (scalar and vector) occurs when the destination register is in one of the vector banks. Figure 23g provides some examples followed by brief descriptions of the type of action being performed and what is actually to be performed. Although VADD is used through these examples, the action is applicable to all VFP arithmetic instructions.

ARM A32 Assembly Language

STR	LEN	Instruction	Result
1	1	VADD.F64 D0,D1,D2	D0=D1+D2. Operation is scalar as destination (D0) is in Bank 0.
1	1	VADD.F32 S4,S8,S20	S4=S8+S20. Operation is scalar as destination (S4) is in Bank 0.
2	4	VADD.F32 S10,S16,S24	S10=S16+S24;S12=S18+S26;S14=S20+S28;S8=S22+ S30. Vectorial and notice wrap around on the last iteration.
2	2	VADD.D64 D4, D8, D0	D4=D8+D0; D6=D10+D2. Mixed as the second source registers is in Bank 0.

Figure 23g. Examples of Scalar, Vector and Mixed operations.

Len and Stride

The bits associated with LEN and STRIDE in the FPSCR can be set up using VMRS and VMSR instructions to transfer the required bit pattern into the FPSCR. This has to be done through an ARM register and is a two-part process, as the FPSCR must be copied across first so that the flag settings may be maintained and a mask applied just to affect the settings of LEN and STRIDE. Any ARM register can be used and the two-way process would look like this:

```
    VMRS R4, FPSCR      @ Copy FPSCR into R4
                        @ carry out bit setting here
    VMSR FPSCR, R4      @ Copy R4 into FPSCR
```

The LEN field occupies three bits (b16-b18) whilst the STRIDE field occupies two bits (b20-b21). Figure 23h (over) shows the various bit combinations for LEN and STRIDE and the outcomes for each as well as their reliability with single and double-precision numbers.

Not all combinations return predictable results and should be avoided. Use the table to select what combination works for the type of values you are dealing with. You will see from this that STRIDE bits are only ever 00 or 11 to represent 1 and 2, respectively. LEN operates so a value of 1 is represented by 000 (ie, the actual binary stored is one less than value).

Program 23b demonstrates how vector addressing delivers the third option listed in Figure 23g. The bulk of the listing is actually given over to first seeding values and then printing them out using printf. The theory behind the latter should be familiar to you now, and as we will ultimately be printing four double-precision values, three of these have to be pushed onto the stack so the main: function begins by reserving 24-bytes for just this purpose (24-bytes being three words).

The actual instruction being actioned is:

```
VADD.F32 S10, S16, S24
```

This involves three vector banks in Bank 1, Bank 2 and Bank 3. As we will be using STRIDE=2, LEN=4 as our vector control settings, Bank 1 is used to hold results (S10, S12, S14, S8), Bank 2 will hold the first set of values (S16, S18, S20, S22) and Bank 3 the second set of values (S24, S26, S28, S30).

Five values have been defined for use. To make things easier to check, a single value is assigned into the Bank 2 registers and then four separate values assigned to each of the registers in Bank 3.

	STR	Bits	LEN	Bits	Single (Sx)	Double (Dx)
1		b00	1	b000	All scalar	All Scalar
2		b11	1	b000	Normal	Normal
3	1	b00	2	b001	Normal	Normal
4	2	b11	2	b001	Normal	Normal
5	1	b00	3	b010	Normal	Unpredictable
6	2	b11	3	b010	Normal	Normal
7	1	b00	4	b011	Normal	Unpredictable
8	2	b11	4	b011	Normal	Unpredictable
9	1	b00	5	b100	Normal	Unpredictable
10	2	b11	5	b100	Unpredictable	Unpredictable
11	1	b00	6	b101	Normal	Unpredictable
12	2	b11	6	b101	Unpredictable	Unpredictable
13	1	b00	7	b110	Normal	Unpredictable
14	2	b11	7	b110	Unpredictable	Unpredictable
15	1	b00	8	b111	Normal	Unpredictable
16	2	b11	8	b111	Unpredictable	Unpredictable

Figure 23h. STRIDE and Vector LEN combinations and their effect on single and double-precision numbers.

The lenstride: entry point marks where the FPSCR is seeded with the settings for STRIDE and LEN. We require settings of 2 and 4 respectively. Looking at Figure 23h we can see in line 8 the binary settings to achieve this for single-precision are 11 and 011 (a 'normal operation for single-precision).

As STRIDE and LEN are separated by a single bit the bit pattern we need to seed is 110011. This in turn needs to be shifted so the leftmost bit starts at b21 in the FPSCR so a LSL #16 achieves this.

Looking at the program listing, the 'convert:' routine transforms the Sx registers in Bank 1 into double-precision values in Bank 0. In this program Bank 0 is not touched so these registers are free, but beware, you must ensure that you have at least one double-precision register that you can use if you plan to utilise printf, otherwise you will be doing a lot of register moving and restoring.

Program 23b is shown overleaf. All source files are available on the companion website at www.brucesmith.info.

Program 23b Using LEN and STRIDE to sum vectors.

```
/*** Using LEN and STRIDE to sum vectors ***/

    .global   main
    .func main
main:

    SUB SP, SP, #24         @ room for printf

    LDR R1, addr_value1     @ Get addr of values
    LDR R2, addr_value2
    LDR R3, addr_value3
    LDR R4, addr_value4
    LDR R5, addr_value5

    VLDR S16, [R1]          @ load values into
    VLDR S18, [R1]          @ registers
    VLDR S20, [R1]
    VLDR S22, [R1]
    VLDR S24, [R2]
    VLDR S26, [R3]
    VLDR S28, [R4]
```

```
        VLDR S30, [R5]

lenstride:
/* Set LEN=4 0b011 and STRIDE=2 0b11 */
        VMRS R3, FPSCR          @ get current FPSCR
        MOV R4, #0b110011       @ bit pattern
        MOV R4, R4, LSL #16     @ move across to b21
        ORR R3, R3, R4          @ keep all 1's
        VMSR FPSCR, R3          @ transfer to FPSCR

        VADD.F32 S10, S16, S24  @ Vector addition
        VADD.F32 S12, S18, S26
        VADD.F32 S14, S20, S28
        VADD.F32 S8, S22, S30

convert:
/* Do conversion for printing, making sure not */
/* to corrupt Sx registers by over writing     */

        VCVT.F64.F32 D0, S10
        VCVT.F64.F32 D1, S12
        VCVT.F64.F32 D2, S14
        VCVT.F64.F32 D3, S8
        LDR R0, =string         @ set up for printf
        VMOV R2, R3, D0
        VSTR D1, [SP]           @ push data on stack
        VSTR D2, [SP, #8]
        VSTR D3, [SP, #16]
        BL  printf
        ADD SP, SP, #24         @ restore stack

_exit:
        MOV R0, #0
        MOV R7, #1
        SWI 0

addr_value1:    .word value1
addr_value2:    .word value2
addr_value3:    .word value3
```

```
addr_value4:    .word value4
addr_value5:    .word value5

    .data
value1:     .float 1.0
value2:     .float 1.25
value3:     .float 1.50
value4:     .float 1.75
value5:     .float 2.0

string:
.asciz " S10 is %f\n S12 is %f\n S14 is %f\n S8 is %f\n"
```

I make no apologies for the simplicity of this program, but it does provide a good way to get to grips with using the FPSCR and the STRIDE and LEN bits. It is worth spending some time making copies of the source and editing the file to look at other combinations. Perhaps try to test the rest of the examples given in Figure 23g.

24: Neon

The Neon subsystem is an Advanced SIMD (Single Instruction, Multiple Data) processing unit. Rather than processing data linearly, one item after the other, it does so in parallel – altogether. This parallel processing ability allows us to achieve more than simple clock speed improvements.

Neon can apply a single action to many pieces of data at one time without the data ever leaving the registers. So much so that it appears that you are simply loading and then storing data which has been transformed by some intervening instructions - we'll look at a good example of this later in this chapter. In this way, you can get more 'speed' (or completed operations) out of Neon than you can a standard SISD (Single Instruction, Single Data) processor running at the same clock rate.

Figure 24a depicts how Neon operations work.

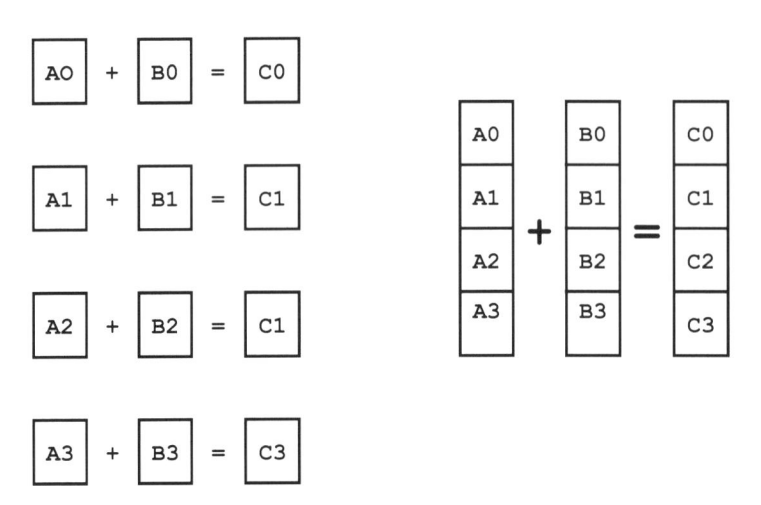

Figure 24a. Neon operations are carried out all at once – in parallel rather than serially.

While a normal processor would do A0+ B0=C0, A1+B1=C1 and so forth the Neon system does this in one instruction producing the same output.

Neon supports several data types:

- 32-bit single precision floating point
- 8, 16, 32 and 64-bit signed and unsigned integers
- 8 and 16-bit polynomials

The convention used to distinguish types is to put the first letter of the type before the size. For example, an unsigned 32-bit integer would be U32, 32-bit floating point would be F32 and so on.

You should take into account a few differences between the Neon and VFP systems:

- Neon does not support double-precision floating point numbers.
- Neon only works on vectors and does not support advanced operations such as square root and divide.
- VFP offers some specialised instructions not supported by the Neon unit (SQRT for example).

Neon is used to crunch lots of numbers and quickly. If you need floating point precision, then use the VFP. However, bear in mind that the Neon hardware shares the same floating-point registers supplied by the VFP, so if you are using both formats together ensure your register management is up-to-scratch.

Devices such as the ARM Cortex-A8 and Cortex-A9 support 128-bit vectors but will execute with 64-bits at a time, whereas Cortex-A15 devices can execute 128-bits at a time. It is important therefore to understand how the Neon is implemented on the architecture you are using. They are not all the same.

Neon Instructions

As illustrated in Figure 24b the Neon system uses a bank of 32 by 64-bit registers which can also be configured as 16 by 128-bit registers. Here the D registers of the VFP are doubled up to make a Q or Quad registers.

- 32 off 64-bit ('double-word') registers: D0-D31
- 16 off 128-bit ('quad-word') registers: Q0-Q15

To enhance Neon performance and reduce code density the Neon instruction set includes structured load and store instructions that can load or store single or multiple values from or to single or multiple 'lanes' in a vector register. As we shall see below, these load and store operations are incredibly versatile and can manipulate data during the load and store operation.

D0	D1	<< >>	Q0
D2	D3		Q1
D4	D5		Q2
D6	D7		Q3
D8	S9		Q4
D10	D11		Q5
D12	D13		Q6
D14	D15		Q7
D16	D17		Q8
D18	D19		Q9
D20	D21		Q10
D22	D23		Q11
D24	D25		Q12
D26	D27		Q13
D28	D29		Q14
D30	D31		Q15

Figure 24b. The Neon register configuration. Compare this to Figure 22b to see how the register structure is built.

Neon also includes instructions that transfer complete data structures between several vector registers and memory. Many of the instructions can operate on different data types, specified in the instruction encoding. The software indicates the data required by appending a suffix to the instruction mnemonic. The number of elements to be operated on is indicated by the specified register size. For example:

```
VADD.I16 Q0, Q1, Q2
```

indicates an operation on 16-bit integer elements stored in 128-bit Q registers. These operations are carried out by dividing the vector into a series of lanes – this means that the operation is on eight 16-bit lanes in parallel. This is illustrated below in Figure 24c which also shows pictorially how 'lanes' are organised. The instruction performs a parallel addition of eight lanes of 16-bit elements from vectors in Q1 and Q2, storing the result in Q0.

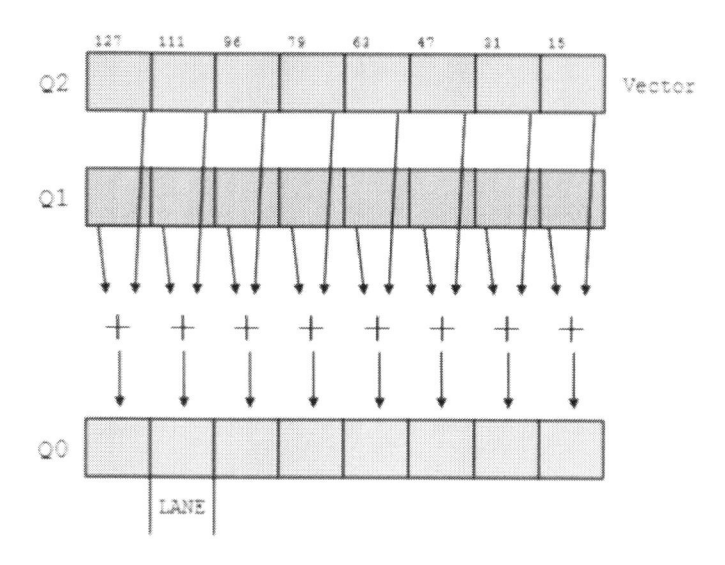

Figure 24c. Manipulating data lanes in Neon.

Some instructions take different size input and output registers. For example:

```
VMULL.S16 Q0, D2, D3
```

multiplies four 16-bit lanes in parallel, producing four 32-bit products in a 128-bit destination vector!

Instructions specify what's in the vectors. Here are a few examples:

```
VADD.I32   Q1, Q2, Q3 @  4x 32-bit integer add
VQADD.S32  Q1, Q2, Q3 @  4x 32-bit integer add with
                         signed saturation
VQADD.U32  Q1, Q2, Q3 @  4x 32-bit integer add with
                         unsigned saturation
```

Instructions can be used to promote and demote datatypes:

```
VMOVL.S32 Q0, D0  @ 2x 32-bit signed promotion to
                    64-bit
```

```
VMOVN.I32    D0, Q0   @ 4x 32-bit narrow to 16-bit
VQMOVN.U32   D0, Q0   @ 4x unsigned 32-bit narrow to
                      @ 16-bit with saturation
VQMOVUN.S32  D0, Q0   @ 4x 32-bit narrow signed
                      @ data to 16-bit unsigned
                      @ saturation
```

The datatype always corresponds to the source – you cannot promote past 64-bit, or demote to less than 8-bit. Some instructions can promote and demote as part of its operation:

```
VADDL.S32   Q0, D0, D1  @ 2x signed 32-bit promotion
                        @ to 64-bit and then add
VADDW.S32   Q0, Q0, D2  @ Promotes d2 to S64 and does
                        @ 2x 64-bit adds with Q0
VADDHN.S32  D0, Q0, Q1  @ 4x signed 32-bit add,
                        @ take the high half, and
                        @ narrow to 16-bit
```

Addressing Modes

Neon instructions have limited ability when used as an addressing mode source. For example, this loads D0 with the contents of the address held in R0:

```
VLD1.64 {D0}, [R0]
```

This next example does the same but adds the size of transfer to R0 after the transfer has taken place, which is handy when you are storing data in sequential blocks of memory.

```
VLD1.64 {D0}, [R0]!
```

Finally, this next instruction adds the contents of R1 to R0 after D0 is loaded with the contents of the address held in R0:

```
VLD1.64 {D0}, [R0], R1
```

Neon Intrinsics

Because of the complexity of Neon applications (decoding video or sound for your smartphone for example), C is invariably used to write code for compiling. However, the most direct way to utilise Neon is by writing assembly code, not least because the code produced by the compiler out of the C file is not always very 'tight' and can be wasteful of resources. Equally, C doesn't always make the best register decisions when compiling.

The term Neon Intrinsic is often used to refer to C compilation of Neon. An intrinsic function is a function available for use in a given programming language whose implementation is handled specially by the compiler. Typically, it substitutes a sequence of automatically generated instructions for the original function call, similar to an inline function. Unlike an inline function, though, the compiler has an intimate knowledge of the intrinsic function and can, therefore, better integrate it and optimise it for the situation.

Intrinsic functions are often used to explicitly implement vectorization and parallelisation in languages which do not address such constructs. The compiler parses the intrinsic functions and converts them into vector math or multiprocessing object code appropriate for the target platform.

Neon intrinsics are a set of definitions that induces use of Neon when compiling the C program. Some programmers love them; some hate them. For performance-critical programs then I am not a fan. It's too easy for the compiler to inject extra register unload/load steps between your intrinsics. The effort to get it to stop doing that is more complicated than just writing the stuff in raw Neon Assembler. At this level, it's good to know what's happening and control it yourself.

There is no support for Neon intrinsics for architectures before ARMv7. When building for earlier architectures, or for ARMv7 architecture profiles that do not include Neon, the compiler treats Neon intrinsics as ordinary function calls. This operation results in an error at link time.

Neon Assembler

Program 24a is a simple example for you to try and ensure that Neon is operating on your system:

Program 24a. A simple neon test.

```
/* Simple Neon test */
.global _start
_start:

LDR R0, =number1
LDR R1, =number2
```

```
VLD1.32   {Q1}, [R0]
VLD1.32   {Q2}, [R1]

VADD.I32  Q0, Q1, Q2

MOV R7, #1
SWI 0

.data
number1:  .word 1,0,0,0,0,0,0,0,0,0,0,0,0,0,0,0
number2:  .word 2,0,0,0,0,0,0,0,0,0,0,0,0,0,0,0
```

To assemble the code remember to use:

```
-mfpu=neon
```

to the assembler command line. This specifies that Neon instructions are permitted. For example:

```
as -mfpu=neon -o prog24a.o prog24a.s
ld -o prog24a prog24a.o
```

If you leave out the mfpu option, then you will almost certainly get an error message of the type:

```
Error: selected FPU does not support instruction.
```

The program simply puts the values 1 and 2 into Q1 and Q2 respectively and then adds them, storing the result in Q0.

Neon Arrays

Because Neon can manipulate large amounts of data with one instruction, it is often used to code graphics software. For example, if you rotate a picture on your smartphone or tablet the process is probably done by manipulating blocks of data using Neon instructions.

The following code will rotate the contents of a block of four Q registers through 90 degrees. Figure 24d shows the matrix before and after. The numbers on the left refer to the Q registers, and the grid numbers are placeholders for each lane so you can see the before and after state.

ARM A32 Assembly Language

```
           Before Position              After Position
    ┌───┬───┬───┬───┐         ┌───┬───┬───┬───┐
Q0  │ 0 │ 1 │ 2 │ 3 │         │12 │ 8 │ 4 │ 0 │
    ├───┼───┼───┼───┤         ├───┼───┼───┼───┤
Q1  │ 4 │ 5 │ 6 │ 7 │         │13 │ 9 │ 5 │ 1 │
    ├───┼───┼───┼───┤         ├───┼───┼───┼───┤
Q2  │ 8 │ 9 │10 │11 │         │14 │10 │ 6 │ 2 │
    ├───┼───┼───┼───┤         ├───┼───┼───┼───┤
Q3  │12 │13 │14 │15 │         │15 │11 │ 7 │ 3 │
    └───┴───┴───┴───┘         └───┴───┴───┴───┘
```

Figure 24d. Rotating data through 90 degrees.

Program 24b lists the assembly code that will produce this. The data used is simple numbers just so that you can visually inspect the start and end results via a GDB register dump.

Program 24b. Rotate a matrix by 90 degrees.

```
/* Rotate 4x4 Matrix Through 90 Degrees */

.global _start
_start:

@ Get data pointers
LDR R0,=matrix0
LDR R1,=matrix1
LDR R2,=matrix2
LDR R3,=matrix3

@ Load Q0-Q1 with the data
VLD1.32 {Q0}, [R0]
VLD1.32    {Q1}, [R1]
VLD1.32    {Q2}, [R2]
VLD1.32    {Q3}, [R3]

@ Transpose Matrix
VZIP.32 Q0, Q1
```

```
VZIP.32 Q2, Q3

@ Interleave inner pairs
VSWP D1, D4
VSWP D3, D6

@ Mirror flip matrix
VREV64.32 Q0, Q0
VREV64.32 Q1, Q1
VREV64.32 Q2, Q2
VREV64.32 Q3, Q3

@ Swap high and low halves
VSWP D0, D1
VSWP D2, D3
VSWP D4, D5
VSWP D6, D7

@ Store result
VST1.32 {Q0}, [R0]
VST1.32 {Q1}, [R1]
VST1.32 {Q2}, [R2]
VST1.32 {Q3}, [R3]

MOV R7, #1
SWI 0

.data
matrix0:    .word 0,1,2,3
matrix1:    .word 4,5,6,7
matrix2:    .word 8,9,10,11
matrix3:    .word 12,13,14,15
```

There are some instructions we have used for the first time here, and if you are interested in digging deeper, you might want to work through these diagrammatically substituting the numbers for colour in a 4 x 4 grid.

VLDn loads one n-element structure from memory into one or more Neon registers. Elements of the register not loaded are unaltered. VZIP interleaves the elements of two vectors. It can take three sizes namely, 8, 16 or 32. The illustration below (Figure 24e) shows the before and after of VZIP.32 as used in the example.

```
        Before VZIP                    After VZIP
Qd  | A3 | A2 | A1 | A0 |          | B1 | A1 | B0 | A0 |
Qm  | B3 | B2 | B1 | B0 |          | B3 | A3 | B2 | A2 |
```

Figure 24e. The effect of VZIP.

The operation is the same as that performed by VST2 before storing, so use VST2 rather than VZIP if you need to zip data immediately before writing back to memory.

VREV can take three forms and will reverse the order of 8-bit, 16-bit, or 32-bit elements within each doubleword of the vector, and places the result in the corresponding destination vector.

VREV16 reverses the order of 8-bit elements within each halfword of the vector. VREV32 reverses the order of 8-bit or 16-bit elements within each word of the vector. VREV64 reverses the order of 8-bit, 16-bit, or 32-bit elements within each doubleword of the vector. VSWP is a simple vector swap exchanging the contents of the two vectors (it can also be used to swap the top upper and lower 64-bits of a Q register, VSWP D0, D1).

Matrix Math

Matrix multiplication often finds its way into primers such as these. I deliberately avoided them in the early part of this text as they are tedious and long winded, and frankly difficult to follow. I have left it until now as with Neon they are simple(ish) to code and relatively short. In these next two examples, we'll see how to add and multiply them together.

To add two matrix you simply add the corresponding elements in each column to create a third answer matrix thus:

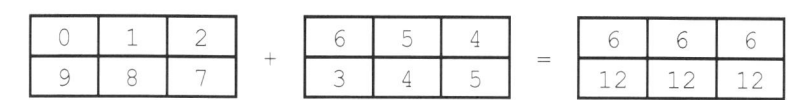

```
| 0 | 1 | 2 |   | 6 | 5 | 4 |   | 6  | 6  | 6  |
| 9 | 8 | 7 | + | 3 | 4 | 5 | = | 12 | 12 | 12 |
```

Figure 24f. Adding two matrices together.

This matrix is a 3x2 matrix – three columns, two rows.

ARM A32 Assembly Language

Program 24c below uses Neon to add the elements of two 4x4 matrices comprising 32-bit values. Neon allows for structured load and store operations which can interleave the data they 'get' for 'free'. The VLD instruction assists with this. In the listing below the VLD instruction takes first a number, 1, 2, 3 or 4, which represents the 'stride' and then a value relating to 8, 16, 32 or 64 bits.

R0 and R1 point to the two arrays, which are loaded into Q0 and Q1 as 32-bit integers. The '1' in the instruction here represents there is a single element structure to the lane.

Program 24c. Adding two 4x4 Matrix together.

```
/* Add two 4x4 matrix together */

.global _start
_start:

LDR R0, =matrix1
LDR R1, =matrix2
LDR R2, =matrix3

VLD1.i32 {Q0}, [R0]   @ Load 4 x 32bit integers, 1st array
VLD1.i32 {Q1}, [R1]   @ Load 4 x 32bit integers, 2nd array
VADD.i32 Q2, Q0, Q1   @ Add the values of 4 int32
VST1.i32 {Q2}, [R2]   @ Store the 4 x 32bit integers

MOV R7, #1
SWI 0

.data
matrix1:   .word 2,0,0,0,0,0,0,0,0,0,0,0,0,0,0,0
matrix2:   .word 4,0,0,0,0,0,0,0,0,0,0,0,0,0,0,0
matrix3:   .word 0,0,0,0,0,0,0,0,0,0,0,0,0,0,0,0
```

Again, if you interrogate the program through GDB, you will see the results.

There are two types of multiplication for matrices: scalar multiplication and matrix multiplication. Scalar multiplication is easy. You just take a regular number (called a "scalar") and multiply it on every entry in the matrix, thus:

ARM A32 Assembly Language

0	1	2
3	4	5

X

2

=

0	2	4
6	8	10

Figure 24g. Multiply a matrix by a scalar.

On matrix multiplication (non-scalar) you multiply each of the elements of a row in the left-hand matrix by the corresponding elements of a column in the right-hand matrix, and then sum the resulting 'n' products to obtain one element in the product matrix. For example:

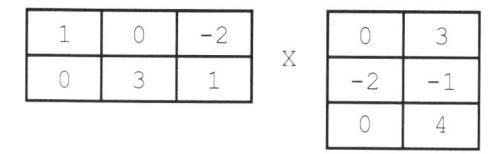

1	0	-2
0	3	1

X

0	3
-2	-1
0	4

Figure 24h. Multiply two 4x4 matrix.

To find the result here I multiply the rows of A by the columns of B. Take the first row of A and the first column of B and multiply the first entries, then the second entries, and then the third entries, and then add the three products. This gives:

0	-5
-6	-1

Figure 24i. The matrix result.

Program 24d given below keeps things simple by using two matrices of equal size and assumes that the matrices are stored in memory in column-major order. The process for multiplication is the same, as illustrated below (Figure 24j), where the math for first column result is shown. The same will be done for the next three columns to give the final result:

241

ARM A32 Assembly Language

Program 24d. Multiply two 4x4 32-bit floating point arrays.

```
/* Floating Point 4x4 Matrix Multiplication */
.global _start
_start:

.macro matrixf32 resultQ, col0_d, col1_d
VMUL.f32 \resultQ, Q8,  \col0_d[0]  @ element 0 by column 0
VMLA.f32 \resultQ, Q9,  \col0_d[1]  @ element 1 by column 1
VMLA.f32 \resultQ, Q10, \col1_d[0]  @ element 2 by column 2
VMLA.f32 \resultQ, Q11, \col1_d[1]  @ element 3 by column 3
.endm

LDR R0, =matrix0
LDR R1, =matrix1
LDR R2, =matrix2

VLD1.32 {D16-D19},[R1]!  @ first 8 elements of matrix 1
VLD1.32 {D20-D23},[R1]!  @ second 8 elements of matrix 1
VLD1.32 {D0-D3},[R2]!    @ first 8 elements of matrix 2
VLD1.32 {D4-D7},[R2]!    @ second 8 elements of matrix 2

matrixf32 Q12, D0, D1    @ matrix 1 * matrix 2 col 0
matrixf32 Q13, D2, D3    @ matrix 1 * matrix 2 col 1
matrixf32 Q14, D4, D5    @ matrix 1 * matrix 2 col 2
matrixf32 Q15, D6, D7    @ matrix 1 * matrix 2 col 3

VST1.32  {D24-D27}, [R0]!  @ store first 8 elements result.
VST1.32  {D28-D31}, [R0]!  @ store 2nd 8 elements result.

MOV R7, #1
SWI 0

.data
matrix0:  .float 0,0,0,0,0,0,0,0,0,0,0,0,0,0,0,0
matrix1:  .float 1.5,1.5,1.5,1.5,1.5,1.5,1.5,1.5,1.5,
1.5,1.5,1.5,1.5,1.5,1.5,1.5
matrix2:  .float 2.5,2.5,2.5,2.5,2.5,2.5,2.5,2.5,2.5,2.5,
2.5,2.5,2.5,2.5,2.5,2.5
```

ARM A32 Assembly Language

(Note: in the listing above the 'matrix1' and 'matrix2' definitions should be on a single line each in your program listing.)

X0	X4	X8	XC
X1	X5	X9	XD
X2	X6	XA	XE
X3	X7	XB	XF

+

Y0	Y4	Y8	YC
Y1	Y5	Y9	YD
Y2	Y6	YA	YE
Y3	Y7	YB	YF

=

X0Y0+X4Y1+X8Y2+XCY3
X1Y0+X5Y1+X9Y2+XDY3
X2Y0+X6Y1+XAY2+XEY3
X3Y0+X7Y1+XBY2+XFY3

Figure 24j. Calculating the first column of a 4 x 4 matrix multiplication.

In the program, each column from the matrix is loaded into a Neon register; we can use the vector-by-scalar multiplication (VMLA) instruction to calculate the result for each column. We must also add the results together for each element of the column, which we do use the accumulating version of the same instruction.

Remember that the D registers are aliased with the Q registers so that we can access the contents of these register, either way, remembering that Q0 is the combination of D0 and D1 and so forth.

The program beings by loading the first eight elements matrix (Matrix 1) into D16-D19, and the second eight elements in D20-D23 which correspond to Q12 and Q13. It then loads the contents of Matrix 2 into D0-D7 (Q0-Q1).

The crux of the program then operates through these instructions which calculate a single column using just four Neon instructions:

```
VMUL.f32    Q12, Q8,  D0[0]
VMLA.f32    Q12, Q9,  D0[1]
VMLA.f32    Q12, Q10, D1[0]
VMLA.f32    Q12, Q11, D1[1]
```

Here, the first instruction (VMUL.F32) takes x0, x1, x2 and x3 (in register Q8) and each is multiplied by y0 (element 0 in D0), and the result is stored in Q12. The three subsequent VMLA.F32 instructions operate on the other three columns of the first matrix, multiplying by corresponding elements of the first column of the second matrix. Results are accumulated into Q12 to give the first column of values for the result matrix.

This set of instructions must be executed three more times to calculate the second, third and fourth columns. Here we use values Y4 to YF from the second matrix in registers Q1 to Q3.

Rather than repeat the four lines three more times the program has this implemented as a macro (called 'matrixf32') that is called with the correct information seeded through to it.

VLD and VST in their Stride

The VLSD instruction provides incredible flexibility in that it can manipulate data as it is loaded. The VST instruction can also be the same before it stores data to memory.

```
VLD 2.8 {D14, D15}, [R0]
```

It is worth breaking the instruction down into its parts:

2:	This is the interleave pattern (stride). It may be 1, 2, 3 or 4.
8:	This is the data type: 8, 16 or 32.
D14,D15	This is the Neon register list, ie, registers to use. Up to four registers can be included.
[R0]	The ARM register containing the address of the data.

```
VLD2.16 {D0, D1},[R0]
```

Would load the D0 and D1 (Q0) registers with four 16-bit elements in the first register (D0), and four 16-bit elements in the second (D1), with adjacent pairs (even and odd) separated to each register.

```
VLD2.16 {D0, D1},[R0]
```

Changing the size to 32-bits loads the same amount of data, but now only two elements make up each vector, again separated into even and odd elements.

Program 24d can be used as the basis of some investigation. This takes some simple visual data and performs a VLD on it. If you compile this with the -g option you can jump into GDB and inspect the registers to see what has happened to your data. You can add to the program simply using different values using additional registers so you can get a good visual idea of what is happening.

ARM A32 Assembly Language

One of the most common uses for this sort of Neon instruction is to read and sort RGB video data. If you imagine that the information was stored as a sequence of R,G,B, R,G,B, R,G,B as 24-bit data then you could sort the three channels into R, G and B using:

```
VLD3.8 {D0, D1, D2}, [R0]
```

Here the red information will be in D0, the green in D1 and the blue in D2.

VLD and VST can also be used to good effect when it comes to sorting data. Consider this command:

```
VLD4.8 {D0[2], D1[2], D2[D2], D3[2]}, [R0]
```

This would take the element in the third lane from the four vectors and store them at the address in R0, leaving the other lanes intact.

In summary VLD1 loads one to four registers of data from memory, with no deinterleaving. Use this when processing an array of non-interleaved data; VLD2 loads two or four registers of data, deinterleaving even and odd elements into those registers; VLD3 loads three registers and deinterleaves and VLD4 loads four registers and deinterleaves. VST supports the same options but interleave the data from registers before writing them to memory.

Load of Others

In addition to structural loads and stores Neon also provides two other formats for the instruction:

VLDR and VSTR to load or store a single register as a 64-bit value.

VLDM and VSTM to load multiple registers as 64-bit values.

The latter can be useful for pushing and pulling registers from the stack.

245

25: Thumb Code

Thumb is the name given to a subset of the ARM instruction set. It was originally introduced with ARMv4-T. Significantly it is a 16-bit (two-byte) implementation, so instructions can in theory be coded in half the space of an equivalent ARM program but in reality achieving the same result in a third less space . This higher code density makes Thumb code popular where memory constraints are tight. You will probably not see a lot of Thumb programs around on the forums. This is mainly because most Thumb code seems to be written and compiled from C. But that isn't to say we can't hand assemble it.

In terms of hardware there is no real difference between the way in which ARM and Thumb instruction sets function — they are one and the same. Although Thumb is a 16-bit implementation register sizes do not change. R0 is still a word wide, as are the other registers. What is different is how they are fetched and interpreted before execution. Thumb instructions are expanded into their 32-bit equivalents internally by the hardware, so it doesn't slow down their execution in any way — ARM speed is maintained. This makes it perfectly acceptable to mix normal sections of ARM and Thumb code and jump from one to the other; in fact jumping from ARM to Thumb is the preferred way to enter Thumb code.

A Thumb-2 instruction set was introduced with ARMv6T2 (and included in subsequent releases) and added more instructions to the base set but also allows most of the new Thumb instructions to be conditionally executed. If you like, Thumb-2 offers a 'best of both worlds' compromise in that it has access to both 16-bit and 32-bit instructions allowing programmers who are tight for space to extract the maximum bang-per-byte by combing the two. Thumb-2 was a step towards the development of a Unified Assembly Language, which is discussed in Chapter 26.

If you flick back to Chapter 6 and look at Figure 5c the diagram shows the Status Register configuration. Bit 5 is the 'T' bit and this is normally clear to indicated ARM State. When the T bit is set (T=1) then the chip is in Thumb State. We'll look how to move between states and write a simple program that can be the shell for any Thumb code you may wish to write. But first....

Differences

The Thumb instruction set will be very familiar to you, but there are differences that need to be borne in mind. If you understand these you should have no difficulties implementing and writing a Thumb program from your existing ARM knowledge (which should be quite extensive at this point). And of course, GCC supports Thumb as does GDB, so the tools to do so are readily available.

The major architectural difference is that your code does not have direct access to all the ARM registers; only R0 to R7 inclusive are available. Registers R8 to R12 inclusive can only be used in conjunction with MOV, ADD, SUB and CMP. There is very limited access to R13 (SP), R14 (LR) and R15 (PC) and only indirect access to the CPSR. There is no access to SPSR and the VFP instructions cannot be accessed from Thumb State.

Thumb	
R0	
R1	
R2	
R3	Registers available to all Thumb instructions. Instructions
R4	assembled in two-bytes (16-bits)
R5	
R6	
R7	

R8	
R9	
R10	Registers only available to a few Thumb instructions. Namely MOV,
R11	ADD, SUB, CMP.
R12	
R13 SP	SP, LR, SP only have limited
R14 LR	access and SP only accessible via
R15 PC	PUSH and POP instructions/

CPSR	Indirectly
SPSR_xxx	None

Figure 25a. Thumb registers accessibility.

The registers and code that are not available can be accessed from the program, but only after ARM State is switched back in. In other words you have to first come out of Thumb State to execute what you want to do and then switch back into Thumb State to continue. Figure 25a summarises these register restrictions. However, the advantage of all this is that when you move between ARM and Thumb State the contents of registers are preserved.

By definition, the other significant difference is that mnemonic representations of Thumb instructions are shorter, often with one less operand. Compare these ARM and Thumb versions of ADD:

```
ADDS R2, R2, #16    @ ARM State immediate addition
ADD R0, #3          @ Thumb equivalent, dest implied
```

The conditional code modifiers for instructions are not available, with only branch relative instructions conditionally executable. Therefore you cannot execute instructions like:

```
ADD CC R0, #3
```

in Thumb State.

The shift and rotate operators ASR, LSL, LSR and ROR are implemented as standalone instructions and are no longer available as a modifying operand. The following code segment illustrates the format for use:

```
LSL R2, R3    @ Shift R2 left number positions in R3
```

In the example above, if R2=4 and R3=1 then R2 would become 8.

Thumb includes just two branch instructions. B and BX. The B variant is the only one that is conditional, but the range here is limited to a label that must be within a signed single byte value, effectively -256 to 254. A non-conditional branch instruction can be extended to a range within an 11-bit signed immediate value, -2048 to +2046 bytes.

The BL instruction is not conditional but because it can be used in an indirect manner the address range can be up to 4Mb in either direction. An example of this is provided at the end of the next section.

There are also significant changes to multiple load-store and stack access instructions and these are covered below separately.

Assembling Thumb

To switch between ARM and Thumb states, you should use the GCC directives:

ARM A32 Assembly Language

```
    .arm
```

or:

```
    .thumb
```

These directives replace the oft seen older versions .code32 and .code16, but these should be considered as old hat now. If necessary, these directives will also automatically insert up to three bytes of padding to align to the next word boundary for ARM, or up to one byte of padding to align to the next half-word boundary for Thumb. Thus use of .align is unnecessary.

Both .arm and .thumb must be used to direct the assembler what to compile. They do not assemble any instructions themselves; they just direct the assembler as to what follows. Rather than having to play with bit 5 directly in the CPSR the state change will be handled directly for you if you follow the correct protocol for doing so which involves using the BX instruction.

Program 25a. How to invoke Thumb State and run Thumb code.

```
@   Use of Thumb code
@   This divide routine is R0/R1
@   with R2=MOD and R3=DIV

        .global main
        .func main
        .arm
main:
        ADR R0, thumbcode+1
        MOV LR, PC
        BX R0

exit:   MOV R0, #0
        MOV R7, #1
        SWI 0

        @ All Thumb code to be placed here
        .thumb
thumbcode:
        MOV R3, #0

loop:
```

```
        ADD R3, #1
        SUB R0, R1
        BGE loop
        SUB R3, #1
        ADD R2, R0, R1
        BX LR                   @ Return to ARM
```

Essentially, if you load the link address of the start of the Thumb code into R0 and set the least significant bit of R0 (that is b0=1) then Thumb State will be invoked automatically when the Thumb code is branched to with BX. This implies that you must always start from ARM state, but that must be the case anyway as that is the state the chip fires up in. Program 25a above shows how this works in practice. (Note the use of '@' for comments. GCC Thumb code does not like the inclusion of '/* */' style comments and these can sometimes cause an error.)

Thumb instructions are located from the thumbcode: label. This address is loaded into R0 at the start of main: and 1 is added to the address to set the least significant bit of R0. The BX (Branch with eXchange) is executed and the address in R0 is swapped into the PC. Because ARM and Thumb instructions are word or half-word-aligned respectively, bits 0 and 1 of the address are ignored because these bits refer to the half-word and byte part of the address.

The instructions at thumbcode perform a division routine (although we have not loaded any data into them to work with!) before the BX LR returns code back to the calling ARM code. ARM state is switched back in due to the requirement to execute an ARM instruction. Note that you have to switch back to ARM State to call a SWI call or a function such as printf.

You must use a BX LR instruction at the end of the ARM subroutine to return to the caller. You cannot use the MOV PC,LR instruction to return in this situation as it will not update the T bit for you thereby delivering the State change.

It is worth having a look at how GDB sees the assembled program as it confirms some of the differences outlined earlier. Figure 25b overleaf shows output from GDB using:

```
    x /12i main
```

As usual the addresses listed in the first column may be different on your board.

ARM A32 Assembly Language

Notice how the 'S' suffix is applied to the data instructions in the thumbcode portion of the listing. When dealing with registers R0-R7 all data processing instructions update the Status Flags and so the S suffix is enforced automatically by the assembler.

You will also note that the BGE instruction has a .N appended to it. In Thumb the .N specifier forces the assembler to generate a 16-bit encoding. In this case, if the instruction cannot be encoded in 16 bits, the assembler generates an error.

```
0x08390   <main>:        add          r0, pc, #13
0x08394   <main+4>:      mov          lr, pc
0x08398   <main+8>:      bx           r0
0x0839c   <exit>:        mov r0, #0
0x083a0   <exit+4>:      mov r7, #1
0x083a4   <exit+8>:      svc          0x00000000
0x083a8   <thumbcode>:   movs         r3, #0
0x083aa   <loop>:        adds         r3, #1
0x083ac   <loop+2>:      subs         r0, r0, r1
0x083ae   <loop+4>:      bge.n        0x83aa <loop>
0x083b0   <loop+6>:      subs         r3, #1
0x083b2   <loop+8>:      adds         r2, r0, r1
0x083b4   <loop+10>:     bx           lr
```

Figure 25b. Disassembling Program 25a.

The process of mingling segments of ARM and Thumb code together is called *interworking* and you are free to write code that moves between the two instructions sets if you so desire. The same ADR-BX process can be used throughout. If for example an ARM routine was located at the label 'armroutine' then it could be called with:

```
ADR R0, armroutine
BX  R0             @ Branch exchange to armroutine
```

Before making any calls that utilise the Link Register you should preserve its contents on the stack so that you can return to the original point of entry, and then recall the program originally entered at main, so that the program can complete its flow correctly.

Although BX is used in the examples above, the BLX instruction can also be used to jump into Thumb code. This instruction automatically saves the PC into the LR, so the MOV LR, PC instruction included in the listing is not needed. The +1 is still required for the entry address to switch State. The BX instruction should still be used to return from any called routine.

```
main:
    ADR R0, thumbcode+1
    BLX R0
```

Program 25b shows how these come together in practice using the printf function to print the result of a division performed in an extended program. Note that the additional ARM code follows the Thumb code. This is necessary otherwise the compiler will create an error when trying to create the relative branch address to the ARM code. Note also that the .arm and .thumb directives should be before the label marking the section of appropriate code.

Program 25b. Using external functions by interworking code.

```
@ Interworking ARM and Thumb code to call printf

    .global main
    .func main
    .arm
main:
    ADR R5, thumbstart+1
    BX R5

    .thumb
thumbstart:
    MOV R0, #9           @ Do 9/3
    MOV R1, #3
    MOV R3, #0
loop:
    ADD R3, #1
    SUB R0, R1
    BGE loop
    SUB R3, #1           @ R2=MOD
    ADD R2, R0, R1       @ R3=DIV
    ADR R5, divprint
    BX  R5
thumbreturn:
    @ Continue adding code as required
    @ Call ARM functions as and when needed
    ADR R5, exit
    BX  R5               @ Return to exit
```

```
        .arm
divprint:
    LDR R0, =string
    MOV R1, R3@ DIV in R3
                            @ MOD in R2 already
    BL printf
    ADR R5, thumbreturn+1
    BX R5

exit:
    MOV R7, #1
    SWI 0

.data
string:    .asciz "Result of 9/3 is: %d MOD %d\n"
```

Accessing High Registers

Only a handful of instructions can access the full set of ARM Registers. As already stated most Thumb instructions are limited to R0-R7 and automatically update the CPSR in doing so. Figure 25c lists the instructions and format use for accessing the higher registers R8-R14 and the PC. Apart from CMP these instructions do not update the CPSR

MOV <Dest>, <Operand1>
ADD <Dest>, <Operand1>
CMP <Operand1>, <Operand2>
ADD <Dest>, <Operand1>|<#Immediate>
ADD <Dest>, <Operand1>, <Operand2>|<#Immediate>
SUB <Dest>, <Operand1>|<#Immediate>
SUB <Dest>, <Operand1>, <Operand2>|<#Immediate>

Figure 25c. Thumb instructions that can access all ARM registers.

Stack Operators

The Thumb stack instructions are the most significant departure from the ARM instruction set, in fact opting to use the more traditional PUSH and

POP terms. We have seen these before as they are provided as pseudo-instructions by the GCC Compiler. In Thumb their action is similar so you should have little difficulties in getting to grips with them. However, there is a significant difference in that there is no stack pointer (SP) available to the instruction. This is because R13 is fixed as the Stack Pointer in Thumb operations and is automatically updated by the instructions. In other words, there is only one stack permissible in Thumb.

```
PUSH {R1-R4}    @ Push R1, R2, R3 & R4 onto stack
POP  (R2-R3}    @ Pop top 2 items into R2 and R3
```

PUSH can include the LR in its list and POP can include the PC, otherwise registers are limited to R0-R7 inclusive. In the first instance the SP address is adjusted by four words; in the second by two words. In ARM terms PUSH performs:

```
STMDB SP!, <REGLIST>
```

and POP performs:

```
LDMIA SP!, <REGLIST>
```

Single and Multi-Register

The LDR and STR instructions are supported by Thumb but not all addressing modes are supported. In fact only three are available for use with these and other associated commands. Figure 25d lists these, which are based on the pre-indexed addressing concept, and supply offset by register or by an immediate operand.

Addressing Mode	Example
Load/Store Register	LDR R0, R1
Base + Offset	LDR R0, [R1, #5] LDR R0, [R1, R2]
Relative	LDR R0, [PC, #8]

Figure 25d Addressing mode samples in Thumb State.

Multi-register access is limited to the use of increment after addressing modes using LDMIA and STMIA instructions. Note also that the ! update operator is not an option as it is in ARM State - it is mandatory::

```
STMIA R1!, {R2, R3, R4}
```

Functions in Thumb

The example given in Program 25b illustrates how an ARM, or more exactly libc, function can be called from Thumb code. Effectively you have to go back to ARM State. There is nothing stopping you creating your own functions in Thumb code — in other words a function consisting entirely of Thumb code that runs exclusively in Thumb State. But when calling the function it must have the least significant bit of the pointer to it set. As the linker in the compiler cannot do this, you yourself must do it within your calling code, especially if you use an absolute address.

In other words when you call any standalone Thumb code from another section of Thumb code, the entry condition is exactly the same as if you were entering Thumb code from ARM State. You add one to the link address.

Interestingly, you can have two functions with the same name — one for ARM and one for Thumb. The linker allows this provided they operate within different instruction sets. However, this shouldn't be considered good practice and should generally be avoided.

New ARMv7 Instructions

As part of the release of ARMv7 architecture, seven new instructions were added to the Thumb instruction set. There are seven new instructions, the most significant of which is Compare and Branch on Zero, or Non Zero. This instruction compares the value in the register with zero and conditionally branches forward a constant value. It does not affect the condition flags.

```
CBNZ R0, newdest    @ R0<>0 then branch to 'newdest'
CBZ R0, next        @ R0=0 then branch to 'next'
```

Both of these instructions can take a 'N' or '.W' modified as follows:

```
CBZ.N R0, next
```

'.N' is 'narrow' and informs the assembler to generate a 16-bit encoding. '.W' is 'wide' and signifies a 32-bit encoding. A 'N' (16-bit) is selected by default, whereas assembling in the A32 state will result in a 32-bit or wide encoding.

```
NOP
```

Is No Operation and does nothing other than providing padding which may be needed to ensure the following instruction sits on a 64-bit boundary. It also delays the program by a cycle.

Other new instructions include YIELD, SEV, WFE and WFI which are concerned with events and interrupts as they happen.

An 'IT'(if-then) instruction was added which permits up to four successive instructions to execute based on a tested condition, or on its inverse. IT is ignored when compiling into ARM code, but when compiling into Thumb, it generates an actual instruction. For example:

```
CMP R0, R1    @ if (R0 == R1)
ITE EQ        @ R0 = R2;
MOVEQ R0, R2  @ Thumb: condition via ITE 'T' (then)
              @ else R0 = R3;
MOVNE R0, R3  @ Thumb: condition via ITE 'E' (else)
```

ARMv8 deprecates the use of the 'IT' instruction.

26: Unified Assembler

Unified Assembler Language (UAL) is a standard syntax model for ARM implemented from ARMv8 onwards. From ARMv4T to ARMv7-A there are two instruction sets: ARM and Thumb. They are both '32-bit' in the sense that they operate on up-to-32-bit-wide data in 32-bit-wide registers with 32-bit addresses. In fact, where they overlap they represent the exact same instructions – it is only the instruction encoding which differs, and the CPU effectively just has two different decode front-ends to its pipeline which it can switch between.

Based on the combined A32 and T32 instruction sets, UAL forms a consistent programming model. This way you should produce the most economical and productive code possible. UAL implements some changes to both ARM and Thumb code to help in this standardisation, as well as the addition of new instructions. Use of this new syntax will affect backwards compatibility of code. UAL is a common syntax for A32 and T32 instructions. It supersedes earlier versions of both the ARM and Thumb assembler languages.

The GCC compiler (and I would assume other compatible compilers) will be able to assemble code written in pre-UAL and UAL syntax. If it is your intention to use UAL then you should make sure that your source code contains the directive:

```
.syntax unified
```

With any other definitions at the start of your code. You may also need to specify the architecture you are utilising – see later.

T32 extends the Thumb instruction set with bit-field manipulation, table branches and conditional execution operations. At the same time, the ARM instruction set is extended in areas to maintain equivalent functionality in both instruction sets. This combination produced a Unified Assembly Language (UAL), which supports assembly of either Thumb or ARM instructions from the same source code; versions of Thumb first seen on ARMV7 processors are essentially as capable as ARM code (including the ability to write interrupt handlers).

With this knowledge, we should re-address the concept of Thumb-2 for clarity. From ARMv6 there are two instruction sets: ARM (A32) and Thumb-2 (T32). They are both '32-bit' in the sense that they operate on up-to-32-bit-wide data in 32-bit-wide registers with 32-bit addresses. Where they overlap they represent the same instructions - it is only the instruction encoding which differs, and the CPU effectively just has two different front-ends to its pipeline which it can switch between to decode the instruction (we'll cover this in a later chapter).

T32 encompassed not just additional instruction (mostly with 4-byte encoding, although there are a few two-byte encoding) to bring it almost to parity with ARM, but also allows conditional execution of most Thumb instructions. A mixed 16/32-bit instruction stream provides the economy of space of Thumb combined with most of the speed of pure ARM code. A stated aim for T32 was to achieve code density similar to Thumb with performance similar to the ARM instruction set on 32-bit memory.

If performance is critical, then it is important to have at least half the instructions encoded as 16-bit to get maximum performance.

The general rules for generating the 16-bit form of the instructions are:

- Use registers in the range R0-R7
- Set the condition flags unless the instruction is conditional wherever possible
- Use immediate constants in the range 0-7 or 0-255

Thumb Changes

Changes have been made to the original Thumb syntax to bring T32 in line with A32. In original Thumb code where the first operand and destination operand were the same, you need only specify it once. Now they must both be specified so:

```
ADD R0, R1     @ Old Thumb format
ADD R0, R0, R1 @ UAL format
```

In a similar fashion, where the instruction sets the condition flags you must enforce this with the standard 'S' suffix:

```
ADD R0, R1, R2  @ Old Thumb format
ADDS R0, R1, R2 @ UAL format
```

Now, the MOV instruction is used as an addition operation with zero as an immediate value:

```
MOV R0, R1      @ Old Thumb format
ADD R0, R1, #0  @ UAL format
```

And to confuse matters, the CPY instruction becomes a MOV instruction:

```
CPY R0, R1   @ Old Thumb format
MOV R0, R1   @ UAL format
```

Increment after becomes the default addressing mode for the LDM instruction:

```
LDMIA R0!, {R0, R1}  @ Old Thumb format
LDM R0!, {R1, R2}    @ UAL format
```

And write-back is not specified in LDM now if the base register is in the register list:

```
LDMIA R0!, {R0, R1}  @ Old Thumb format
LDM R0, {R0, R1}     @ UAL format
```

New A32 Instructions

Figure 26a lists the new instructions added to the A32 instruction set as part of UAL.

For T32 the BL and BLX instructions are confirmed 32-bit operations. Below are a few examples, and all can be used with an optional condition if required. Use of narrow and wide directives are also permitted.

BFC clears any number of adjacent bits at any position in a register and does so without affecting any of the other bits:

```
BFC R0, #5, #3
```

Clears bits 5,6, and 7 of the value held in R0.

BFI copies any number of low order bits from a register into the same bits of the specified destination register:

```
BFI R0, R1, #5, #3
```

Copy bits 5, 6 and 7 from R1 into bits 5, 6, and 7 of R0.

ARM A32 Assembly Language

MLS multiplies two register values and then subtracts the least significant 32-bits of the result from a third register and writes the result to a destination register:

```
MLS R0, R1, R2, R3
```

Multiply the contents of R1 and R2, subtract the least significant 32-bits from R3 and place into R0.

Mnemonic	Action
BFC	Bit Field Clear
BFI	Bit Field Insert
MLS	Multiply and Subtract
MOV	New wide variant that loads a 16-bit immediate value t bits 0:15 of a register
MOVT	Move Top. Load a 16-bit immediate value to bits 16:31 of a register
RBIT	Reverse bits in a word
SBFX	Signed Bitfield extract
UBFX	Unsigned Bitfield Extract

Figure 26a. New A32 instructions.

Compare by Zero

One of the most common cases is a comparison by zero. The table below (Figure 26b) illustrates the differences between ARM, T32 and T16 for this operation:

State	Mnemonics	Length
ARM	CMP r0,#0 BEQ <label>	8 bytes
T32	CMP r0,#0 BEQ <label>	4 bytes
T16	CBZ r0,<label>	2 bytes

Figure 26b. Compare by Zero – code options.

As we can see, in T16, CBZ has replaced CMP+BEQ from the ARM and Thumb states and condensed it into one instruction which is two bytes long.

Assembling UAL

The ARM processor can only work in either ARM state or Thumb state. It's the case even in pre-UAL supporting processors. You cannot intermix A32 and T32 code. To use A32 and T32 code in the same program, you must do so in blocks and switch between states at the appropriate point. Called 'interworking' the technique was introduced in Chapter 24 – nothing has changed.

However, you should use the directive:

```
.syntax unified
```

At the top of your source along with your other directives to invoke UAL. When you compile the source you should also specify the architecture you are compiling for, for example:

```
march=armv8-a
```

Code written using UAL can be assembled for A32 or T32 for any ARM processor using this technique.

As we have seen some T32 instructions can have either a 16-bit encoding or a 32-bit encoding. If you do not specify the instruction size, by default:

- For forward reference LDR, ADR, and B instructions, the compiler should generate a 16-bit instruction, even if that results in failure for a target that could be reached using a 32-bit instruction.

- For external reference LDR and B instructions, the compiler should generate a 32-bit instruction.

- In all other cases, the compiler should generate the smallest size encoding that can be output.

If you want to override these defaults, then you should use the .W or .N to specify instruction width (wide or narrow) to ensure a particular instruction size.

The .W post-fix is ignored when assembling A32 code, so you can safely use this specifier in programs that might assemble as A32 or T32 code.

Because instruction may be a mix of 16-bit and 32-bit wide, it is important to monitor address alignment. From ARMv7 architecture on, the A bit in the System Control Register (SCTLR) controls whether alignment checking is enabled or disabled. The exception is in ARMv7-M, the UNALIGN_TRP bit, bit 3, in the Configuration and Control Register (CCR) controls this. (See Chapter 28 regarding these registers.)

If set alignment checking is enabled, all unaligned word and halfword transfers cause an alignment exception. If disabled, unaligned accesses are permitted for the LDR, LDRH, STR, STRH, LDRSH, LDRT, STRT, LDRSHT, LDRHT, STRHT, and TBH instructions. Other data-accessing instructions always cause an alignment exception for unaligned data. For STRD and LDRD, the specified address must be word-aligned.

27: Connectivity

Single Board Computers and development boards offer the ability to connect the outside 'real' world for control. The range of projects or 'makes' is extensive and there is a well established hobbyist industry able to supply a wide range of electronics allowing the control of just about anything that has an electrical signal applied to it.

Most single boards computers and development boards are fitted with some form of standard interface that allows input and output. One of the most popular is GPIO, which is what I will discuss here. Other interfaces can be treated in largely the same way, although you will need to decode and substitute the correct information. The same concepts will apply.

Figure 27a. A wide variety of controllers and devices can be connected to your board and controlled via assembly language.

Many interface boards come with their own software which is often written in a high level language such as C or Python. As a start I would recommend you connect everything together and run these programs first to ensure that everything is in working order and the connections are correct!

You will need to locate the GPIO datasheet for your interface. Chances are this is available via the board's website or through one of the many on-line forums that exist. These datasheets can be a little daunting if you have not looked at one before, but if you look at it in conjunction with the examples worked below, you will be able to follow it clearly enough, and that will enable you to investigate the numerous other GPIO functions for yourself. You will also need to obtain a schematic or similar of your board so you can identify the pin numbers on the GPIO.

The GPIO Controller

The GPIO has its own controller chip and this contains no less than 41 registers. The first five of these registers deal with reading and writing to the GPIO pins. These pins are numbered GPIO 0 through to GPIO 53 although only a handful or so of these are available to us to connect to on the GPIO expansion port itself – these is the pins on your board. The first five of these registers, their names and the pins they are associated with are listed in Figure 27b.

No	Name	Off	Pins
0	GPIO Function Select 0 (GPSEL0)	#0	0-9
1	GPIO Function Select 1 (GPSEL1)	#4	10-19
2	GPIO Function Select 2 (GPSEL2)	#8	20-29
3	GPIO Function Select 3 (GPSEL3)	#12	30-39
4	GPIO Function Select 4 (GPSEL4)	#16	40-49
5	GPIO Function Select 5 (GPSEL5)	#20	50-53

Figure 27b. GPIO registers and pin control.

It should be noted also that the GPIO Controller pin numbers do not rnormally run concurrently on the GPIO main GPIO header connector and may differ again on any expansion board you have attached. Please ensure you familiarise yourself with the system you are using as the pin numbers here relate specifically to the numbers assigned by chip designer.

Each of these registers is 32-bits (one word) wide and each pin has three bits assigned to it within each register. In GPSEL0 GPIO Pin 0 has bits 0,

1 and 2 assigned to it. GPIO 1 has bits 3, 4 and 5 and so on. In GPSEL1, then the first three bits (0, 1 and 2) are assigned to GPIO 10. In GPSEL2, then the first three bits (0, 1 and 2) are assigned to GPIO 20. Figure 27c illustrates the arrangement for GPSEL2.

(You may have noticed above that not all the bits in Register 5 are used. This is correct. Only the first 12 bits are used and the others are classed as 'reserved'. Likewise bits 30 and 31 in each of the other registers are unused)

Pin 29	Pin 28	Pin 27	Pin 26	Pin 25	Pin 24	Pin 23	Pin 22	Pin 21	Pin 20
31 30	29 28 27	26 25 24	23 22 21	20 19 18	17 16 15	14 13 12	11 10	9 8 7	6 5 4 3 2 1 0

Figure 27c. Bit association with GPSEL2.

It is important to understand how these bits are assigned as we will need to address them individually at various times to make things happen in their associated registers.

To assign a pin as an input we must store a 0 in the three associated bits (000). To make the same pin an output we must write a 1 in those same three bits (001). For example, to make GPIO 21 an output we must place 001 in bits 3, 4 and 5. To achieve this we could write the binary value:

    001000

(decimal 8) to GPSEL2. Of course we must preserve and not overwrite any other bits that may be set or clear so we would do this using a bitwise operator as we shall see in due course. (Other bit combinations assign other functions to the pins, so it is important to get this right.)

The base address for the GPIO controller in your operating system depends on the system you are using. You will need to locate this – a good option, if you can not obtain it from your board's website, is to examine any programs available for the board to demonstrate the capabilities of the GPIO. It is likely it will have this base address within the program file at some point.

For purpose of illustration we will assume that the GPIO base address is:

    0x3F200000

This is the address where the first register is located — GPSEL0. If we want to get to the second register, GPFEL1, then we need to add four to the controller's base address. Figure 27d also contains a column called 'off'. This is the number of bytes offset from the GPIO Controller start address where that particular register starts. GPSEL2 has an offset of 8, so its address would be:

```
0x3F200000+8
```

So far we have looked at configuring a pin as an input or an output. To turn the pin on (set) or off (clear) we have to write some values into another register. (In this case I am talking about turning a LED on or turning an LED off.)

There are four registers associated with setting and clearing pins and these are detailed in Figure 27d.

No	Name	Off	Pins
7	GPIO Pin Set 0(GPSET0)	#28	0-31
8	GPIO Pin Set 1(GPSET1)	#32	32-53
10	GPIO Output Clear 0(GPCLR0)	#40	0-31
11	GPIO Output Clear 1(GPCLR1)	#44	32-53

Figure 27d. GPIO registers for setting and clearing.

There is a single bit associated with each pin for the purpose of setting and clearing. For example, to set GPIO 22 we would write a '1' into bit 22 of GPSET0. To clear the same bit, we would need to write a '1' into bit 22 of GPCLR0.

If you were to write a 1 to bit 22 in GPSET0 but GPIO 22 was defined as an input nothing would happen. If you then set GPIO 22 to an output, an attached LED would light. The last value written to either GPSET0 or GPCLR0 in this case is remembered and actioned when the status of the pin is changed.

As we can see from Figure 27d the offset for GPSET0 is 28 and for GPCLR0 is 40 and this value added to the base address to the GPIO controller is where we need to write to.

Building the Code

That's quite a lot to take in, so let's work through an example. Here we'll assume that we are dealing with GPIO 22. We have an LED attached to it which we want to turn on. Before we can do that we have to initialise the

ARM A32 Assembly Language

pin by first setting it as an input, then as an output. Finally we can turn the LED on by setting the bit associated with the pin. The toggling of the input/output status of the pin enables it to record what the last action was (by order) when we set or clear its status.

The code segment that follows is pseudo-code just for illustrative purposes — if you try and use it 'as is' it will not work, for reasons which I'll explain shortly!

```
.input
LDR R3, .gpiobase       @ get GPIO Base address
MOV R5, R3              @ save copy for later use
ADD R3, R3, #8          @ pin 22 in register 2 so add 8 offset
MOV R2, R3              @ move address into R2
LDR R2, [R2, #0]        @ get value in Register 2
BIC R2, R2, #0b111<<6   @ clear 3 bits assoc with pin 22
STR R2, [R3, #0]        @ and write value back to GPIO Base

.output:
MOV R2, R3              @ write GPIO addr to R2
LDR R2, [R2, #0]        @ get value at R2
ORR R2, R2, #1<<6       @ set lsb as output for pin 22
STR R2, [R3, #0]        @ and write to Register 2

.set
MOV R3, R5              @ get base addr
ADD R3, R3, #28         @ set GPSET0 address for set
MOV R4, #1              @ set bit
MOV R2, R4, LSL #22     @ rotate to pin 22 and place in R2
STR R2, [R3, #0]        @ write to memory to set
```

The comments should help you follow this through. The key thing to remember here is that, for GPIO 22, we are dealing with Register 2 which has an offset of 8. This means that 8 must be added to the GPIO base address at 0x3F200000. In Register 2 bits 3, 4 and 5 are associated with pin 22. Thus we must shift left any value we want to write into those bits by six places. Take a look at the BIC instruction below which is taken from the input part of the segment:

```
BIC R2, R2, #0b111<<6
```

267

R2 contains the address of Register 2. If we shift the binary value 111 left by six places we get 111000000. The result is that these three bits are cleared when we store this value back in the register. Remember BIC performs a logical bit clear or AND NOT on the value in R2. By effectively placing 000 in the three bits we have assigned the pin as an input. (We have used a slightly different way to perform the LSL here using '<<' which is one of many shortcuts that GCC provides.)

The .output: routine now programs the same pin as an output by writing a 1 into bits 3, 4 and 5 of Register 2. It does this with:

```
ORR R2, R2, #1<<6
```

We have now initialised the pin by getting it ready to act as an output.

Now we just have to place a 1 in the bit associated with the pin in the GPSET0 register. GPIO 22 is pin 22 so we have to place a 1 in bit 22 of GPSET0. GPSET0 is offset 28 bytes from the start of the GPIO Controller, so the 28 is added to the base controller address and then the left shifted bit stored there.

As I said, this program won't work, but assuming the LED attached was now illuminated, to turn it off we would use:

```
MOV R3, R5              @ get base addr
ADD R3, R3, #40         @ get GPCLR0 address for set
MOV R4, #1              @ set bit
MOV R2, R4, LSL #22     @ rotate to pin 22 and place in R2
STR R2, [R3, #0]        @ write to memory to set
```

So why won't the program work? Because most operating systems will not allow us to write directly to the GPIO Controller (or other I/O space for that matter)! It is a self-protect mechanism that is built into it to try and ensure we don't do anything that might otherwise cause it to crash. So we have to get around that.

Virtual Memory

The way we get around this problem is to use a technique that allows us to create an area of memory that mirrors the protected space we want to access. We can then access this *virtual memory* space to read and write information using libc calls. In fact what we do is treat the process as a file operation for which there are three parts:

- Open the file
- Create the virtual file map
- Read and write what we want to do and close the file for it to take effect.

a three part process which is straightforward enough, and much of what we discussed in the pseudo-program above is part of the final step.

Program 27a shows how this all comes together for the example we have worked above — GPIO 22. You can run and compile this one!

Program 27a. Setting GPIO 22 to turn on an attached LED.

```
/* GPIO PIN access via memory mapping file to Controller */
/* This example sets GPIO 22                             */
/* change gpiobase number to suit your board             */

        .global main
  main:
        SUB    sp, sp, #16          @ Create 16 bytes storage
        LDR    R0, .addr_file       @ get GPIO Controller addr
        LDR    R1, .flags           @ set flag permissions
        BL     open                 @ call to get file handle

        STR    R0, [SP, #12]        @ File handle number
        LDR    R3, [SP, #12]        @ Get File handle
        STR    R3, [sp, #0]         @ Store file handle on top stack
        LDR    R3, .gpiobase        @ get GPIO_Base address
        STR    R3, [sp, #4]         @ store on SP+4
        MOV    R0, #0               @ R0=0
        MOV    R1, #4096            @ R1=page
        MOV    R2, #3               @ R2=3
        MOV    R3, #1               @ R3=1 (stdouts)
        BL     mmap

        STR    R0, [SP, #16]        @ store virtual mem addr
        LDR    R3, [SP, #16]        @ get virtual mem addr
        ADD    R3, R3, #8           @ add 8 for block 2
        LDR    R2, [SP, #16]        @ get virtual mem addr
```

```
        ADD    R2, R2, #8            @ add 8 for block 2
        LDR    R2, [R2, #0]          @ load R2 with value at R2
        BIC    R2, R2, #0b111<<6     @ Bitwise clear of three bits
        STR    R2, [R3, #0]          @ Store result [set input]
        LDR    R3, [SP, #16]         @ Get virtual mem address
        ADD    R3, R3, #8            @ Add 8 for block 2
        LDR    R2, [SP, #16]         @ Get virtual mem addr
        ADD    R2, R2, #8            @ add 8 for block 2
        LDR    R2, [R2, #0]          @ Load R2 with value at R2
        ORR    R2, R2, #1<<6         @ Set bit....
        STR    R2, [R3, #0]          @ ...and make output
        LDR    R3, [SP, #16]         @ get virt mem addr
        ADD    R3, R3, #28           @ add 28 offset to GPIO_Base
        MOV    R4, #1                @ get 1
        MOV    R2, R4, LSL#22        @ Shift by pin number
        STR    R2, [R3, #0]          @ write to memory
        LDR    R0, [SP, #12]         @ get file handle
        BL     close                 @ close file

        ADD    SP, SP, #16           @ restore SP
        MOV    R7, #1
        SWI    0

.addr_file:  .word    .file
.flags:      .word    1576962
.gpiobase:   .word    0x3F200000 @ GPIO_Base address

.data
.file:       .ascii  "/dev/mem\000"
```

Remember to edit the program to reflect the GPIO base address you require.

Both the open and close calls in Program 27a can be performed using the appropriate Syscalls if you desire. Just load the Syscall number into R7 (5 for open and 6 for close) and call SWI 0. The mmap call is more problematic and in theory a call to Syscall 192 should work; but it doesn't, so in the interim we will have to make do with the libc call.

The virtual map file we are opening is called:

```
/dev/mem
```

The address of this string is placed in R0 and what we require from it in terms of read/write access etc. is seeded into R1. The flags setting work as provided and can be reliably used as we have not discussed file operations in any detail here. (If you wish to investigate further we are allowing O_RDWR, O_SYNC and O_CLOEXEC operations on the file — without which we wouldn't be able to use it sensibly anyway!)

The call to 'open' creates the file and returns a file handle or file descriptor (a unique number identifying the file) in R0. We need this number whenever we wish to access the file, so it is placed on the stack for safe keeping.

The call to libc mmap required the address we are looking to virtualise and the handle for the open file placed on the top of the stack. The output and file size in bytes are set before mmap is called (these are known constants, ie. page size and block size).

The close routine implements what we did earlier to define the GPIO pin for input/output before setting it. The stack is used to hold and pass data around to ensure no corruption of the information when calling libc functions. The close routine is also a little more long winded than the original pseudo-program version. That is because I have deliberately avoided using 'scratch' registers for saving information as these might get corrupted by libc.

Using and Adapting

I tend to compile these files into machine code using a name indicative of the pin. For example, for Program 27a I would compile and save the executable using the name, 'on22'. I would also create a complementary file to clear the pin using the filename 'off22'. Creating a pair for each file gives you the immediate ability to set and clear individual pins as you wish. The downside is that you must run the files as a Root User otherwise they will fail with an error. A Root User is what you might call an administrator — it means you have total access privileges on your system. You can set yourself up to be a Root User on your system if you wish to make this always the case. Alternatively, you will need to run the programs using the sudo command, thus:

```
sudo ./on22
```

If you want to debug these files using GDB then you must also run GDB as a root user, and you can do this using sudo again. Ensuring you have compiled your source file using the –g option with GDB :

```
sudo gdb on22
```

and you should be able to step through the operation of the code that we have created to further develop your understanding of what is going on.

You only require minimal changes to adapt the program to work on other pins, and you should have more than enough information to do this. As an extra example, Program 27b has been adapted to set GPIO 17 and the comments in the assembler identify exactly what has changed. You will notice that the only changes are in the close routine. Referring back to Figure 27a we can see that GPIO 17 is in GPIO Function Select 1 (GPSEL1) and the offset here is 4. This is the first change we must make.

Bits 21, 22 and 23 within GPSEL1 are linked to GPIO 17 so the logical shift left value associated with writing bx111 and bx001 is 21. Finally GPIO 17 is associated with bit 17 in GPSET0 so this is the final shift value we need to change in the assembler. Thus to adapt this program to assemble as a set routine for any GPIO pin you need to make a maximum of seven changes to values. To turn the file into a clear routine for GPIO 17 just change the 28 to 40 in the line towards the end as indicated.

Program 27b. Adapting for GPIO 17.

```
/* GPIO PIN access via memory mapping file to Controller */
/* This example sets GPIO 17 after first initialising   */

        .global main
main:
        SUB     sp, sp, #16
        LDR     R0, .addr_file
        LDR     R1, .flags
        BL      open

        STR     R0, [SP, #12]
        LDR     R3, [SP, #12]
        STR     R3, [SP, #0]
        LDR     R3, .gpiobase
        STR     R3, [SP, #4]
        MOV     R0, #0
        MOV     R1, #4096
        MOV     R2, #3
        MOV     R3, #1
        BL      mmap
```

```
        STR   R0, [SP, #16]
        LDR   R3, [SP, #16]
        ADD   R3, R3, #4         @ add 4 for block 1
        LDR   R2, [SP, #16]
        ADD   R2, R2, #4         @ add 4 for block 1
        LDR   R2, [R2, #0]
        BIC   R2, R2, #0b111<<21 @ Bitwise clear of three bits
        STR   R2, [R3, #0]
        LDR   R3, [SP, #16]
        ADD   R3, R3, #4         @ Add 4 for block 1
        LDR   R2, [SP, #16]
        ADD   R2, R2, #4         @ add 4 for block 1
        LDR   R2, [R2, #0]
        ORR   R2, R2, #1<<21     @ Set bit....
        STR   R2, [R3, #0]
        LDR   R3, [SP, #16]
        ADD   R3, R3, #28        @ add 28 - use 40 to clear
        MOV   R4, #1
        MOV   R2, R4, LSL#17     @ Shift by pin no for bit location
        STR   R2, [R3, #0]
        LDR   R0, [SP, #12]
        BL    close

        ADD   SP, SP, #16

        MOV R7, #1
        SWI 0

.addr_file:   .word    .file
.flags:       .word    1576962
.gpiobase:    .word    0x3F200000 @ GPIO_Base for board
.data
.file:        .ascii "/dev/mem\000"
```

Other GPIO Functions

There are a number of other registers that form part of the GPIO Controller that can be used and programmed using these methods. As already mentioned you will need to get a copy of the relevant peripherals datasheet to get the specific detail that you need relating to the other registers, their functions and what you need to do to use them. It is all there.

One final thing in relation to the datasheet: If you look at the memory maps at the start of the document you will see that the ARM peripherals are mapped as starting at an address different from the one you used for .gpiobase for instance.

All operating systems implement their own memory addressing systems which overlay the ones provided by default by the CPU. This allows the OS in question to implement virtual memory mapping — a technique that allows program and applications to use more memory than is actually available to them by swapping data in and out of memory from the SD Card in use or the hard drive attached.

Finally a word of warning. The GPIO pins will probably control a whole host of functions on your board and if you are not careful you can crash your OS causing everything to freeze and necessitating a hard reset. Always save your work before you try to execute any machine code file for the first time.

28: Exception Handing

This chapter provides an overview of exception handling, the various modes of ARM operation, vectors and interrupts. This is a fundamental design aspect of the ARM chip and provides a clever and versatile way to customise the manner in which your chosen operating system works. It should be considered an advanced topic and as such its detail is beyond the scope of this book. However, it is fascinating as is the whole concept of interrupts which are fundamental to everyday operation. As such an overview here is provided which will certainly help you should you delve into areas such as bare metal programming, or look at writing your own OS. And these are all tasks you should consider as a next step in the learning curve.

Most operating system are defensive in the way they are configured, and their core, the kernel memory management, prevents you from accessing something that is not mapped into the process memory map. In other words, it will not let you just read and write to arbitrary memory locations. It is for this reason that the GPIO pins and other hardware components of most boards cannot be accessed from a standard machine code program running under a local OS.

Each operating system has a method that allows you to access its more vulnerable parts and tries to do so in such a way that the end result is not fatal! The first operating system written for ARM was by Acorn, and not surprisingly it was called RISC OS. In RISC OS the whole system is deployed in a way to make it easy to configure and reconfigure for the programmer's needs. Indeed a whole wave of SYS calls are provided in RISC OS just for this purpose. I say this just to indicate that it is an OS worth trying if you wish to play with interrupts and events in a controlled manner. (RISC OS is free as a downloadable OS and you can find out more by going to www.brucesmith.info.)

Direct memory access can only be performed by operating as a root user or by writing a standalone OS — bare metal programming in effect.

Modes of Operation

In Chapter 5, we examined the Current Program Status Register and saw how the individual bits within it were used as flags to denote certain conditions. The figure presented then is shown again as Figure 28a.

31	30	29	28	27...8	7	6	5	4	3	2	1	0
N	Z	C	V		I	F	T	MODE				

Figure 28a. The Status Register configuration.

The N, Z, C and V flags should be very familiar by now. The ones we are concerned with now are held in the low byte of the register in bits 0 to 7.

The Mode bits are located from 0 to 4 (five in total), and their setting determines which of the six operating modes the ARM operates in. Figure 28b summarises these modes. Any of them can be entered by changing the CPSR. Except for User Mode and Supervisor Mode all modes can be entered when an exception occurs.

Mode	Description
FIQ	Entered when a high priority (fast) interrupt is raised
IRQ	Entered when a low priority (normal) interrupt is raised
Supervisor and Reset	Entered on reset and when a Software Interrupt instruction is executed
Abort	Used to handle memory access violations
Undef	Used to handle undefined instructions
User	Unprivileged mode under which most tasks run

Figure 28b. The ARM's six modes of operation.

User Mode is the one used by default by programs and applications. This is the environment we work in, and in truth, we as programmers never have to leave it, unless we are looking to be more adventurous and take over total control of the ARM chip itself. This is not for the novice and care needs to be taken when that line is stepped over.

Referring back again to Figure 28a, bits 7 and 6 are used for enabling and disabling IRQ and FIQ interrupts respectively. If a bit is set the associated interrupt is disabled. If the bit is clear then the interrupt is enabled. Bit 5 is the Thumb mode bit and is discussed in Chapter 25. For all interrupts this bit is clear and the processor is operating in ARM State.

Vectors

Vectors play an important role in the operation of the ARM chip. A vector is a known location in memory that is exactly one word, or 32-bits wide. (Not to be confused with vectors in VFP.)

There are two types of vectors: hardware vectors and software vectors. Hardware vectors are hardwired to the ARM chip itself and they never change, and as Figure 28c shows, they are located at the very beginning of the memory map. However, the vector table can be located at a higher address in memory, here starting at 0xFFFF0000.

Hardware vectors control the ultimate flow of information and are a set of memory addresses that are 'known' to the ARM chip. The term 'known' here means that they are physically 'hard-wired' and are thus termed hardware vectors. Hardware vectors typically control the flow of abnormal events which the chip itself cannot deal with. They are often referred to as exception vectors and they reside smack bang at the start of the memory map from 0x00000000 to 0x0000001C. Figure 28c lists the hardware vectors.

```
Address          Hi Address       Vector
0x00000000       0xFFFF0000       ARM reset
0x00000004       0xFFFF0004       Undefined Instruction
0x00000008       0xFFFF0008       Software Interrupt (SWI)
0x0000000C       0xFFFF000C       Abort (pre-fetch)
0x00000010       0xFFFF0010       Abort (data)
0x00000014       0xFFFF0014       Address exception
0x00000018       0xFFFF0018       IRQ
0x0000001C       0xFFFF001C       FIRQ (or FIQ)
```

Figure 28c. The ARM Hardware vectors.

One common reason for manipulating the hardware vectors is to change the machine's response to memory access faults. If some non-existent memory is accessed then one of the memory fault vectors, 0x0000000C to

0x00000014, is called. The normal effect of this is for the Operating System to report a fatal error and stop executing the current task. Sometimes, for example when writing a memory editor, this is not a very desirable thing to happen. It would be better simply to warn the user that a particular location is invalid and allow editing to continue for the rest of memory.

Vectors are useful to the programmer as they allow programs to access standard routines without directly calling the physical address where the machine code for the routine is stored.

In the early days of computers operating systems were small and everything was 'hard-coded', meaning addresses where used in absolute terms. The problem with using absolute addresses and by this I mean a real physical address rather than a branch offset for example, is that you are always tied to that address. If the OS is updated then, a pound to a pinch of salt, that address will change. Now any external or third-party code that uses that absolute address might be snookered. If the code is updated and its execution point is changed, all that needs to happen is for the address in the vector to be changed.

Instruction	Description
B <address>	Jump to an address given as a relative offset to the PC.
LDR PC, [PC, #offset]	Load address from memory to the PC. This address is a 32-bit value stored close to the vector table. This is slightly slower than the previous method due to extra memory access. The bonus is that you can branch to any address in the memory map.
LDR PC, [PC, #-0xFF0]	Load address of a specific interrupt service routine from 0xFFFFF030 to the PC.
MOV PC, #value	Copies an immediate value into the PC. This will normally be a single byte value that is rotated right by an even number of bits. Thus provides access to the full memory map but with gaps.

Figure 28d. Instructions that may be used in a vector.

The second advantage to using vectors is that we, as the programmer, can also change the address in the vector — we can intercept it. By intercepting vectors we can modify and even change the way the computer operates. This is not easy but if you plan to write bare metal code then you will be required to take control of the vector table yourself and manage its requirements.

When an exception interrupt occurs the processor stops what it is doing and jumps to the appropriate location in the vector table. Each location contains an instruction pointing to the start of a specific handling routine. These instructions normally take one of three forms as shown in Figure 28d.

For example, when an IRQ interrupt occurs it ultimately goes via the IRQ vector. This location is 32-bits wide (a word), and is just big enough to contain an instruction that facilitates an instruction to branch to another memory location.

Register Arrangements

Each of the modes has an associated set of registers available to it. The registers available to the programmer vary according to the current CPU operating mode. The arrangement pictured below is illustrative only as a concept.

Other architectures implement processor modes differently and may have additional modes to those illustrated here. Please refer to the reference manual for the architecture you are interested in.

When executing in User Mode the full set of registers, R0 to R15, are available for use. However, when the CPU switches into another operation mode, this all changes. Figure 28e shows the register arrangement depending on the mode of operation. All modes have dedicated stack pointers and link registers associated with them. Whilst all modes except for User Mode have a new register, the Saved Program Status Register, available to them, only FIQ mode has several dedicated registers from R8-R12. Otherwise registers remain unchanged.

The SPSR is used to hold a copy of the User Mode Status Register when one of the other modes is entered. The User Mode does not have and it does not need an SPSR. An important point to note here is that the CPSR is only copied into the SPSR when an exception or interrupt is raised; it is not changed if you physically write to the CPSR to change mode.

User	FIQ	IRQ	SVC	UND	ABT
R0					
R1					
R2					
R3					
R4					
R5					
R6					
R7					
R8	R8_fiq				
R9	R9_fiq				
R10	R10_fiq				
R11	R11_fiq				
R12	R12_fiq				
R13 SP	R13_fiq	R13_irq	R13_svc	R13_und	R13_abt
R14 LR	R14_fiq	R14_irq	R14_svc	R14_und	R14_abt
R15 PC					

CPSR					
	SPSR_fiq	SPSR_irq	SPSR_svc	SPSR_und	SPSR-abt

Figure 28e. The ARM programmer's model.

The idea behind this banked register system is that each processor mode has some private registers which it can make use of without affecting the values of the normal registers, thus ensuring that the programmer does not have to worry about saving the contents of their own User Mode registers when an alternative mode is entered.

Figure 28f shows how the low byte of the CSPR looks when one of the modes is invoked. With the exception of User Mode, all modes are privileged. When power is first applied to the ARM chip it starts off in Supervisor Mode.

	I	F	T	MODE				
	7	6	5	4	3	2	1	0
Abort	1	1	0	1	0	1	1	1
FIQ	1	1	0	1	0	0	0	1
IRQ	1	uc	0	1	0	0	1	0
Supervisor	1	uc	0	1	0	0	1	1
System	1	1	0	1	1	1	1	1
Undefined	1	uc	0	1	1	0	1	1
User	0	0	0	1	0	0	0	0

Figure 28f. Bit settings for Mode changes in CPSR.

Interrupts can be enabled and disabled very easily in ARM — using masking. Bits 7 and 6 enable or disable IRQ and FIQ interrupts respectively. If either bit is set then the associated interrupt is disabled and will not be processed. When an exception or interrupt occurs, the interrupt mask bit will normally be set by the chip. For a number of modes the FIQ bit remains unchanged (uc).

Exception Handling

An exception is a condition that requires the halting, temporary or otherwise, of whatever code is executing. A segment of code called an exception handler is called at this point. It identifies the condition and passes control to the appropriate route to handle the exception. When an exception causes a mode change the following sequence of events needs to happen:

- The address of next instruction is copied into the appropriate LR
- The CPSR is copied into the SPSR of the new mode
- The appropriate mode is set by modifying bits in the CPSR
- The next instruction is fetched from the vector table.

When the exception has been dealt with, control can be returned to the code that was executing when the exception occurred. This is done as follows:

- The LR (minus an offset) is moved into the PC

- The SPSR is copied back into CPSR and by default this automatically changes the mode back to the previous one
- If set, the interrupt disable flags are cleared. Clear the interrupt disable flags to re-enable interrupts.

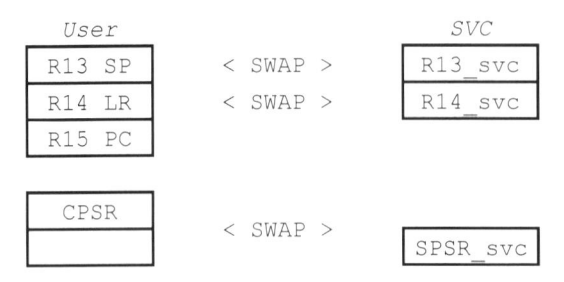

```
         User                              SVC
      R13 SP        < SWAP >            R13_svc
      R14 LR        < SWAP >            R14_svc
      R15 PC

      CPSR          < SWAP >
                                        SPSR_svc
```

Figure 28g. Swapping registers on at a privileged exception.

The illustration above in Figure 28g illustrates what happens at a register level when a SWI call is made. The concept is the same for any of the privileged mode exceptions. The SP and LR of the accessing Mode are switched in over the User Mode ones to allow the exception to be serviced, whilst preserving the status of the interrupted program. The return address is copied from the User Mode PC and stored in the LR of the privileged mode being invoked. R14_svc in the example above.

By preserving the status of the three User Mode registers shown, the status quo of program execution can be maintained when the SVC Mode call has been serviced simply by swapping them back. As stated earlier the CPSR is only saved into the requesting mode's SPSR when an exception occurs. It does not happen when the mode is changed by flipping the Mode bits.

MRS and MSR

There are two instructions which can be used directly to control the contents of the CPSR and SPSR and they can be used on the whole contents or at bit level.

The MRS instruction transfers the contents of either the CPSR or SPSR into a register. The MSR instruction works the opposite way and transfer the contents of a register into either the CSPR or SPSR. The instruction syntax is as follows:

```
MRS (<suffix>) <Operand1>, <CSPR|SPSR>
MSR (<suffix>) <CSPR|SPSR|Flags>, <Operand1>
MSR (<suffix>) <CSPR|SPSR|Flags>, #immediate
```

ARM A32 Assembly Language

Some examples will make their operation clearer. The following three lines of code could be used to enable IRQ Mode:

```
MRS R1, CPSR
BIC R1, R1, #0x80
MSR CPSR_C, R1
```

First the CPSR is copied into R1 where it is then masked with 10000000 to clear the bit at b7 — the position of the I flag. (see Figure 26a). R1 is then written back to CPSR. Note the use of the _C as an addition to the CPSR operand. For the purpose of programming, the CPSR and SPSR are divided into four different sectors. These are illustrated below in Figure 28h.

Flags (F) [24:31]	Status (S) [16:25]	Extension (X) [8:15]	Control (C) [0:7]
N Z C V Q			I F T Mode

Figure 28h. The CPSR/SPSR segments to control updating.

By using the correct adjunct(s) on the appropriate instruction we can ensure that only the correct bits of the associated register are updated. The F, S, X and C suffixes may be used in like fashion.

To disable the IRQ, the following segment of code would suffice:

```
MRS R1, CPSR
ORR R1, R1, #x080
MSR CPSR_C, R1
```

The same commands can be used to effect a mode change thus:

```
MRS R0,CPSR          @  copy the CPSR
BIC R0,R0,#0x1F      @  clear mode bits
ORR R0,R0,#new_mode  @  select new mode
MSR CPSR,R0          @  write CPSR back
```

In User Mode you can read all the bits of the CPSR but you can only update the condition of the field flag, ie, CPSR_F.

In Chapter 12 we briefly introduced the concept of saturation and the Q flag. The MRS RN,CPSR instruction can be used to to read the CPSR, then test the value of the Q flag. If it is 0, the saturation or overflow did not occur when an operation took place. Otherwise, at least one instance of saturation or overflow occurred. Use an MSR CPSR_f,#0 instruction to clear the Q flag (this also clears the condition code flags).

Interrupts When?

Interrupt Request Mode (IRQ) and Fast Interrupt Mode (FIQ) are called when an external device pages the ARM chip and demands its attention. For example, the keyboard generates an interrupt whenever a key is pressed. This is a signal to the CPU that the keyboard interface (matrix) should be read, and the ASCII value of the key entered into the keyboard buffer. If the ASCII value is 0x0D (RETURN), the keyboard buffer must be interpreted.

The analogy here can be you, sitting at your own keyboard learning Assembly Language. At some point your phone starts to ring. You have been interrupted. So, you stop what you are doing (you may make a quick note to remind you or you may save your work) and answer the phone (you deal with or process the interruption). When you have completed the phone call, you hang up and return to what you were doing before the interruption.

The process with the ARM chip is much the same. It receives an interrupt signal at which point it saves what it is doing in line with what we have already discussed and then hands control to the calling interrupt routine by invoking the appropriate mode of operation. When the interrupt has finished its work (in the keyboard example this would be reading the key press and placing the ASCII code in the keyboard buffer) it hands control back to the ARM which restores all its previously saved information and returns to User Mode, picking up where it left off.

So here the interrupt is a function of the ARM chip itself, but how it is dealt with and what happens thereafter is a feature of the software handling it.

Without an effective interrupt system, the ARM at software level would have to spend a lot of its time checking all attached components just to see if anything has happened, taking up time and resources. Think of all the connections to your computer — keyboard, mouse, USB ports, disk drives... They all require servicing, and often.

Fast Interrupts (FIQs) are deemed to be ones that have the highest priority and are the ones that must be serviced first. For example, any disk drive connected, otherwise data might be lost. The only time a FIQ is not serviced first is when another FIQ is in the process of being serviced. The Interrupt Request (IRQ) line is deemed to be of lower priority where a slight delay will not create any problems.

The need for speed in processing an FIQ interrupt is signified by its position in the hardware vector table. It is the last in the list. This is because it actually begins executing right at that point — the other vectors all perform other branch instructions further into the system software. The FIQ code resides in the space after the vector at 0x1C. It is then the job of the appropriate interrupt coding to identify which device caused the interrupt and process it accordingly and as quickly as possible.

Your Interrupt Decisions

When dealing with interrupts you need to make the decision about other interrupts. For example what happens if a new interrupt occurs whilst you are handling an existing interrupt? The easiest method is to invoke what is called a non-nested interrupt handling scheme. In this all interrupts are disabled until control is handled back to the interrupted task. The downside of this is that only one interrupt can be serviced at a time, and if a succession of interrupts are occurring you may lose some of the requests. This could have consequences.

A nested interrupt scheme allows more than one interrupt to be handled at a time and in this case you would look to re-enable interrupts before fully servicing the current interrupt. This is more complex but it solves the problems that can occur with interrupt latency, which is the interval of time from an external interrupt signal being raised to the first fetch of an instruction of the raised interrupt signal.

For an FIQ, the IRQs are disabled as the FIQ is deemed critical in relation.

In all cases the implementation of a stack for interrupt handling (interrupt stack) should be considered essential for context switching between the modes and preserving information. If several interrupts occur at the same time the details need to be stored somewhere for processing as the sequence is dealt with.

Returning From Interrupts

When the interrupt service routine has been performed, the operating system must return to the original program which was interrupted by the FIQ or IRQ. This is done by using the following instruction:

```
SUBS R15, R14, #4
```

This restores the program counter so that the interrupted program can be resumed from exactly the point at which it was suspended. The 'subtract 4' calculation is required to correct for the effects of pipelining. Providing that the interrupt handling routine has not corrupted any shared registers or workspace, the program will continue executing as if the interrupt had never happened. On most computers interrupts are occurring and being serviced all the time without the user even realising it.

The System Control Register

The System Control Register – SCTLR – is a 32-bit register that controls standard memory and system facilities. It provides monitoring and configuration of:

- memory alignment and endianness
- memory protection and fault behaviour
- MMU and cache enables
- interrupts and behaviour of interrupt latency
- location for exception vectors
- program flow prediction.

The SCTLR is only accessible in privileged modes. The format of the SCTRL differs in architectures, so it is advisable to review your processor documentation to retrieve the correct map. Other architectures may also use different registers to convey information – again please refer to your processor reference manual to ascertain the right source.

Writing Interrupt Routines

Usually, you will not need to create interrupt service routines of your own because the OS provides a well-defined system for doing so.

If you intend to write direct interrupt handling routines, you should observe the following rule to avoid potential disasters:

- Do not re-enable interrupts in the handling routine. If this is done, a second IRQ/FIQ could interrupt the processor before it has finished handling the first. Sometimes this may be permissible, but you could be walking on thin ice if you do it. Be very aware!
- The interrupt routine must be written as economically as possible. Processing the interrupt at maximum speed should be a major goal. If it keeps interrupts disabled for too long, then the normal background activities will grind to a halt. The keyboard will lock, various software clocks will lose time, and the mouse pointer will freeze.

- All shared processor registers should be preserved. They should contain the same values on exit from the interrupt routine as they did on entry to the interrupt. This is absolutely vital if the interrupted task is to be resumed correctly.
- The interrupt handling routine should avoid calling OS routines. It is possible that one of these routines would be only half executed when it is interrupted by IRQ/FIQ. If re-entered in the interrupt routine, workspace could be disturbed, causing the routine to corrupt when resumed.

29: Opcodes and Pipelines

We have been dealing with assembly language throughout this book; we can easily forget that this is not what the ARM chip operates on. The assembler generates opcodes. These opcodes are hexadecimal numbers, which can be decoded by the hardware inside the chip, and the action represented by them performed. These numbers have been cleverly thought out, and the bit patterns hidden in the numbers convey very specific information.

The Unified Assembly Language defines two separate instruction sets:

- A32 ARM instruction set – 32-bit wide
- T32 Thumb instruction set – 32 and 16-bits wide.

The features of the instruction set are:

- 3-address data processing instructions
- Condition execution of each instruction
- Shift and ALU operations in single instruction
- Load-Store and Load-Store multiple instructions
- Single cycle execution of all instructions
- Instruction extension through co-processor and core hardware.

From the above list, we can see that there are five basic types of instruction:

Data Operations
These instructions have, and they have very similar formats. Examples are ADD and CMP, which add and compare two numbers respectively. The operands of these instructions are always in registers (or an immediate number), and never in memory. This group of instructions will do most of the work in your programs.

Load and Save
Load and save registers may be byte or word specific. The memory location used is determined by the addressing mode.

Multiple Load and Save
Allows word transfers between processor and memory and vice versa.

Branching
The branch instruction provides a convenient way of reaching any part of the address space in a single instruction. The PC address has a displacement added to it. The instruction holds the displacement value and can be either forward (+) or backwards (-).

SVC
This one instruction group provides the way for user's programs to access routines provided by the operating system. Examples include writing to the screen, reading from the keyboard and accessing I/O memory. By issuing SVC instructions, the user's program may utilise this operating system software.

Floating Point and Neon
A co-processor or core extension adds these instructions to the overall instruction set. They are not part of the base ARM set so when the ARM cannot identify them it passes them to any other attached unit that may want to identify them. In such cases, they are 'caught' by the VFP or Neon unit.

I have provided an example from the ARM and Thumb instruction sets below. This information can be very specific to the architecture you are using, especially with the more recent releases. If this interests you then go to the ARM website and download the processor-specific manual that interests you. These are in PDF format and can run to well over 2000 pages!

A Data Processing Example

These instructions obtain a result by performing an operation on one or two operands. The first operand is always a register, and the second may be a shifted register (Rm) or an immediate value. Figure 29a illustrates the binary encoding of the three basic types of data processing instruction. To recap the syntax for this type of instruction is:

```
<opcode> {<cond>} {S} Rd, Rn, n
```

Where:

<Cond>:   Is the condition field and indicates the flags to test.

S: Set condition flags in CPSR

n: May be 'Rm', '#constant' or 'Rs' <shifts | rotate> N.'

Rd: Is destination register

Rn: Is first operand, Rn/Rm. Rs remains unchanged

Immediate Operand

31 30 29 28	27 26 25	24 23 22 21	20	19 18 17 16
COND	0 0 1	OPCODE	S	Rn

15 14 13 12	11 10 9 8	7 6 5 4 3 2 1 0
Rd	Rotate	Immediate

Immediate Shift Operand

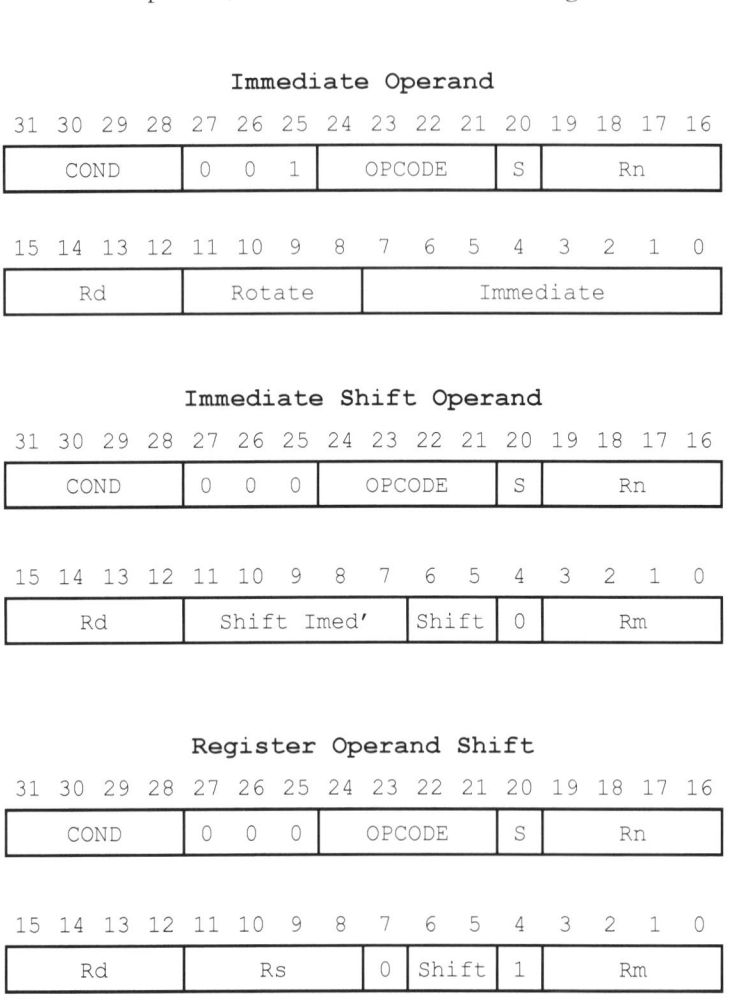

31 30 29 28	27 26 25	24 23 22 21	20	19 18 17 16
COND	0 0 0	OPCODE	S	Rn

15 14 13 12	11 10 9 8 7	6 5	4	3 2 1 0
Rd	Shift Imed'	Shift	0	Rm

Register Operand Shift

31 30 29 28	27 26 25	24 23 22 21	20	19 18 17 16
COND	0 0 0	OPCODE	S	Rn

15 14 13 12	11 10 9 8	7	6 5	4	3 2 1 0
Rd	Rs	0	Shift	1	Rm

Figure 29a. Binary encoding for ARM data processing instructions.

In A32, all instructions can be conditionally executed. The first four bits, 31-28, (<cond>) is a bit pattern representing these conditions as shown in Figure 29b. If the state of the C, N, Z and V flags meets the condition, the instruction is executed. Otherwise it is ignored. Being four bits there are 16 possible conditions, although in practice 15 different codes are used –1111 is 'reserved' and not for use. Chapter 9 has details on these codes and their use.

ARM A32 Assembly Language

Code	Suffix	Flags
0000	EQ	Z set
0001	NE	Z clear
0010	CS	C set
0011	CC	C clear
0100	MI	N set
0101	PL	N clear
0110	VS	V set
0111	VC	V clear
1000	HI	C set and Z clear
1001	LS	C clear or Z set
1010	GE	N equals V
1011	LT	N not equal to V
1100	GT	Z clear AND (N equals V)
1101	LE	Z set OR (N not equal to V)
1110	AL	(Ignore)

Figure 29b. Condition codes.

Bit 25 is either '0' or '1'. If '0' the operand two is a register, if it is a '1' then operand two is an immediate value.

Bits 24-21 are the Opcode and again the bit pattern determines the opcode as listed in Figure 29c.

Bit 20 is the Set condition flag. If this is a '0' then the CSPR flags are not updated. If it is a '1' then the flags are updated.

Bits 19 to 12 hold details of the Rn (data) and Rd (destination) resisters.

Bits 11 to 0 hold information relating to 'operand 2'. If it is an immediate value (bit 25) then the bits specify an 8-bit immediate value and the rotation required - refer to Chapter 11 for the specifics for this. If it is a shift type operation, then the second operation register is defined in bits 0-3 and the shift information in the remaining bits.

All other opcodes are encoded in a similar fashion with the bits determining the type of information contained. Remember that the instruction set varies across ARM architectures so if you are interested in pursuing this further, obtain the data instruction set for the relevant processor, from the ARM website, to investigate further.

Code	Mnemonic	Result
0000	AND	Rd= Op1 AND Op2
0001	EOR	Rd= Op1 EOR Op2
0010	SUB	Rd= Op1-Op2
0011	RSB	Rd= Op2-Op1
0100	ADD	Rd= Op1+Op2
0101	ADC	Rd= Op1+Op2+C
0110	SBC	Rd= Op1-Op2+c-1
0111	RSC	Td= Op2-Op1+C+1
1000	TST	Set cond codes on Op1 AND Op2
1001	TEQ	Set cond codes on Op1 EOR Op2
1010	CMP	Set cond codes on Op1-Op2
1011	CMN	Set cond codes on Op1+Op2
1100	ORR	Rd= Op1 OR Op2
1101	MOV	Rd= Op2
1110	BIC	Rd= Op1 AND NOT Op2
1111	MVN	Rd= NOT Op2

Figure 29c. Data opcodes to act upon.

Thumb Examples

Thumb instructions are encoded in 16-bits or 32-bits. Each Thumb instruction is either a single 16-bit half-word, or two consecutive half-words making up a 32-bit instruction. The first five bits of the instruction that the PC points to determine this. These patterns identify a 32-bit instruction:

```
0b11101
0b11110
0b11111
```

ARM A32 Assembly Language

Figure 29d shows the encoding for three T32 data processing instructions.

T32 Data Processing, 12-bit Immediate

Hw1: bits 15-11 = `1 1 1 1 0`, bit 10 = `i`, bit 9 = `0`, bits 8-5 = OP, bit 4 = S, bits 3-0 = Rn

Hw2: bits 15-12 = imm3, bits 11-8 = Rd, bits 7-0 = imm8

T32 Add, Subtract, Plain 12-bit Immediate

Hw1: bits 15-11 = `1 1 1 1 0`, bit 10 = `i`, bit 9 = `1`, bit 8 = `0`, bit 7 = OP, bit 6 = `0`, bits 5-4 = OP2, bits 3-0 = Rn

Hw2: bits 15-12 = imm3, bits 11-8 = Rd, bits 7-0 = imm8

T32 Move, Plain 16-bit Immediate

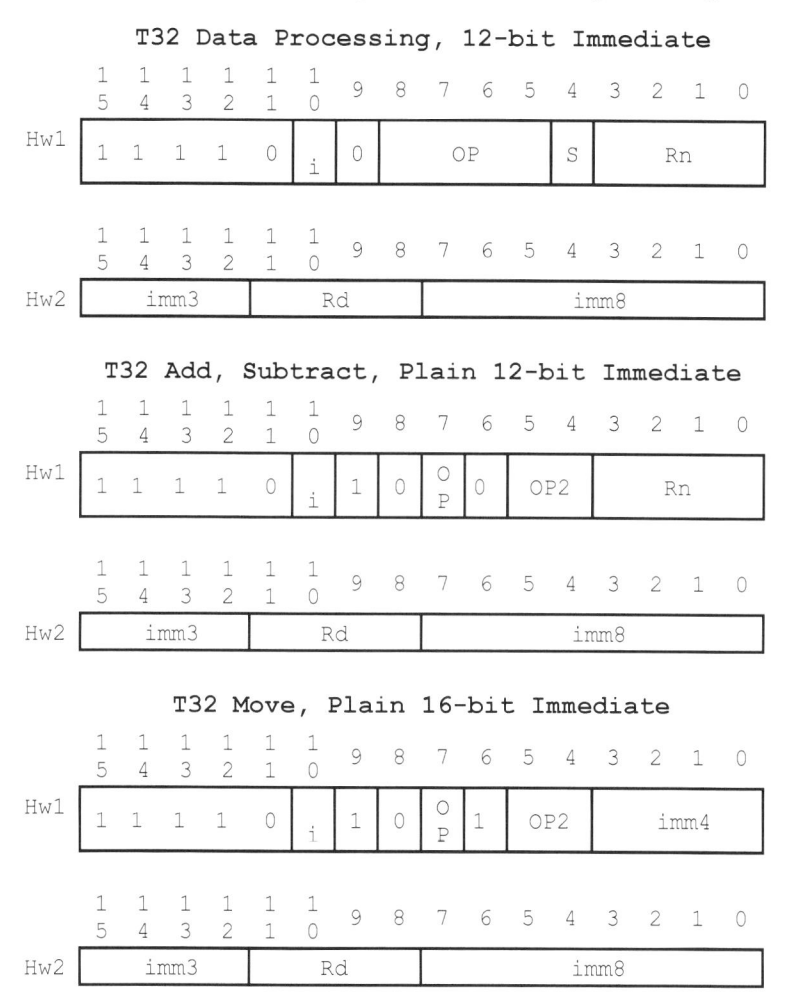

Hw1: bits 15-11 = `1 1 1 1 0`, bit 10 = `i`, bit 9 = `1`, bit 8 = `0`, bit 7 = OP, bit 6 = `1`, bits 5-4 = OP2, bits 3-0 = imm4

Hw2: bits 15-12 = imm3, bits 11-8 = Rd, bits 7-0 = imm8

Figure 29d. T32 data processing encodings.

In the first instance, 'Data Processing, 12-bit Immediate' bits 8:5 in HW1 define the instruction. For example 0b1010 is ADC while ADD is 0b0000. In these instructions if the S bit is set, the instruction updates the condition code flags according to the results of the instruction.

For instructions with plain 12-bit immediate the value is found in the i, imm3 and imm8 fields. The OP and OP2 fields define the instruction. For example OP=0 and OP2=00 is ADD immediate, while OP=1, OP2=10 is SUB immediate.

293

For MOV instruction with plain 16-bit immediate, the value is stored in imm4, i, imm3 and imm8.

Figure 29e shows a couple of 16-bit Thumb encodings:

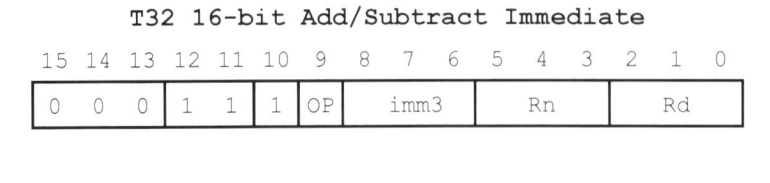

T32 16-bit Add/Subtract Immediate

15	14	13	12	11	10	9	8	7	6	5	4	3	2	1	0
0	0	0	1	1	1	OP	imm3			Rn			Rd		

T32 16-bit Add/Subtract Register

15	14	13	12	11	10	9	8	7	6	5	4	3	2	1	0
0	0	0	1	1	0	OP	Rm			Rn			Rd		

Figure 29e. T32 16-bit encoding examples.

In 16-bit Add/Subtract Immediate OP is 0b0 for ADD Immediate and 0b1 for SUB Immediate. The same OP code values are used for 16-bit Add/Subtract Register values.

Pipeline

We examined the pipeline in Chapter 13. At that point we looked at the original generic three-stage process and hinted then that ARMv6 has an 8-stage operation. The eight stages are described in Figure 29f. During operation, dependent on the instruction being performed the pipeline will route one of three different ways to process stages 5, 6 and 7 and so will further maximise the instruction process prowess of the chip.

There are three blocks of operation that can be switched in at stages 5, 6 and 7 depending on the operation taking place. For example, if a multiply instruction is being processed then these stages are induced in place of the other parallel stages. This allows the ARM to deliver just about one instruction for each cycle.

The Fetch stages can hold up to four instructions, while the Execute, Memory, and Write stages can contain a predicted branch, an ALU or multiply instruction, a load/store multiple instruction and a coprocessor instruction in parallel execution. By overlapping the various stages of operation, the processor maximizes the clock rate achievable to execute each instruction. It delivers a throughput greater than one instruction for each cycle.

Stage	Name	Description
1	Fe1	This is first stage of the instruction fetch where the address is sent to memory and an instruction returned.
2	Fe2	Second stage of instruction fetch. The ARM will try to predict the destination of any branch at this point.
3	De	Decode instruction.
4	Iss	Read registers and issue instruction action.
5	Sh	Perform shift operations as required.
6	ALU	Perform integer operations
7	Sat	Saturate integer results
5	MAC1	First stage of the multiply-accumulate pipeline.
6	MAC2	Second stage of the multiply-accumulate pipeline.
7	MAC3	Third stage of the multiply-accumulate pipeline.
5	ADD	Address generation stage.
6	DC1	First stage of data cache access.
7	DC2	Second stage of data cache access.
8	WBi	Write back of data from the multiply or main execution pipelines (Load Store Unit).

Figure 29f. The eight-stage pipeline of the ARMv 11 includes sub-pipelines which can be banked in for maximum efficiency.

Newer architectures may implement the pipeline differently but they tend to stick to the same processing length. However, there are exceptions for example, the ARM Cortex-A72 uses a 15 stage pipeline, while the Cortex-A73 uses an 11 stage pipeline. Increasing the pipeline increases power consumption and creates heat. This could have a devastating effect on small systems because bigger power supplies and more space between components would be required and perhaps even aided cooling by fans.

It is important to be aware of this pipeline process. As your programs evolve and become more complex, the pipeline can have an effect on instruction operation and timing.

Branch operations and changes to the PC can cause delays in your pipeline. If for example, there are 12 instructions in the pipeline, some branches won't be determined until the end or near the end of the pipe. If the branch is actioned, then you have to discard the cluster of instructions that are no long required. The pipeline with the branch destination will now have to wait for several instruction cycles for the pipeline to catch up as instructions feed through it.

Data can provide its hazards as well. Consider this snippet:

```
ADD R1, R2, R3
SUB R4, R5, R1
```

The SUB instruction follows ADD in the pipeline. However, SUB requires a result from the ADD instruction (as is often the case). In some cases, this can result in the pipeline stalling while it waits for the result of the ADD to be made available to it. If fact this could but doesn't happen as there is specific 'forwarding' mechanism built into the ARM chip that expedites the result should it be needed.

Neon Pipeline

Neon instructions execute in their own 10-stage pipeline. ARM can dispatch two Neon instructions per cycle. The Neon pipeline has a pre-processing holding area where a 16-instruction entry queue holds them until they are due to enter the pipeline. This means that ARM>Neon transfers are fast, but Neon>ARM transfers are slow. Neon instructions will, therefore, execute much later than they appear in the code. The ARM pipeline won't stall until the Neon queue fills, this means you can dispatch a set of Neon instructions, then carry on doing other work while Neon catches up.

This type of minutiae only becomes important when you are looking to make code function as quickly and efficiently as possible.

Instruction Cycles

There was a time when the clock speed of a CPU was the only topic on computer people's tongues. However, the clock cycle isn't the most important thing when discussing speed. There are many factors that determine the overall performance of a processor core including the number of instructions it can execute per clock cycle. Instructions Per Cycle (IPC) is a key aspect of a processor's design, and it affects performance.

When I started to code, the world was dominated by 8-bit processors, and they executed all instructions sequentially. As one instruction completed, the next instruction was executed and so on. Fetch, decode, execute and write-back (the result). Thus it would take four clock cycles to execute an instruction or 0.25 instructions per clock. In this respect to increase the performance, you would need to increase the clock speed. If a processor pipeline can operate the fetch, decode, execute and write-back as one it can complete one instruction in a single clock cycle bumping the IPC from 0.25 to 1.

Nowadays, we are used to multi-tasking, and working on computations in parallel. A company production line will not work on one product but many at the same time as they pass down a conveyor belt from start to finish with a bit in the build process done at each point.

The shortest stage in a pipeline indicates the maximum speed of the instruction operation. You can alleviate any bottlenecks in the pipeline by turning one complex stage into several simpler, but faster, ones. These often operate concurrently.

It is important to remember also that not all instructions are the same. The ARM has different classes of instructions. For example, reading a value from memory is a different class of instruction than adding two integer numbers, which is in turn different to multiplying two floating point numbers, which is again different to testing if a condition is true, and so on.

Multiplying two floating point numbers in the FPU is slower than adding two integers in the ALU, or loading a value into a register. So, the next step to improving performance is to split the execution engine into separate units which can run in parallel. So, while a slow floating point multiply is occurring, a quick integer operation can be dispatched and completed. This is certainly the case with Neon, where the ARM can be made to wait ('stall') until the Neon has returned its result – this all takes time.

We have seen that different ARM architectures have different length pipelines and again this has a big effect on speed. A program that is written specifically for a 15-stage pipeline will not run as well on a 9-stage pipeline. The more stages a pipeline has, the higher its operating frequency and the better the performance. However, the latency of the pipeline increases as it takes more cycles to fill the pipeline before it can execute an instruction (it's a bigger bucket!). On start-up, this may not be an issue, however as we discussed earlier, if a branch takes place, the whole contents of the pipeline may require flushing and refilling with the new instructions. To minimise this, the processor needs to predict what will happen at the next branch – branch prediction. The better the branch prediction, the better the performance.

In complex situations where timing is critical, the programmer may need to utilise a technique called instruction scheduling to reduce or eradicate stalls. Load instructions account for about a third of the instructions of all programs and execution time can often be saved by rationalising where the load operation occurs in the program.

The pipeline has a big effect on the timing of instructions. Take this snippet of code:

```
ADD R0, R0, R2
ADD R0, R0, R2
```

ALU operations take one cycle, so these two instructions together take two-cycles. The second line requires the result from the first, but there is no delay in operation as, after the first cycle, the result is available for the second instruction.

```
LDR R1, [R2, #1]
ADD R0, R0, R1
```

These two instructions take three cycles, as R2+1 must first be calculated - one cycle while decoding the ADD instruction in parallel – but ADD cannot proceed through the pipeline on the second cycle as the LDR still needs to be performed. So, the pipeline has effectively stalled for a cycle. This stall in the pipeline means that the IPC will drop, in fact, it is very rare (if not impossible) that a processor will run at its full theoretical IPC.

Since there can be stalls in the pipeline, then it would be good if the processor could scan ahead and see if there are any instructions it could use to fill those stall gaps (and look for potential upcoming branches). This out-of-order execution is okay as long as it does not affect the program. Therefore the processor must run dependency analysis on potential out-of-order instructions. If one of these instructions loads a new value into a register that is still in use by a previous group of instructions, then the processor needs to create a copy of the registers and work on both sets separately. This process is known as register renaming.

The problem with this 'out-of-order' execution, dependency analysis and register renaming is that it is complex. It takes a lot of processor 'effort' and can be power consuming when applied to every instruction. Thus, not all ARM architectures have these out-of-order capabilities. For example, the ARM Cortex-A53 and the Cortex-A35 are 'in order' processors and use less power than the Cortex-A57 or Cortex-A73, but they also have lower performance levels.

When looking for instructions to execute out of order, the processor must scan the pipeline. How far ahead it scans is known as the instruction window. A larger instruction window gives a higher performance per clock cycle, a greater IPC. However, it also means more memory and more power and potential issues with instruction timings. These are real problems, so designers opt to work with smaller instruction windows and aim for better clock frequencies.

Passing data from Neon (and VFP) back to ARM takes at least 20 cycles, however, there are some gains you can make. The VMOV instruction that is passing the data will not cause any stalls (provided the needed Neon register is already available), the stall will actually happen on any ARM instruction that follows instead (including branches). This means that: multiple VMOV instruction can be done back-to-back with only one stall after the whole sequence. Equally, additional Neon instructions can be issued after the last VMOV without stalling (and with enough instructions the stall can be completely avoided).

Note that the VFP is not pipelined, but the VLDR instructions are. So:

```
VLDR S0, [R0]
```

is one cycle faster than:

```
VLF1.32 {D0[0]}, [R0]
```

More information and data relating to the cycle speed of execution of ARM instructions can be found on the ARM Manual datasheets.

30: System on a Chip

The ARM chip is a CPU; however, the CPU alone is not a computer. A computer requires a whole host of other chip-like devices to make it function. For example, the computer needs memory where data is can be manipulated, an audio chip to decode and amplify your music, a graphics processor to draw and display images on your monitor, an interface chip to handle input and output from the board, and many others, each of which has an important and task. As you bring these individual components together on a computer board, they occupy more and more space, effectively making the proposed device bigger and generating more heat in the process, which requires ventilating.

Figure 30a. A Broadcom System-on-Chip – BCM2837.

In a masterstroke of engineering, a System On Chip (SoC) device brings many of these together and integrates them into one single chip. Typically, a SoC will contain a CPU, a GPU (a graphics processor), memory, USB controller, power management circuits, Bluetooth and probably much more.

SoC devices are custom made and therefore the companies designing and manufacturing them have them made for specific applications.

Clearly, the number one advantage of a SoC is its size: A SoC is only a little larger than a standard ARM microprocessor, and yet it contains much more functionality. If you use a CPU, it's very hard to make a computer that's smaller than 10cm (4 inches) squared, purely because of the number of individual chips that you need to squeeze in. Using a SoC, we can put a complete computer inside a smartphone or tablet, and still have plenty of space for batteries. Nowadays, SoC's form the basis of most single board computers.

By integrating everything together on a single chip, you create impressive gains in operating speed. By including memory on the processor chip, operations take place many times faster than having to access it the information in main memory via an external address-bus. Due to its very high level of integration and much shorter 'wiring', a SoC also uses considerably less power – again, this is a big bonus when it comes to mobile computing. Cutting down on the number of physical chips means that it's much cheaper to build a computer using a SoC, too.

There is a downside to SoC technology from the consumer point of view and a reason why those devices do not easily dominate the market. Being permanently fixed in one configuration, they are difficult, if not impossible, to upgrade, so you can't readily add new memory or upgrade the core processor. What you brought is what you're stuck with!

Many companies, like Apple, Broadcom and Qualcomm license the ARM chip technology from ARM. They then develop their SoC systems and include their requirements onto the silicon and utilise the cores the chip provides as they require.

Co-Processors

The ARM design allows for additional processing hardware to be connected. As these are intended to support the ARM, they are called co-processors. Up to 16, numbered 0-15, can be connected. Instructions such as MCR and MRC can be used to communicate with them, and many co-processors add their instruction sets which are worth investigating.

However, co-processors are becoming a thing of the past, with the integration of Neon and VFP into newer A64-based chips. Older architectures – many of which are still current and fully utilised - continue to use co-processors. In ARMv6 co-processor technology is installed. In fact, the VFP occupies two slots, CP10 and CP11 in the system. CP14 and CP15 are for system use alone, but the others are all free for use.

(Interestingly this was a unique design structure introduced by Acorn as early as 1983 with the launch of its Second Processor Tube interface which allowed additional CPU's to be plugged into the side of the BBC Micro, allowing another processor dependent operating system such as CP/M to be run. An ARM, Second Processor unit, was one of the last released for the BBC Micro!)

Memory & Caches

The ARM also has an area of very fast memory called a cache. The development of caches and caching is one of the most significant developments in computer and chip design. In the early days of computing, main memory was slow and expensive – but CPUs weren't particularly fast, either. As processor clock speeds increased significantly, the gap began to widen very quickly. However, memory struggled to keep up and access times were far slower than processors, so the processor was always stalling waiting to gain memory access. It was a problem needing a solution. Caching was invented to solve this problem.

CPU caches are small sections of memory that store information the processor is most likely to need next. The data loaded into the cache depends on algorithms employed by the designer and a set of underlying assumptions about programming code. The purpose of the cache is to ensure the processor has the next bit of data it will need already loaded into the cache by the time it goes looking for it (also called a cache hit). In this way, the processor is not stalling waiting for information.

Some processors, and indeed most SoC systems, utilise at least two caches, called L1 and L2. The second cache, L2, is larger than L1 and the two work in tandem to ensure the flow of data is constant, and that cache misses don't happen. Sometimes this means that the data held in L1 is duplicated in L2, while some systems never share data. Third and fourth caches (L3 and L4) can exist on some systems, and their pecking order remains in numerical order.

The size of the cache increases performance but at the cost of power and heat dissipation which can be an issue. Some SoC designers dedicate the L2 cache with a particular function, such as on-board memory for a videocore.

The Neon often has access to L2 as a scratchpad to speed things up. It all depends on the SoC in question.

The GPU

The Graphics Processing Unit is the other major component of the SoC configuration. With the advent of high-end gaming and virtual reality systems, the GPU can become quite complicated. While a CPU might only have four cores, a GPU can have over 100 cores that can handle thousands of code threads concurrently with the aim of speeding up the rendering of real-time graphic displays.

It is unlikely that a SoC would contain a GPU of this level of capability, but even for the simplest graphics tasks, like drawing a square on the screen, a graphics processor will outperform a CPU.

You can use the CPU or the GPU for video and photo processing, but the dedicated hardware will get the job done with less power than either of those. That is why video encoding/decoding and photo processing often have their hardware. The SoC device can have this built into it.

Single Board Computers

SoC's form the heart of most, if not all, of the single board computers available today. Indeed were it not for the needs of humans to interact with them, the SBC could be virtually the size of the SoC. But physical restrictions mean that we need places – ports – to plug in keyboards, mice and display devices, and a variety of pins and tags where we can connect other purpose built hardware. To paraphrase the old joke: "Did you hear the one about ARM? They were so successful they had to move into smaller premises".

31: ARMv8 Overview

The concept behind ARMv8 was to provide ARM with a clean slate with which to design and encode an entirely new instruction set. The brief was for it to be 64-bit instruction set while adhering as much as possible to keeping mnemonics and processes familiar.

Because of the sheer weight of numbers 32-bit ARM will remain accessible and a processor of choice for existing designers and developers. Not least because the programmers have vast experience in 32-bit code. For this reason part of the brief was, as much as possible, to maintain compatibility with older architectures while streamlining both ARM and Thumb instruction sets. Thus the Unified Assembly Language was developed.

A64 provides a new start. Hopefully, the new instruction set will remain consistent across architectures to allow stability for the development and continuity in implementation.

As you may have already concluded working through this book, it's hard to provide a comprehensive coverage of all options and architectures with ARM simply because they can differ so much. This makes writing about ARM generically difficult and possibly a reason why the number of texts on the subject is few and far between. What I have tried to do is stick to the fundamentals and point out differences in the major architecture releases where they occur. It is by no means comprehensive and a reason I suggest that you furbish yourself with the appropriate architecture manual and start to refer to this. The knowledge you have at this stage should be more than adequate to understand the manuals.

So, this chapter finishes off by providing a general overview of what is on offer when AArch64 state is selected. It highlights some of the major features and differences.

Different Compatibility

ARMv8 architecture implements two instruction sets – UAL which comprises A32 and T32, and A64. The state the processor is placed in at reset determines the instruction set selected – AArch32 State (A32 and T32) or AArch64 State (A64). It is not possible to interwork between the two instruction sets and therefore not possible to switch from A32 to A64 during a program operation. It is one or the other. The operating system in force determines the instruction state. A64 is not UAL.

Code written in A64 for the ARMv8 processors cannot run on ARMv7 Cortex-A series processors. However, code written for ARMv7-A processors can run on ARMv8 processors in the AArch32 execution state.

A64 provides similar functionality to the A32 and T32 instruction sets in AArch32 or ARMv7. However, the design of the new A64 instruction set allowed several improvements to be made just due to the fact the designers were starting from scratch. For example:

- consistency in the encoding – many A32 instructions had to be fitted in to make UAL possible.
- a wide range of flexible constants designed for the purpose. For example, MOV accepts a 16-bit immediate, which can be shifted to any 16-bit boundary
- easier data types – by providing more concise and efficient ways of manipulating 64-bit integers.
- long offsets – A64 instructions provide longer offsets, both for PC-relative branches and for offset addressing.
- Fixed length instruction – A64 instructions are the same length, unlike T32, which is a variable-length instruction set.

A64 Register Set

The AArch64 execution state provides 31 × 64-bit general-purpose registers which are accessible at all times and in all exception levels. Each register is 64 bits wide and referred to as registers X0-X30. The lower half of each of this set can be accessed as 32-bit registers and are known as W0-W30. For example, W0 maps onto the lower word of X0, and W1 maps onto the lower word of X1. Figure 31a illustrates this. Note that this is a different arrangement from what we have seen in FPU and Neon register sets where the two 32-bit registers map to a single 64-bit register. Register 30 also maps to the Link Register (LR) which we'll discuss below.

Most integer instructions in the A64 instruction set have two forms, which operate on either 32-bit or 64-bit values. Any write operation to a W register will affect the content of the lower word in the corresponding X register.

There is no X31 or W31 register. Many instructions are encoded such that the number 31 represents the Zero Register, ZR (WZR/XZR). There is a restricted group of instructions where one or more of the arguments are encoded such that number 31 represents the Stack Pointer (SP). Figure 31b lists the special registers found in AArch64.

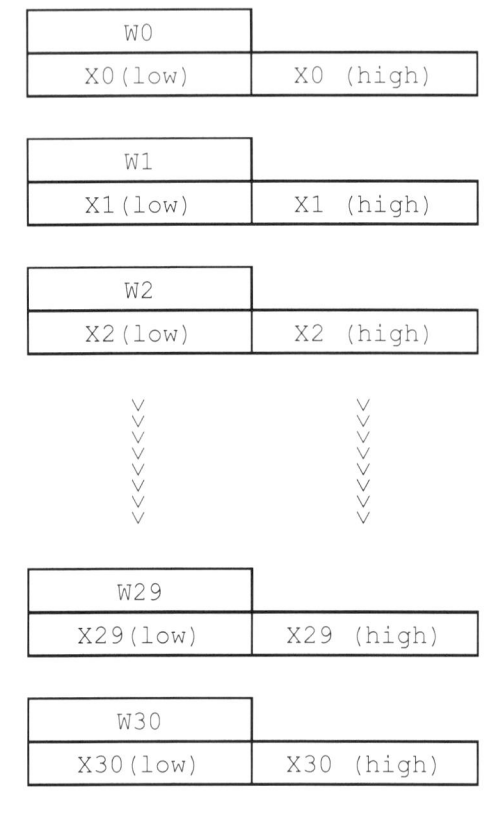

```
        W0
     X0(low)         X0  (high)

        W1
     X1(low)         X1  (high)

        W2
     X2(low)         X2  (high)

         v                v
         v                v
         v                v
         v                v
         v                v
         v                v

        W29
     X29(low)        X29 (high)

        W30
     X30(low)        X30 (high)
```

Figure 31a. AArch64 provides 31 'W' registers with 30 'X' registers mapped into their lower 32-bits.

The Zero Register is only useful as a source for loading a zero. Writes to it are ignored, and all reads return 0. Note that the 64-bit form of the SP register does not use an X prefix. You can use the zero register in most, but not all, instructions.

ARM A32 Assembly Language

Direct access to the PC has been removed to make return prediction easier. The PC can no longer be specify as the destination of a data processing instruction or load instruction. Its use is implicit in certain instructions such as PC-relative load and address generation.

In AArch64 state, the Link Register (LR), which maps to register 30, stores the return address when a subroutine call is made. It can also be used as a general-purpose register if the return address is stored on the stack. Unlike in AArch32 state, the LR is distinct from the Exception Link Registers (ELRs) and is therefore not banked.

Flag	Width	Name
WZR	32-bits	Zero Register
XZR	64-bits	Zero Register
WSP	32-bits	Current Stack Pointer
SP	64-bits	Current Stack Pointer
PC	64-bits	Program Counter

Figure 31a. Special registers in AArch64

In AArch64 state, there is no Current Program Status Register (CPSR). You can access the different components of the traditional CPSR independently as Process State fields:

- N, Z, C, and V condition flags (NZCV).
- Current register width (nRW).
- Stack pointer selection bit (SPSel).
- Interrupt disable flags (DAIF).
- Current exception level (EL).
- Single step process state bit (SS).
- Illegal exception return state bit (IL).

You can use the MSR instruction to write to the:

- N, Z, C, and V flags in the NZCV register.
- interrupt disable flags in the DAIF register.
- SP selection bit in the SPSEL register, in EL1 or higher.

You can use the MRS instruction to read:

- N, Z, C, and V flags in the NZCV register.
- interrupt disable flags in the DAIF register.
- exception level bits in the CurrentEL register, in EL1 or higher.
- SP selection bit in the SPSel register, in EL1 or higher.

The order in which information is stored in memory is called endianness, or byte-ordering. There are two ways to do this. Little-Endian (LE) or Big-Endian (BE). For Big-Endian, the most significant byte is stored at the lowest address, that is the address closest to zero. Little-Endian puts the least significant byte at the lowest address.

Endianness is controlled separately for each execution level. For EL3, EL2 and EL1, the relevant register of SCTLR_ELn.EE sets the endianness. The additional bit at EL1, SCTLR_EL1.E0E controls the endian setting for EL0. In the AArch64 execution state, data accesses can be LE or BE, while instruction fetches are always LE.

Syntax Differences

When comparing UAL with A64, there are differences in syntax and assembler structure. Here are a few of the major differences.

In UAL you can make an instruction conditional by appending a condition suffix directly to the mnemonic. For example:

```
BEQ label
```

In A64 the condition code suffix is separated from the mnemonic using a '.' delimiter. For example:

```
B.EQ label
```

A64 provides several unconditionally executed instructions that use a condition code as an operand. For these instructions, you specify the condition code to test for in the final operand position. For example:

```
CSEL w1,w2,w3,EQ
```

In UAL the '.W' and '.N' instruction width specifiers control whether the assembler generates a 32-bit or 16-bit encoding for a T32 instruction. As A64 is a fixed width 32-bit instruction set, it has no need for the use of .W and .N qualifiers.

A32 has no equivalent of the extend operators. In A64 you can specify an extend operator in several instructions to control how a portion of the second source register value is signed or zero extended. For example:

```
ADD X1, X2, W3, UXTB #2
```

Here, the instruction, UXTB is the extend type (zero extend, byte) and #2 is an optional left shift amount.

Other differences are inherent in the fact that the registers and their sizes are different between the two states. These have been highlighted previously in this chapter.

Exceptions

When executing in AArch64, the following registers hold the exception return state:

- Exception Link Register (ELR).
- Saved Processor State Register (SPSR).

There is a dedicated SP for each exception level, but it is not used to hold return state: SP_EL0, SP_EL1, SP_EL2, and SP_EL3. When in AArch64 at an exception level other than EL0, the processor can use either:

- A dedicated 64-bit stack pointer associated with that Exception level (SP_ELn).
- The stack pointer associated with EL0 (SP_EL0).

EL0 can only ever access SP_EL0.

In Figure 31c, the 't' suffix indicates that the SP_EL0 stack pointer is selected. The 'h' suffix indicates that the SP_ELn stack pointer is selected.

While most instructions don't access the SP, some instructions, ADD for example, can read and write to the current stack pointer to adjust it in a function. For example:

```
ADD SP, SP, #0x10    @ Adjust SP to be 0x10 bytes
                                before its current value
```

When taking an exception, the processor state is stored in the relevant Saved Program Status Register (SPSR), in a similar way to the CPSR in the pre-AArch64 models. The SPSR holds the value of PSTATE before taking an exception and is used to restore the value of PSTATE when executing an exception return.

Exception	Options
EL0	EL0t
EL1	EL1t, EL1h
EL2	EL2t, EL2h
EL3	EL3t, EL3h

Figure 31c. AArch64 Stack pointer options.

In AArch64, the system configuration is controlled through system registers and accessed using MSR and MRS instructions (as with pre-AArch64 ARMs). The name of a register tells you the lowest Exception level that it can be viewed from. For example:

- TTBR0_EL1 is accessible from EL1, EL2, and EL3.
- TTBR0_EL2 is accessible from EL2 and EL3.

Except for EL0, registers that have the suffix _ELn have a separate, banked copy in the levels.

Previous versions of the ARM architecture have used coprocessors for system configuration. However, AArch64 does not include support for coprocessors but does implement a number of new system registers.

AArch64 does not have a direct equivalent of the Current Program Status Register (CPSR). In AArch64, the components of the traditional CPSR are supplied as fields that are accessible independently. These are now referred to collectively as Processor State (PSTATE).

In AArch64, you return from an exception with the ERET instruction. This copies the SPSR_ELn into PSTATE (where 'n' is the level number) and restores the ALU flags, execution state, exception level, and the processor branches.

The PSTATE.{N, Z, C, V} fields can be accessed at EL0. All other PSTATE fields can be executed at EL1 or higher and are undefined at EL0.

There are three Exception Link Registers, ELR_EL1, ELR_EL2, and ELR_EL3, which corresponds to each of the exception levels. When an exception is taken, the Exception Link Register for the target exception level stores the return address to jump to after the handling of that exception completes. If the exception was taken from AArch32 state, the top 32 bits in the ELR are all set to zero. Subroutine calls within the exception level use the LR to store the return address from the subroutine. For example when the exception level changes from EL0 to EL1, the return address is stored in ELR_EL1.

When in an exception level, if you enable interrupts that use the same exception level, you must ensure you store the ELR on the stack because it will be overwritten with a new return address when the interrupt is taken.

AArch32 Processor Modes

In ARMv8 running in AArch32 State the architecture provides nine modes and these are illustrated in Figure 31d.

Processor Mode	Mode Number
User	0b10000
FIQ	0b10001
IRQ	0b10010
Supervisor	0b10011
Monitor	0b10110
Abort	0b10111
Hyp	0b11010
Undefined	0b11011
System	0b11111

Figure 31d. AArch32 Processor Modes.

As an unprivileged mode, User mode has restricted access to system resources. All other modes have total access to the system and are able to change mode freely, and execute software as privileged.

The following registers are available and accessible in any processor mode:

- 15 general-purpose registers R0-R12, the Stack Pointer (SP), and Link Register (LR).
- Program Counter (PC).
- Application Program Status Register (APSR).

Additional registers are available in privileged software execution. ARM processors have a total of 43 registers. The registers are arranged in partially overlapping banks. There is a different register bank for each processor mode. In privileged software execution, CPSR is an alias for APSR and gives access to additional bits.

The additional registers are:

- Two Supervisor Mode registers for banked SP and LR.
- Two Abort Mode registers for banked SP and LR.
- Two Undefined Mode registers for banked SP and LR.
- Two Interrupt Mode registers for banked SP and LR.
- Seven FIQ Mode registers for banked R8-R12, SP and LR.
- Two Monitor mode registers for banked SP and LR.
- One Hyp Mode register for banked SP.
- Seven Saved Program Status Register (SPSRs), one for each exception mode.
- One Hyp Mode register for ELR_Hyp to store the preferred return address from Hyp mode.

Code can run in either a Secure state or in a Non-secure state. Hypervisor (Hyp) mode has privileged execution in Non-secure state.

AArch32 State Exceptions

The introduction of ARMv8 architecture brought with it a change in system control. The exception model defines four levels EL0-EL3. The architecture does not specify how software can use the different exception levels, but the following (Figure 31e) is a typical usage model for them:

Exception	Utilised For
EL0	Applications
EL1	OS kernel and associated functions typically described as privileged.
EL2	Hypervisor - support for processor virtualisation
EL3	Secure monitor - provides support for two security states

Figure 31e. Exception Levels.

The numeric value specifies the level of the exception. Thus, EL0 is the lowest exception level, and EL3 is the highest. The code at EL3 cannot take exception to a higher exception level, so cannot change execution state. If a change is required then the system must reset.

The execution state is backwards-compatible with ARMv7-A architecture that includes security extensions. This features:

- 13 times 32-bit general purpose registers, and a 32-bit PC, SP, and Link Register (LR). Some of these registers have multiple Banked instances for use in different processor modes.
- 32 times 64-bit registers for Neon/Advanced SIMD and Floating-point support.
- two instruction sets, A32 and T32.

It provides an exception model that maps the ARMv7 model onto the ARMv8 model and levels collecting the processor state into the Current Processor State Register (CPSR).

Movement between exception levels follows some rules:

- The change to a higher exception level indicates increased software execution privilege.
- You cannot change an exception to a lower level.
- There is no exception handling at level EL0; exceptions must be taken to a higher level.

An exception causes a change of program flow. Execution of an exception handler starts, at an Exception level greater than EL0, from a defined vector that relates to the exception taken. Exceptions include:

- Interrupts such as IRQ and FIQ.
- Memory system aborts.
- Undefined instructions.
- System calls. These permit unprivileged software to make a system call to an operating system.
- Secure monitor or hypervisor traps.

To return from an exception, the processor must execute an exception return instruction – ERET. The processor state when an exception return instruction is committed must be restored.

EL1 is used for most processor modes interrupt handling. User (EL0) and Hypervisor (EL2) being the exceptions.

The processing of exceptions in AArch32 State is directly linked to AArch64 state which we will take this up further in Chapter 31.

AArch32 Exceptions in AArch64

For backwards compatibility, AArch32 must match earlier architectures (viz ARMv7) privilege levels. It also means that AArch32 only deals with the 32-bit general-purpose registers. To enable this there must be some communication between the ARMv8 architecture, and the view of it provided by the AArch32 execution state.

Referring to Figure 28e (Chapter 28), there are 16 x 32-bit general-purpose registers (R0-R15) for software use. Fifteen of them (R0-R14) can be utilised for general-purpose data storage. The remaining register, R15, is the program counter (PC). The software can also access the CPSR, and the saved copy of the CPSR from the previously executed mode is the SPSR. On taking an exception, the CPSR is copied to the SPSR of the mode to which the exception is made.

The registers accessed will be determined by the processor mode the software is executing in at the time of the exception and the register itself. This is called banking and these registers are only accessible only when a process is executing in that particular mode.

In contrast, the AArch64 execution state has 31 x 64-bit general-purpose registers accessible at all times and in all exception levels. A change in execution state between AArch64 and AArch32 means that the AArch64 registers must necessarily map onto the AArch32 (ARMv7) register set.

The upper 32 bits of the AArch64 registers are inaccessible when executing in AArch32. If the processor is operating in the AArch32 state, it uses the 32-bit W registers, which are equivalent to the 32-bit ARMv7 registers.

AArch32 maps the banked registers to AArch64 registers that would otherwise be inaccessible.

The SPSR and ELR_Hyp registers in AArch32 are additional registers that are accessible using system instructions only. They are not mapped into the general-purpose register space of the AArch64 architecture. Some of these registers are mapped between AArch32 and AArch64:

  SPSR_svc maps to SPSR_EL1.

SPSR_hyp maps to SPSR_EL2.

ELR_hyp maps to ELR_EL2.

The following registers are only used during AArch32 execution, however, because of the execution at EL1 using AArch64, they retain their state despite them being inaccessible during AArch64 execution at that Exception level.

SPSR_abt.

SPSR_und.

SPSR_irq.

SPSR_fiq.

The SPSR registers are only accessible during AArch64 execution at higher exception levels for context switching.

Again, if an exception is taken to an Exception level in AArch64 from an Exception level in AArch32, the top 32 bits of the AArch64 ELR_ELn are all zero.

Finally

Just a quick overview of ARMv8 with the introduction of AArch64 and AArch32 so that you might get a flavour of what the new architecture and instructions offers. I will have more information appearing on my website about developments in this area.

As mentioned elsewhere in this book ARM is a vast subject, and every architecture brings its differences. Whatever architecture you might go forward with remember to ensure you have the latest Reference Manuals from ARM to provide you with precise detail about the programmers model, system registers and instruction sets. I hope that these pages have, up to this point, provided you with the fundamentals of ARM programming and will allow you to attack the Reference Manuals with confidence.

Please give me your feedback if you desire at 'feedback@brucesmith.info' or via the link on my website.

a: GCC Updates

If you are planning to work at the sharp end of ARM code, then it makes sense to have the latest version of the GCC software available. If you are using a Linux-based system, then the best way to do this is to compile it for yourself. The process is not difficult but requires some time, and dependent on the system you are running it can take several hours, so it is something worth doing overnight or before you go out for the day.

To check what the latest stable release of GCC is, go to:

```
https://gcc.gnu.org/
```

Under the heading 'Supported Releases', you will see the supported stable versions, You will also seed a 'Development' version listed. 'Development' indicates a beta version under testing and will probably contain issues. But you can have a look to see what is coming up.

When I checked (at the time of writing this) the latest supported release was 6.3, and the Development version was 7.0. It will have undoubtedly progressed past this by the time you read this.

You will need a good amount of free space on your drive to compile the program. I would suggest about 8GB as a minimum and ideally, double this. You will also need to know what version ARM chip you are using and what architecture it uses.

In a Terminal window from the root prompt enter:

```
cd
mkdir code
cd code

wget http://nl.mirror.babylon.network/gcc/releases/gcc-6.3.0/gcc-6.3.0.tar.bz2
```

(Note you should enter from wget onwards as a single line - not two lines as shown here.)

The last line will download the compressed file. Substitute the version number you require to download at the two specific points in the line. Next uncompress the file you downloaded and extract files from the archive with::

```
tar xvf gcc-6.3.0.tar.bz2
```

Again, use the version number you are using. After five minutes or so of screen activity the prompt will return. Now enter:

```
cd gcc-6.3.0
contrib/download_prerequisites
mkdir obj
cd obj
```

```
../configure -v --enable-languages=c,c++ --with-cpu=cortex-a53 \
  --with-fpu=neon-fp-armv8 --with-float=hard --build=arm-linux-gnueabihf \
  --host=arm-linux-gnueabihf --target=arm-linux-gnueabihf
```

The last three lines above are in fact one command line, the '\' character at the end of the first two of the three lines tells the command line interpreter that more is to come. Note in the first of these three lines that the 'cpu' specified is 'cortex-a53' and on the second line, the 'fpu' is specified as 'armv8'. You will need to edit these with the values you require for your processor.

This process takes about 10 minutes or so.

To assist the compilation and so as to keep the time required to a manageable level you should ensure a swap space of at least 1024mb. Anything less can drastically increase the time required, and if you are using an SD Card as your medium, the constant writing to it it can drastically reduce the life of the card. Enter:

```
dd if=/dev/zero of=/swapfile1GB bs=1M count=1024
mkswap /swapfile1GB
swapon /swapfile1GB
```

You are now ready to compile:

```
make -j5
```

It is good to keep and eye on the process for the first 15 minutes or so. In my experience, this is when errors occur if they are going to. The '-j5' option ensures all cores of the ARM are used to undertake the compilation.

When the prompt finally appears, install it using:

```
make install
```

Type 'gcc -v' to check everything is ok.

b: ASCII Character Set

Binary	Dec	Hex	ASC	Binary	Dec	Hex	ASC
010 0000	32	20		011 1111	63	3F	?
010 0001	33	21	!	100 0000	64	40	@
010 0010	34	22	"	100 0001	65	41	A
010 0011	35	23	#	100 0010	66	42	B
010 0100	36	24	$	100 0011	67	43	C
010 0101	37	25	%	100 0100	68	44	D
010 0110	38	26	&	100 0101	69	45	E
010 0111	39	27	'	100 0110	70	46	F
010 1000	40	28	(	100 0111	71	47	G
010 1001	41	29	)	100 1000	72	48	H
010 1010	42	2A	*	100 1001	73	49	I
010 1011	43	2B	+	100 1010	74	4A	J
010 1100	44	2C	,	100 1011	75	4B	K
010 1101	45	2D	-	100 1100	76	4C	L
010 1110	46	2E	.	100 1101	77	4D	M
010 1111	47	2F	/	100 1110	78	4E	N
011 0000	48	30	0	100 1111	79	4F	O
011 0001	49	31	1	101 0000	80	50	P
011 0010	50	32	2	101 0001	81	51	Q
011 0011	51	33	3	101 0010	82	52	R
011 0100	52	34	4	101 0011	83	53	S
011 0101	53	35	5	101 0100	84	54	T
011 0110	54	36	6	101 0101	85	55	U
011 0111	55	37	7	101 0110	86	56	V
011 1000	56	38	8	101 0111	87	57	W
011 1001	57	39	9	101 1000	88	58	X
011 1010	58	3A	:	101 1001	89	59	Y
011 1011	59	3B	;	101 1010	90	5A	Z
011 1100	60	3C	<	101 1011	91	5B	[
011 1101	61	3D	=	101 1100	92	5C	\

Binary	Dec	Hex	ASC	Binary	Dec	Hex	ASC
011 1110	62	3E	>	101 1101	93	5D	]
101 1110	94	5E	^	110 1111	111	6F	o
101 1111	95	5F	_	111 0000	112	70	p
110 0000	96	60	`	111 0001	113	71	q
110 0001	97	61	a	111 0010	114	72	r
110 0010	98	62	b	111 0011	115	73	s
110 0011	99	63	c	111 0100	116	74	t
110 0100	100	64	d	111 0101	117	75	u
110 0101	101	65	e	111 0110	118	76	v
110 0110	102	66	f	111 0111	119	77	w
110 0111	103	67	g	111 1000	120	78	x
110 1000	104	68	h	111 1001	121	79	y
110 1001	105	69	i	111 1010	122	7A	z
110 1010	106	6A	j	111 1011	123	7B	{
110 1011	107	6B	k	111 1100	124	7C	|
110 1100	108	6C	l	111 1101	125	7D	}
110 1101	109	6D	m	111 1110	126	7E	~
110 1110	110	6E	n				

C: Companion Website

A companion website exists in support of this book. Go to *www.brucesmith.info* and click on the book cover icon to locate additional information and downloads for this book. Or select the *Book Resource Pages* option from the drop-down ARM menu.

The support pages on the website include but are not limited to the following information:

- Source files for all programs in the book
- Updates to programs and information in the book
- Errata data and corrections
- Links to websites and additional downloads mentioned in the book
- Links to instruction ARM Reference Manuals
- Links to free retro computing book PDFs.

The website also contains details of other books written by Bruce Smith and his Techno Blog: *Alan Turing Rocks*.

www.brucesmith.info

Index

! Operator 154
.align directive 169
.align, in Thumb 249
.arm directive 252
.ascii 80, 82, 166
.asciz 166
.byte directive 167
.data 81
.equ directive 167
.macro directive 169
.size main directive 195
.syntax unified 261
.text 81
.thumb directive 252
.word directive 168
\ options 166
_start, lack of 42
128-bit vectors 231
12-bit field in constant range 116
15-stage pipeline 295
16-bit Thumb 246
26-bit ARM 59
32-bit multiplication 74
32-bit multiplication with accumulate 75
32-bit numbers, add 69
32-bit processors 17
64-bit instruction set 304
64-bit numbers, add 70
64-bit vectors 231
8-stage pipeline 294

A32 .... 19, 257, 288, 304
A32, new instructions 259
A64 .... 19, 304
AAPCS standard 185
AArch32 19
AArch32 processor modes 311
AArch32State 305
AArch64 19
AARch64 stack pointer options 310
AARch64 State 305
AArch64 State registers 307
ABI 184

Abort	276
accessing bytes	146
accumulation, long	120
Acorn Computers	13
ADC	68
ADCS	71
ADD	68
add 32-bit numbers	69
add 64-bit numbers	70
add with carry	68
addition instructions	68
addition, binary	53
addition, matrix	240
address write back	148
addresses, word aligned	60
addressing	59
addressing mode	61, 140
addressing mode, PC relative	151
addressing mode, pre-indexed	140, 145
addressing mode, write back	148
addressing modes, Neon	234
addressing modes, Thumb	254
addressing, indirect	140, 143
addressing, post-indexed	140, 149
ADDS	69
administrator	271
ADR	140
AL	101
aligning data	169
alignment, word	59
AND	89
Application Binary Interface	184
applications, stack	164
APSR register	219, 311
architecture	15, 58
arithmetic shift right	113
ARM 32-bit processors	17
ARM early chips	59
ARM instructions	26
ARM licence	14
ARM state	246
ARM, 26-bit	59
ARM, operand breakdown	290
ARM, registers	60
ARMv7	205
ARMv8	205, 304
arrays, Neon	236
As	38, 42

ascending stack	161
ASCII code	80, 90
ASR	113
assemble	28, 42
assembler errors	38
assembler source	42
assembler structure	30, 34
assembler, generating source from C	193
assembler, -mfpu option	212
assembling UAL	261
assembly, GDB	131

B	65, 105
backslash options	166
backwards compatibility, AArch64	314
bad joke	47
bare metal programming	78, 18
base address, GPIO	265, 267
BBC BASIC	27
BBC Micro	13
BEQ	63
BFC	259
BFI	259
BIC	92
big-endian	308
Binary	25
binary addition	53
binary numbers, weights	48
binary string, print	93
binary subtraction	53
binary to decimal	48
bit settings, modes	281
bit, clear	92
Bits	47
bits, CPSR	283
BL	65, 105
BNE	63
book pdf	23
books, free	23
branch calculation	126
branch exchange	110
branch instruction	63, 65, 105
branch predication	297
branch, pipeline effect	127
branches, Thumb	248
breakpoint commands	138
breakpoints	135
breakpoints, deleting	135

breakpoints, setting	135
BX	110
Bytes	47
bytes, accessing	146
C	173
C programming	18
C, generating assembler source file	193
Caches	302
calculate branch	126
calculation, immediate operands	117
Carry (C) flag	62
CC	101
characters, convert case	90
clear bits	92
CLI	33
CMN	64, 77
CMP	64, 77
code, ASCII	80
code, loops	107
codes, condition	97, 290
condition codes, VFP	220
command line	33
command, echo	40
command, sudo	271
commands, breakpoint	138
comments	41, 45
comments, in Thumb	250
compare instructions	64, 77
compiler	18
compiling C source files	191
condition code	97, 297
AL	101
CC	101
CS	101
EQ	99
GE	103
GT	103
HI	102
HS	101
LE	103
LO	101
LS	103
LT	103
MI	100
NE	99
NV	102
PL	100

- VC 100
- VS 100
  - multiple flags 102
  - single flags 97
  - with S suffix 105
- conditional execution 97
- conditional execution, floating point 219
- constants, immediate 144
- control-characters 80
- controller chip, GPIO 264
- conversion numbers 50
  - binary to decimal 48
  - binary to hex 50
  - decimal to binary 49
  - decimal to hex 52
  - hex to decimal 52
- convert character case 90
- co-processor 289, 301
- copy link register to program counter 66
- Core 14
- CPSR 62, 276
- CPSR bits 283
- CPU 25
- create new directory, mkdir 199
- CS 101
- CubeStats 29
- cycle, instructions per 296
- cycles, instruction 296

- D registers 209
- DA option 154
- data processing 67
- data types, Neon 231
- data, aligning 169
- datatype 234
- datatype, promote and demote 234
- DB option 154
- debugging 129
  - floating point 216
  - breakpoints 135
  - hex dump 139
  - register values 136
  - screen output 130
- decimal numbers, weights 48
- Decode 125
- decrement after 154
- decrement before 154
- deleting breakpoints 135

descending stack..161
development boards..16
DGB, hex dump...139
directive .ascii..81, 82
directive .text..81
directive, data storage...166
directives .data..81
disassembler...131
disassembler switches...134
disassembling C...190
disassembling syscalls..199
disassembling, Thumb...251
division and remainder...122
double precision numbers, format..207
dump, registers..136

EA option...161
eabi_attributes..195
Eax 85
Ececute stage...294
Echo 40, 168
ED option...161
editor, graphical..39
editor, text...35
Endian..308
EOR 89
EQ 99
error messages..34
error, assembler..28
errors, twos complement..57
exception handling...275
exception link register..309
executable file...45
Execute..125
exiting programs...79
extended rotate...115

FA option...161
FD option...161
Fetch 125
Fetch stage..294
file structure..174
FIQ 276, 281, 284
Flag
        Zero..62
        Carry...62
        Negative...62

ARM A32 Assembly Language

Overflow	62
Q	123
saturation	123
status	62
test	92
setting	64
updating	65
floating point, conditional execution	219
floating point, debugging	216
floating point, -mfpu	212
floating point, printing	213
FP	195
FPSCR register	217
Frame Pointer	195
Frame Pointer variable	198
free books	23
frozen programs	129
function standard, ABI	184
function, scanf	178
functions	184
functions, passing more than three values	186
functions, preserving status flags	189
functions, register designations	185
functions, thumb	255
-g option, assembler	131
GCC compiler	18
GCC directive	80
GCC updates	316
GDB	129
GDB, assembling for	131
GDB, floating point	216
GE	103
General Public Licence	19
GNU	18
GPCLR register	266
GPIO	263
GPIO base address	265
GPIO pins	264
GPIO registers	264
GPSEL registers	264
GPU	03
graphical editor	39
GT	103
gvim	39
hardware vectors	277
hex dump	139
HI	102

327

high-level languages 28
HS 101
IA option 154
IB option 154
immediate constants 144
immediate constants range 116
immediate operands calculation 117
increment after 154
increment before 154
indirect addressing 140, 143
input from keyboard 82
input size 233
Instruction
    64-bit 304
    A32 new instructions 259
    ADC 68
    ADCS 71
    ADD 68
    ADDS 69
    ADR 140
    AND 89
    ASR 113
    B 65, 105
    BEQ 63
    BFC 259
    BFI 259
    BL 65, 105
    BIC 92
    BNE 63
    BX 110
    CMN 64, 77
    CMP 64, 77
    cycles 296
    division 122
    EOR 89
    JSR 106
    LDBR 146
    LDM 153
    LDR 61, 81, 144, 151
    LSL 94, 111
    LSL 111
    memory load 153
    memory store 153
    MLA 74
    MLS 260
    MOV 66, 75
    MOVT 260
    MRS 282

MSR	282
MUL	73
MVN	75
narrow	308
ORR	89
POP	178
PUSH	178
RBIT	260
ROR	114
RRX	115
RSB	72
RSC	72
SBC	72
SBFX	260
shift	111
signed multiply wide	121
SMLAL	120
SMUAD	121
SMULL	119
SMUSD	121
STM	61, 153
STR	145
SUB	72
SVR	78
SWI	78
TEQ	40, 93
TST	93
UBFX	260
UMALA	120
UMULL	119
VABS	216
VADD	216
VCVT	211
VLD	244
VLDR	210, 212, 215
VLSR	212
VMOV	211, 214
VMUL	216
VNEG	216
VNMUL	216
VPUSH	211, 214
VREV	239
VSQRT	216
VSTR	212, 239, 244
VSUB	216
VZIP	239
wide	308
instructions per cycle	296

instructions, ARM ... 26
interpreter, command line ... 33
interrupts ... 276
interrupts, returning from ... 285
interrupts, serving ... 284
interworking ... 252
intrinsics, Neon ... 234
IPC ... 295
IRG ... 276
IRQ ... 281, 284
IRQ disable ... 283
IRQ mode enabling ... 283

JSR ... 106

Kernel ... 173
keyboard input, scanf ... 178
keyboard, reading from ... 82

L1, L2 caches ... 302
Label ... 40
lanes, Neon ... 232
languages, high level ... 28
languages, low level ... 28
Ld ... 38, 42
LDM ... 153
LDR ... 61, 81, 144, 151
LE ... 103
LED, turn on ... 266
LEN ... 222-229
Libc ... 173
libc, mmap call ... 270
Link ... 42
link code ... 35
link command ... 35
link files ... 43
Link register ... 65, 105, 305
link source ... 42
linking programs ... 43
little endian ... 308
LO ... 101
load register ... 81
logical AND ... 87
logical EOR ... 89
logical NOT ... 77
logical OR ... 88
logical shift left ... 94, 111
logical shift right ... 112

long accumulation	120
long multiplication	119
loop control	107
loops code	107
low level languages	28
LS	103
LSL	94, 111
LSR	112
LSRB	146
LT	103
machine code	25
macro parameters	171
macros	169
makefiles	84
makefiles	84
mathematics, saturation	123
matrix addition	240
matrix, multiplication	241
matrix, multiply by scalar	241
matrix, rotate 90 degrees	237
memory store instructions	153
Memory,	
addressing	59
block copy	157
DA option	154
DB option	154
IA option	154
IB option	154
virtual	268, 304
-mfpu option	212
MI	100
microprocessor definition	14
mkdir, create directory	199
MLA	74
MLS	260
Mmap	270
mnemonics	26
mode, AArch32 processor	311
model, ARM programmers	280
modes of operation	276
modes, bit settings	281
Morse code	25
MOV	66, 75
move instructions	75
Move Negative	76
MOVT	260
MRS	282

MSR	282
MUL	73
multiplication instructions	73
multiplication, long	119
multiplication, matrix	241
MVN	75
NaN	208
Nano	35
narrow instructions (.N)	308
NE	99
Negative (N) flag	62
Neon	205, 289
Neon addressing modes	234
Neon data types	231
Neon lanes	232
Neon operations	230
Neon pipeline	296
Neon, STRIDE	244
Not a Number format	208
number input, scanf	178
Numbers	
32-bit multiplication with accumulate	75
32-bit multiplication	74
binary addition	53
binary subtraction	53
binary to decimal	48
binary weights	48
decimal to binary	49
decimal to hex	52
decimal weights	48
hex to decimal	52
twos complement	55
NV	102
object file	45
opcode	47
opcode breakdown, T16	294
opcodes, data	292
operand	47
operand breakdown, ARM	290
operand breakdown, Thumb	293
operating system call	40
operation, modes of	276
ORR	89
output size	233
Overflow (V) flag	62

parameters, macro..171
PC in instructions..124
PC relative addressing..151
pins, GPIO...264
pipeline, branch effect..127
pipeline, eight stage..294
pipeline, Neon...296
pipeline, VFP...299
Pipelining..125
PL 100
POP 178
post-indexed addressing..140, 149
predication, branch..297
pre-indexed addressing..140, 145
print binary string...93
printf 176, 196
printf, passing parameters..177
printing floating point numbers..213
privileged exceptions..281
program comments..41
program counter, R15...62, 124
program label..41
program naming...37
programmers model..60, 280
programs, frozen..129
promoting and demoting datatypes...234
pseudo code..31
PSTATE...309
Pull 159
PUSH..158, 178

Q flag...123, 283
Q registers...231
Quad registers..231

R, register..40
R14 124
R15, program counter..62
R7 79
range restriction, PC addressing..152
range, immediate constant...116
RBIT 260
read from keyboard..82
registers...40, 60
    AArch64 state..207
    APSR..219, 311
    bank..61
    CPSR..62, 64, 276

    D............209
    dump............136
    exception link............309
    FPSCR............217
    function designations............185
    GPCLR............266
    GPIO............264
    GPSEL............264
    link............65, 105, 305
    R15............62
    SCTRL............286
    SPSR............279, 309
    stack pointer............66
    swapping, privileged exceptions............282
    Q............231
    Quad............231
    saving on stack............164, 208
    Thumb............247
    Thumb high access............253
    VFP............208
    W............305
    X............305
    Zero............306
RISC OS............27, 275
Root User............271
ROR 114
rotate right............114
Rotates............111
RRX 115
RSB 72
RSC 72

S Registers............208
S suffix............65, 77, 105
S, updating flags............65
saturation maths............123, 283
SBC 72
SBFX 260
scalar operations............222
scanf function............178
screen output, debugging............130
screen, writing to............80
SCTRL............286
second processor............15
setting breakpoints............135
setting flags............64
shift instructions............111
Shifts 111

signed multiplication..119
signed multiply wide..121
signed multiply with subtraction...121
SIMD 205
SIMD, Advanced..205
single board computer...16, 303
Single Instruction Multiple Data..205
single precision numbers, format...207
SMLAL..120
SMUAD...121
SMULL..119
SMUSD...121
SOC 15, 204, 300
SOC technology..301
Software Interrupt call..78
software vectors..277
source file..34
source file, assemble...42
source files, compiling C 191
SP, adjusting value for stack use..188
SPSR register..279, 309
Stack Pointer..66, 160
Stack
       applications..164
       adjusting SP...188
       AArch64 pointer options..310
       ascending...161
       descending...161
       EA option...161
       ED option..161
       FA option...161
       FD option..161
       implementing..160
       saving registers on..164
       Thumb..254
       use to pass function values...186
status flags...62, 64
Status Register...62, 64
STM 61, 153
STR 145
STRIDE..222-229
STRIDE, in Neon...244
structure, assembler..30
SUB 72
subtraction instructions..72
subtractions, binary..53
sudo command...271

suffix, S..65, 105
summing vectors...227
Supervisor..276
Supervisor call..79
SVC mode..282
SVR 78
SWI 40, 78
SWI call in exceptions..282
Syscall 79, 80
syscall 3..82
syscall 4..80
syscall 4 parameters...80
syscall registers..96
syscalls, disassembling..199
System Control Registers...286
System on a chip...15, 204, 300

T16, opcode breakdown...294
T32 ....288, 304
T32 new instruction...255, 257
technology, SoC...301
TEQ 93
test bits instructions...93
text editors..34
three-stage pipeline..125
Thumb
    Thumb 2..246, 258
    addressing modes..254
    functions...255
    registers..247
    State..246
    branches...248
    comments..250
    disassembling..251
    executing..252
    high register access 253
    interworking..252
    operand breakdown...293
    stack..254
    T32 changes...258
TST   93
twos complement issues...57
twos complement numbers..55

UAL   20, 246, 304
UAL, assembling..261
UBFX 260
UMALA..120

UMULL	119
Underf	276
Unified Assembly Language	20, 246
unsigned multiplication	119
User Mode	58
User Mode register bank	61
User, Root	271, 276
VABS	216
VADD	216
variables, Frame Pointer	198
VC	100
VCVT	211, 215
VDIV	216
Vector Floating Point	204
vector operations	222
vector wrap	222
vectors, hardware	277
vectors, instruction used in	278
vectors, summing	229, 277
VFP	204
VFP condition codes	220
VFP control register	217
VFP pipeline	299
VFP register file	208
VFP types	206
VFPLite	205
videocore	302
Vim	34
Vim commands	35
virtual file map	269
virtual file, open	269
virtual memory	268
VLD	244
VLDR	210, 212
VMOV	211, 214
VMUL	216
VNEG	216
VNMUL	216
VPUSH	211, 214
VREV	239
VS	100
VSQRT	216
VST	239, 244
VSTR	212
VSUB	216
VZIP	239

W registers	305
wide instruction (.W)	308
word length	58
word-alignment	59
write back	155
write-back, addresses	148
writing to screen	80
X registers	305
Zero (Z) flag	62, 77
Zero register	306

www.brucesmith.info/blog

Printed in Great Britain
by Amazon